FIJI COMMANDOS

Major Carl Heinmiller's Experience During World War Two

Robert H. Sabet

Fiji Commandos
Copyright © 2025 by Robert H. Sabet

ISBN 978-1-300-54952-9

Dedication

For the Commando "Types"

Table of Contents

Foreword 6

Introduction 10

Commando "Type" Training 12

Carl Heinmiller, Boy Scout 33

Fiji Scouts 45

Wilson's Promontory 56

Commandos From Oz 65

Pacific Commandos 85

Carl Heinmiller and the Commandos 103

Charles Tripp 114

Heinmiller's Article in American Rifleman 136

Chalk Marks the Spot..................................... 146

Comparing Two Unarmed Combat Systems 162

Boxing, Rugby and Training By Competition 195

Fieldcraft... 209

Colonel Logan E. Weston 217

The Pacific Knife-Fighter................................ 256

David D. Duncan 276

An Unfortunate Incident 287

Postwar Venture.. 297

A Legendary White Warrior................................ 314

Forgotten Warriors and Nice Fellows...................... 322

Carl Heinmiller's Photographs............................ 335

Foreword

In 1984, while serving in El Salvador as a Green Beret adviser, I met a Salvadoran infantryman, a sergeant, who taught me a wonderful lesson about Combatives.

I had been told he had killed seventeen communist guerrillas using only his knife. Naturally, I was very interested. When we met I asked him if what I had heard was true. He nodded. He then showed me the knife he had used. It was a German issued bayonet cut down, as well as the issue scabbard, to a blade length of about six ½ inches.

And it was razor sharp.

His expertise with it did not come from specialized training but rather from growing up using a machete.

When I offered to trade him my Gerber MK-I boot knife for his modified bayonet he declined with a small smile. "I'm very happy with this one," he said, "but thank you."

That is when I knew for sure his story was true.

Military application Combatives remain rooted in the adage "Kill or be Killed." Every culture has its own unique brand of hand-to-hand fighting with the tactics and techniques of that brand, or style, being absorbed into military application and training. I have been privileged to train with a number of allied military units to include the Salvadorans, the Malaysians, the British, and Indonesians. All of these were special operations units whose mission statement included close quarters fighting, prisoner snatches, and sentry removal. We all learned from each other, sharing our systems and styles, and not worrying too awful much about the tools or weapons involved. The universal commonality shared by all of us was first and foremost Attitude. "Kill or be Killed."

I am in full agreement with the author of this fine book, Mr. Bob Sabet, when he shared with me the following. "The subject matter after all, it is people going into the gutter so by its very nature military Combatives instruction must be down to earth (KISS - keep it simple stupid). But even then it can be highly intelligent content wise and on a certain level and used to connect with people. I suppose it is the premise of the whole thing; the camaraderie and brotherhood of these military units and the intense mission sets they must be fully trained in to accomplish the mission and come home in one piece."

De Oppresso Liber,
Greg Walker (ret)
USA Special Forces

The story of the Fiji Guerillas is unique in the Second World War. In no other theatre did Pacific Island troops from Fiji, Tonga and the Solomon Islands train and serve together with New Zealand officers and non-commissioned officers, and operate with American forces, often on extended patrols behind Japanese lines.

The success of the various commandos of the Fiji Guerillas owed much to familiarity of the Fijians and New Zealanders with dense bush and a shared knowledge of bushcraft. Added to this was the discipline and initiative inspired by the military training in Fiji, matched with the newly acquired skills of marksmanship and hand-to-hand combat. Once in action, the scouts proved beyond doubt that the only reliable information which could be obtained in jungle conditions was from observation at close quarters.

The origins of the force can be found in their nomenclature. The company-sized units were designated as Commandos (reminiscent of the mobile Boer infantry units during the First and Second South African Wars) of the Fiji Guerillas (from the Spanish and Portuguese irregular troops who helped to drive the French from the Iberian Peninsula during the Peninsula Wars). Mindful of the experience of guerilla warfare in the Philippine-American War, American commanders preferred the term 'South Pacific Scouts'.

Following the Japanese attack on Pearl Harbor in December 1941, Fiji Commando units were trained to operate behind Japanese lines in the event that the Japanese invaded Fiji. Similar units had been trained in Australia and Singapore to operate as stay-behind parties and independent commandos and operated with varying success behind the lines after the Japanese invasions of Singapore, Rabaul, Ambon and Timor.

Only in Fiji, however, did Pacific Island, New Zealand and American troops come together to create highly trained jungle scouting units. What also emerged during the creation of the Fiji Guerillas were the essential principles of aggressive jungle patrols –planning, reconnaissance, undetected movement through thick jungle and successful ambushes.

The story of Carl Heinmiller and the Fiji Guerillas exemplifies how the Second World War brought people together from across the globe. Fijian customs and bushcraft, New Zealand ingenuity and common sense, and the American tradition of the frontiersman and American Boy Scout all combined in Eastern Fiji in 1942, and again in the Solomon Islands the following year. The result was a scouting force which earned the highest respect from American divisional commanders for the scouts' skillful reconnaissance in the most hazardous circumstances, from Mount Austen on Guadalcanal to Bougainville.

I commend Robert Sabet's story of Carl Heinmiller and the Fiji Commandos to anyone who wants to understand what makes a commando a commando. Certainly in Fiji and again in the Solomons, the Fiji Guerillas proved the value of natural aptitude, initiative, training and discipline in taking the fight to the enemy.

Aaron Fox BA (Hons) (Otago), PhD (Otago)
Independent Military Historian
Palmerston North
New Zealand

Introduction

In 2020 I wrote my first book, The Battle-Fighting Combatives of Allan Corstorphin Smith. At the time it was my intention to bring some exposure to Smith who had played an integral role in bringing judo to the United States. He taught it to the troops stationed at various locations during both World Wars and also during the Interwar period. Smith was an important piece of the puzzle concerning the history of the development of Combatives in the United States of America.

During the course of my research there were other individuals who I encountered doing the same thing; but from varying backgrounds. I wrote about them as well. After a few years of researching the subject, I decided I would take a bird's eye view to see how all that fit in with the overall training of troops and the populace; in Commando type tactics. I took a look at what occurred in the United States, but globally as well.

The training of unarmed combat tactics fit within the larger plan, by the powers that be, of making the local populace and the military, battle-ready, for any invasion; or to take the fight to the enemy. Subjects such as physical conditioning, fieldcraft, demolitions, were just as relevant if not more so. In writing the book, Commando Craze, I also explored something about the mindset that went along with that type of training and what organizations had been tasked with it, such as the Office of Strategic Services.

From taking a look at those specific parameters, I soon had enough to fill another book. The story of the Fijian Commandos provided me with the ideal opportunity to do a deep dive on how someone who had been tasked with training individuals in commando tactics and guerilla warfare, specifically natives from another country, may have approached it.

I wanted to tell their story by taking a look at the individuals who had been embedded with them. One of those individuals was Major Carl W. Heinmiller, who is the main subject of this book.

The underlying question was, what made a Commando a Commando? Were people playing at being Commandos with their Commando "type" training, or did their training which mimicked the training of the actual Commandos of the time period, the ones who had been trained in Scotland, make them also bonafide Commandos?

Was Commando more about a state of mind? As a researcher had pointed out, at a certain point in time the military's thinking was, if that type of training was good for some then why shouldn't it be good for all? Eventually everyone was getting some of that Commando type training.

I also wanted to discuss some of the things that have interested me in writing my previous books, all of them being rather niche. Depending on whether people are more interested in context or action, they may prefer only certain sections of the book, or they may prefer the whole book overall. As with my previous books, it has always been my goal to provide the reader with a bit of both.

Although this book is not specifically a martial arts book, unarmed combat training played an important role in what a Commando was, or did it?

This book is the result of my findings.

Commando "Type" Training

Major James Roosevelt

Regarding the origins of the concept of Commando type training in the United States we have to explore some of the thinking as to the "why" behind it all. One of the main proponents of the Commando concept, early on, was William J. Donovan, aka "Wild Bill" Donovan of the Office of Strategic Services. A lot of the information for this chapter came from the history section of the Marine Corps Counterintelligence Association.

Donovan was a man of great discipline and during World War I he had distinguished himself in the Battle of Champagne – Marne and Saint Mihiel and Argonne Campaigns. He was wounded three times, and for his gallant efforts was awarded the Medal of Honor, Distinguished Service Cross as well as the Distinguished Service Medal Croix de Guerre. He earned his nickname "Wild Bill" in France as a battalion commander. Donovan later became the regimental Commanding Officer of the 165th Infantry-better known as the "Fighting 69th."

In 1905 Donovan had received his B. A. from Columbia College and by combining his final college year with pre-law studies at Columbia Law School, he had been able to graduate in two years. During that time period one of his classmates was Franklin D. Roosevelt, who would later become President Franklin D. Roosevelt. It was Roosevelt who proved to have Donovan's ear concerning the formalization of an intelligence gathering network for the United States.

In 1912, despite the pressures of legal work from his law practice, Donovan became instrumental in founding Troop "I" 1st New York Cavalry, of the New York National Guard. He was elected the Troop's Captain and when it had been called out in support of operations along the Mexican border, he put aside his law books. Prior to the outbreak of the First World War, Donovan was promoted to the rank of Major.

During the interwar years, Donovan served as an unofficial U.S. military observer in Asia for a short time period and then resumed his law practice. He was appointed U.S. District Attorney for Western New York in 1921 and in 1925 he became the Assistant U.S. Attorney General for the same area. It was also during this time period that Donovan became active in politics, with the Republican Party.

Another contact from Columbia, Harlan F. Stone, played an important role in Donovan's later career in establishing a national intelligence organization. Stone was an adjunct professor of law, who had been appointed in 1924 by President Calvin Coolidge as the United States Attorney General. Stone had invited Donovan to be his assistant in charge of the Justice Department's Criminal Division.

In 1928, many government insiders presumed that Donovan would be the heir-apparent to become the next U.S. Attorney General, but his appointment was opposed by party conservatives largely due to his Irish-Catholic background. It had been the one position that Donovan wanted the most.

President Hoover offered Donovan the post of Governor of the Philippines which he declined. In 1932 Donovan ran unsuccessfully for Governor of New York. He returned to his law practice thereafter.

In 1936, President Roosevelt, as a symbol of national harmony brought into the Cabinet one of Donovan's close friends, Knox who had been the Republican Vice-President nominee. Knox recognized Donovan's talents in his endeavors in developing an intelligence agency for the United States. Churchill's Canadian Emissary, William Stephenson, also recognized those same talents. It was those two individuals who were instrumental in securing Donovan's appointment as, the Director of Coordinator of Information (COI).

Prior to the United States becoming involved in the Second World War, Donovan had been fascinated with the British Secret Intelligence Service (SIS). Having that fascination, Donovan was invited to SIS headquarters, where he was shown things that no other American had seen before. Some of those things were the then, Top Secret invention of Radar, as well as the newest interceptor planes, amongst other things. SIS had unlocked their safes and initiated Donovan into the mysteries of SIS techniques of unorthodox warfare. He had been particularly intrigued by the methods which SIS used in capturing German Spies in order to use them as a counteragent. All the things Donovan observed later proved important and they were to be incorporated into the United States' own intelligence structure.

On the basis of what Donovan had seen, he stated unequivocally to the President, that "America needs to form such an organization that would report directly to the President of the United States on all intelligence matters outside the boundaries of the United States." Roosevelt welcomed the suggestion of a single agency which would serve as a clearing house for all intelligence and establishing a training center for what were euphemistically called "Special Operations."

Five months before the United States became involved in World War II, by Executive Order on July 11th 1941, President Roosevelt appointed Donovan the Director, Coordinator of Information. Donovan's duties as defined by Roosevelt's own words were:

> To collect and analyze all information and data which may bear upon national security, to correlate such information and data and make the same available to the President and to such departments and/or officials of the government as the President may determine, and to carry out when requested by the President, such supplementary activities as may facilitate the securing of information important to national security, not now available to the government

It was inevitable that there would be turf wars with other governmental and military organizations tasked with similar operations. Roosevelt's directive was purposely obscure in its wording, due to the secret and potentially offensive nature of the new agency and its functions, and the other intelligence organizations that might become jealous and upset that it was stepping on their toes.

Roosevelt reiterated that Donovan's work was not intended to supersede, duplicate or interfere with the ongoing activities of the General Staff, the Federal Bureau of Investigation, or other existing intelligence agencies. J. Edgar Hoover of the FBI, perhaps fearing that the new intelligence organization would steal the spotlight, was not completely satisfied until Roosevelt assured him that the new agency was forbidden to conduct its activities within the United States. Major General George V. Strong, also felt that there was a conflict of interest in the military arena, by the establishment of the COI. It was Strong's belief that the Army G-2 represented tactical military intelligence and COI represented strategic intelligence of all kinds and that they could not coexist in both a military and a civilian working environment.

In the early years of the war it was Donovan who recommended that the United States establish a "commando military element," independent of the Army and Navy. He submitted a Memorandum to the President stating its overall purpose and function.

The next day, Roosevelt, in non-committal language, indicated that Donovan's proposal for the development and deployment of a "commando military element" had merit and would consider the idea. He then initiated a letter to the Commandant of the Marine Corps (Major General Holcomb) for consideration of Donovan's proposal. Roosevelt who was in constant communication with Prime Minister Winston Churchill, discussed the "commando concept" and Churchill favored the idea.

One of the biggest questions which arose concerning the issue, was where would the notional organization be placed. Donovan's Memorandum to Roosevelt only noted the purpose of the "commando military element", he did not address where it should be placed or its organizational structure.

A number of circumstances pointed directly towards the Marine Corps as the best place.

Around the same time that Roosevelt forwarded a letter to the Commandant of the Marine Corps, concerning the notional "commando" organization, Captain James Roosevelt, his son, prepared a letter describing a notional makeup of a "commando element." That letter also listed both the personnel and equipment needs in order for the structure to operate in the true commando environment. Captain Roosevelt's letter was forwarded through the Chain of Command to the Commandant of the Marine Corps. It is also worth mentioning that Captain Roosevelt had recently served as Donovan's military aid to the COI.

On January 14th Captain Roosevelt's letter had been prepared and forwarded to Major General Clayton B. Vogel, Commanding General at Camp Elliot, San Diego, California. The letter which had been strongly endorsed by Vogel was sent to the Commandant of the Marine Corps. Vogel fully supported Captain Roosevelt's proposal for the creation of a "commandos unit" that was similar to that of the British Commandos and the Chinese Guerrillas and presented further details in personnel and equipment needs for the establishment of the unit.

Upon receipt of both letters, Major General Thomas Holcomb, reviewed the President's letter and made comments on the commando concept. It had been evident right from the start that General Holcomb was faced with two issues which needed to be resolved if he was going to put things into play. The first issue, centered on bringing in Donovan and promoting him to a Brigadier General in the Marine Corp, in order for him to head the "commando force.' The second issue, was to determine if an alternative course could be developed to resolve the first issue that would be in the best interest of the Corp.

According to the history section of the Counterintelligence Association website, regarding the first issue, after considerable consultation with his senior Marine Corps generals, they all recommended against bringing Donovan into the Corps and promoting him a general to run the proposed commando unit. It should be noted that Holcomb, purposefully withheld who had originated the proposal for his senior generals. Also, General Holcomb fully understood that if Donovan got his foot in the door due to his direct link to the president, it would present a force to be reckoned with, which he probably could not control. Not acting upon the issue immediately, the issue still remained unsolved, until after lengthy communications between the Commandant, his generals, Admiral King – Commander in Chief, U.S. Fleet, Admiral Stark – Chief of Naval Operations and Admiral Nimitz – then flying his flag aboard the U.S.S. Pennsylvania. Admiral King sent a directive to Admiral Nimitz directing him to:

> Develop an organization and training of Marines and Naval units of "commando-type" for use in connection with expeditions of raid character for demolition and other destruction of shore installations in enemy held islands and bases. Employment of some small units embarked in submarines appears practicable by use of rubber boats.

Admiral Nimitz in turn passed the problem on to Brigadier General Clayton Vogel of the Joint Training Force and noted that "it appears that four such units may be organized within an infantry battalion without appreciably altering present organization."

Captain Roosevelt's letter had been reviewed and turned over to the War Plans Section at Headquarters Marine Corps. In order to support the general's task in dealing with both documents, the War Plans Section drafted a message for Admiral King's signature. It highlighted the scarcity of specialized personnel on the west coast and directed transfer of infantry, machine gun, and mortar troops from the First Separate Battalion to San Diego, California. This would form the center piece of a Pacific Fleet "commando-type unit."

The events that transpired in the formation of a commando-type unit demonstrated that what President Roosevelt really wanted was the establishment of a commando military unit. In June of 1942 Donovan's COI was redesignated as the Office of Strategic Services (OSS). The new purpose for the OSS was to identify outdated concepts of international espionage, and update them with techniques never previously employed by the United States. Executive Order 9812, delineated the responsibilities of the OSS in matters relating to intelligence and para-military operations.

On a strategic level, the OSS encouraged the Resistance groups in France, supported partisan operations in Italy and the Balkans, and parachuted some of its agents, which included Marines, into Nazi Germany.

Regarding Commando type operations, Churchill along with Roosevelt had endorsed raids on Japanese controlled areas in the Pacific. Donovan seemed to have no desire in having the OSS engage its operations in the Pacific Theater, not to mention Admiral Nimitz's dislike for the OSS and Donovan. It seemed that Donovan's primary concern was exclusively oriented towards Europe rather than the Pacific theater of operations.

Regarding the Marines involvement with Commando type operations, throughout the decade of the thirties, it had been experimenting with the concept of raider-type forces as part of a larger unit in exercise support. The continuing interest in that concept was demonstrated by the formation of the Provisional Rubber Boat Companies from the companies "A", "E", and "I" of the Seventh Marines during Fleet Exercise-7, which occurred in February 1941. The Tentative Landing Manual from 1935 discussed that concept in limited detail.

Through some organizational redesignation, the 1st and 2nd Raider Battalions were formed. The commander of the 1st Raider Battalion was Lieutenant Colonel Merritt A. Edson and the commander of the 2nd Raider Battalion was Lieutenant Colonel Evans F. Carlson. The specific operations were directed in the Pacific Theater.

The basic mission of the new Raider Battalions were to be the spearhead of amphibious landings by larger forces on beaches generally thought to be inaccessible. To conduct raiding expeditions requiring elements of surprise and high speed; and to conduct guerrilla type operations for protracted periods behind enemy lines.

Several Raider Battalion Operations were conducted in the Pacific. Captain James Roosevelt was assigned as the Executive Officer of the 2nd Raider Battalion. He would participate in the famous raid on Makin Atoll in the Gilbert Islands in August of 1942, and for his action, then a Major, he would receive the Navy Cross, the highest Marine Corps award for valor.

In November of 1943 he won the Silver Star and was subsequently promoted to Lieutenant Colonel. During that same year he was given command of the 4th Raider Battalion. He spent 26 months in combat, participating in such battles against Japanese forces on Tawara and Guadalcanal. Later he became a Brigadier General in the Marine Corps Reserves.

An article in the Amarillo Daily News, June 5th 1942 titled "Marines Ready for Debate on Commando Tactics" stated:

> Now that Lord Louis Mountbatten top officer of the British Commandos, is in the United States for consultations with American military leaders, he may find the United States Marines ready to debate a point or two with him—principally about the marines.
> According to a press release received in the Amarillo substation yesterday from marine corps headquarters, district of Oklahoma, Oklahoma City, "the United States Marines resent the headlines which proclaim they are being taught commando tactics."

The English Commandos and the U. S. Marines have come in for a lot of comparison lately and will continue to do as the commandos duplicate raids such as the one at St. Nazaire several weeks ago, when they crippled a German submarine base.

Comparison stops, however, when origination of commando tactics is brought up, according to the marine publicity department.

"It is true the Commandos and marines are trained along similar lines," the release states, "but it is the marine corps that originated these tactics.

"The United States Marines resent the headlines which proclaim that they are being taught commando tactics.

"They have been making landing parties ever since first organized as 'Soldiers of the Sea' in 1775 and this maneuver is the first in which the marine of today becomes proficient," the story continues.

Sgt. F. M. Bell, in charge of marine recruiting here, added that the expediency of successful ship-to-shore landings and the use and transportation of motorized equipment are all included in the marines' basic training.

There is an August 1942 document titled "Functions Of The Office Of Strategic Services—Organized Sabotage And Guerilla Warfare" which outlined that organization's thinking on Commando type training and the importance of that type of training for the natives from overseas allies. I will include the document at the end of this chapter.

This book however, is not about the Marines or the OSS, their Commando type training, or even their operations in the Pacific. It concerns another group who already lived in a country in the South Pacific, the Fijians. It is also about the individuals who organized them into Commando units.

James Roosevelt, Marine Corps Major, helped lead a detachment which raided Makin island. F. D. R.'s other sons are also in service.

Source: Monrovia News Post, November 6th 1943.

S E C R E T

J.P.S. 35/7 (2nd Draft)   COPY NO. 28

AUGUST 10, 1942

JOINT U.S. STAFF PLANNERS

FUNCTIONS OF THE OFFICE OF STRATEGIC SERVICES—
ORGANIZED SABOTAGE AND GUERILLA WARFARE

(Previous references: J.P.S. 35/7; and J.P.S. 26th Mtg., Item 2)

Note by the Secretaries

L.   The enclosure, revised in accordance with J.P.S. 26th Meeting, Item 2, is presented for consideration by the Joint U.S. Staff Planners.

R.L. VITTRUP,

J.E. REID,

Joint Secretariat.

ENCLOSURE

FUNCTIONS OF THE OFFICE OF STRATEGIC SERVICES -
ORGANIZED SABOTAGE AND GUERILLA WARFARE

1. Pursuant to the directive from the Chief of Staff, United States Army, dated July 14, 1942 (J.P.W.C. 21/D), the Joint Psychological Warfare Committee has investigated the subjects listed therein and makes the following report:

A. NATURE OF OPERATIONS AND TRAINING.

    (1) Organized Sabotage and Guerilla Warfare.

        (a) Organized Sabotage. Conduct of organized sabotage in areas occupied by the enemy has become an important if not an essential mode of warfare.

        Usually a representative, called an organizer (either a native or a person knowing the language of the country into which he is sent, and trained in the use of radio) enters a designated area to do, among other things, any or all of the following:

        (i) To organize and to incite to action native groups in enemy occupied territory.

        (ii) To arrange for the entry of arms and equipment for these groups.

        (iii) To distribute seditious pamphlets.

(iv)   To give instruction in the character and use of demolition material.

(v)   To direct, supervise or to conduct sabotage activities.

(vi)   To set up "reception committees" to meet and to aid our armed forces.

All this is done as a means of preparing an area for offensive operations by our armed forces. Instruction in this method of warfare has been undertaken by the Office of Strategic Services and in certain areas (either alone or in conjunction with the British) operations are now being carried on.

(b)   Guerilla Warfare. Guerilla units should be made up in whole or in part of individuals of foreign birth or foreign descent who are already in the armed forces and have had at least three months training. These units, composed of personnel of tested loyalty to the United States, should be organized into language guerilla groups, and should be made available to theater commanders conducting operations in countries to which such groups are native. It is conceived that these units, trained and conditioned for such service, could be employed by the theater commander,

> (i)   Either by being part of his invading wave, or
>
> (ii)   by being placed behind the enemy lines through parachute or glider to join up with the "reception committees" already organized among the native population.

These guerilla groups should be centralized and specially trained with full advantage taken of their knowledge of the language and acquaintance with the various countries, and assigned as needed to various theater commanders, could be made an effective auxiliary force.

(2) Type of Training.

(a)   Organized Sabotage. As carried on by the Office of Strategic Services saboteur candidates are put through a seven-week course which embraces preliminary, basic, and advanced training, in addition to parachute and marine training. Special courses for certain type operations, such as industrial, railroad, and communications sabotage are also given. The subjects of instruction for these

courses have been planned in advance and are given by
officers who themselves have been through schools of instruction in these subjects. The Joint Psychological
Warfare Subcommittee has questioned the Office of Strategic Services officers in charge of the training, and
certain members of that Subcommittee have observed the
operations of one camp, including the work given in the
priliminary and basic schedules. It has compared this
training with the accounts of British training and with
the report of the training in Germany given to the saboteurs now on trial before the Military Commission. From
these reports and this observance, it is believed that the
type of training being given is suitable for saboteurs and
for the "organizers" of saboteurs.

(b) <u>Guerilla Warfare</u>. It is proposed that the
training of guerilla units will include training in demolition and in the prepartation of demolition material. Emphasis will be placed upon physical conditioning. Attention will be given to scouting and patrolling, to instruction in the infantry weapons and, since the guerilla company is completely free of administrative and supply units,
it will be trained to fend for itself and live off the country.

(3) <u>Type of Individual to be trained</u>.

(a)   <u>Organized Sabotage</u>. Individuals have been recruited by the Office of Strategic Services from men sent
by the Army or Navy, from foreigners who have been living
in this country and also from members of Allied armies in
England recruited by the British S.O.E.

(b)   <u>Guerilla Warfare</u>. Personnel for guerilla units
is to be recruited from foreign nationals in the United
States Army who volunteer for service and who meet the
necessary physical and mental requirements for such work.

(4) <u>Training as Individual Saboteurs or Guerilla
Warfare Units or Both</u>.

Statements have been received as to the desired use
of both individual saboteurs and guerilla warfare units. It
is apparent that the services of those two agencies are com-
plementary to each other, and that both can be used under the
direction of theater commanders to good advantage, saboteurs
as immediate and continued agents of attrition, and guerilla
units behind enemy lines on special missions assigned by the
theater commander to synchronize with his offensive or with
the first attacking waves. The Joint Psychological Warfare
Committee believes that training by the Office of Strategic
Services in both types of subversive warfare is desirable.

(5) Method of Allocating Graduates from Schools.

Officers experienced in sabotage training have already been sent to several areas, with the consent or at the
request of theater commanders. It is planned to allocate
militarized guerilla units to theaters of operation to imple-
ment basic directives from the Joint U.S. Chiefs of Staff or
in accordance with requests from theater commanders, and to
have these units operate solely under the direction of such
commanders.

B.   ARMY AND NAVY INSTRUCTOR PERSONNEL FOR SCHOOLS.

The type of training given makes it apparent that Army
and Navy personnel are needed for instructional purposes both in
the military field and in the technical field. Approval of the
recent request for 416 more Army grades and ratings will meet the
immediate emergency, but should the organization of militarized
guerilla units be authorized, additional increments of Army and
Navy instructors will be needed, dependent upon the exigencies of
the demand.

C.   CONTROL OF SUBERSIVE OPERATIONS

(1) In theaters of operations.

In theaters of operation, or in operational areas of
task forces, officers, agents and functions of the Office of

Strategic Services will be under the direct control of theater
or task force commanders and will comply with the provisions of
J.C.S. 67/3, except when the theater commander is an officer
of another nation. In this case direct control will be exercised
by the senior American commander if such exists, otherwise as
directed by the Joint U.S. Chiefs of Staff.

    (2) In areas outside of theaters of operations

        When operating outside a theater of operations,
officers, agents, and functions of the Office of Strategic
Services will be under the control of the Joint U.S. Chiefs
of Staff through such officer or agency as may be designated
by the Joint U.S. Chiefs of Staff.

D.   LIAISON.

    (1) Theaters of Operations

        In theaters of operation, liaison between the Office
of Strategic Services and other agencies, either foreign or
United States, will be as directed by the officer or agency
exercising control of Office of Strategic Services officers,
agents and functions.

    (2) In areas outside of a theater of military operations:

        Plans for subversive operations to be conducted in areas
outside theaters of military operations must be approved by the
Joint U.S. Chiefs of Staff.

The Joint U.S. Chiefs of Staff will exercise general
control over such operations and will delegate direct control
to the Director of the Office of Strategic Services or such
other officer or agency as they may designate.

2. RECOMMENDATIONS

A.   That the Joint U.S. Chiefs of Staff accept in principle
the functions of the Office of Strategic Services as indicated
herein; further study will be made by the Joint Psychological
Warfare Committee as to training, type of men used and organization, and that committee will make further recommendations to the
Joint U.S. Chiefs of Staff.

B.   That in the meantime the present system of the Office of
Strategic Services in the training and use of saboteurs be continued, with such necessary changes as will meet progressive
standards; and that the method of allocating saboteurs, viz.,
assignment by direction of the Joing U.S. Chiefs of Staff or at
the request of theater commanders through the Joint U.S. Chiefs
of Staff, remain in force.

C.   That decisions as to establishment, organization, training and use of guerilla units await the study and report recommended in paragraph 2-A above.

D.   That the Army and Navy furnish instructor personnel for
these schools in the numbers authorized by the Joint U.S. Chiefs

of Staff, in accordance with tables of organization to be submitted for approval later.

E.   That control of subversive operations, including guerilla warfare units, be in accordance with the provisions of paragraph 1 C.

F.   That liaison between the Office of Strategic Services and other agencies be in accordance with the provisions of paragraph 1 D.

Carl Heinmiller, Boy Scout

As stated, my current general area of interest is in taking a look at Commando type tactics and training; but my primary concern has always been the history of unarmed combat systems and the individuals who taught them. I tend to focus on the instructors from both World Wars.

One individual who I encountered in my research was Carl W. Heinmiller. I had located an article showing Heinmiller demonstrating hand-to-hand combat tactics, when he had been stationed in Alabama in 1945. The photograph which accompanied the article was of interest to me because it showed Heinmiller demonstrating a sentry removal technique with the use of a hatchet.

I used that photograph in my book about Skeeter Vaughan, another WW2 Veteran and an unarmed combat instructor from World War Two. It was an important image in my opinion, because there is scant information available concerning the use of hatchets or tomahawks for warfare during that particular conflict.

That article "Bond Program At 8 P.M. Set For Auditorium" in the Birmingham News, June 8th 1945 stated:

> Featuring a five-bout boxing card, one wrestling match and a demonstration of judo, the sports world will make its contribution to the Seventh War Loan drive tonight at the Municipal Auditorium. Opening event on the program, a one-fall wrestling match between Sailor Watkins and Jack Bloomfield, will get underway at 8 o'clock.
>
> The event is sponsored by Gen. Gorgas Post No. 1, American Legion, Veterans of Foreign Wars, Disabled Army Veterans and the Jefferson County war finance committee. Admission is by War Bond purchase only.
>
> Capt. Carl W. Heinmiller, veteran of the South Pacific and knife and dirty fighting expert, will meet Lt. John Archer, Ft. McClellan, in a judo exhibition. Capt. Heinmiller's demonstration will include death blows, paralytic blows, knife, club and bayonet fighting, and hand-to-hand combat.

That one article and photograph piqued my interest and sent me down the rabbit hole. Who was Captain Heinmiller? The article noted that he was a knife and dirty fighting expert and a veteran of the South Pacific. What made him an such an expert? Why hadn't I heard of him before?

I put that photo in the book and put my questions aside, fully intending on revisiting them again someday. That was not the only photo I had uncovered of Heinmiller demoing a sentry removal technique. There had been another one in an article from the same newspaper, which had been written a few days earlier on June 5th.

That photo is of Heinmiller this time demonstrating the use of a large knife for a sentry removal technique. That article "To Be At Bond Show" has a caption accompanying it which stated:

> Capt. Carl W. Heinmiller, famous South Pacific knife fighter, is shown above practicing one of his throat-sticking thrust on Sgt. Louis A. Sahley at Ft. McClellan, Ala. Capt. Heinmiller will meet judo expert Lt. John Archer in a thrilling contest at the Municipal Auditorium Friday night, June 8 at 8:30 p.m., a feature of the Seventh War Bond sports show.

Again, I had never heard of this "famous South Pacific knife fighter" and I wanted to know more.

After the war Heinmiller also had an interesting story. He bought a fort in a small town in Haines, Alaska with several other veterans and decided to start a colony there.

I was able to gather more information from an article "Reawakening at the Beachhead" written by an associate of Heinmiller's after doing an internet search. In that article the historian Daniel Lee Henry described Heinmiller's time in Alaska and mentioned events from Heinmiller's past. He wrote:

Defending Fiji compelled Carl Heinmiller's first efforts to organize indigenous people. The twenty-one-year-old Cleveland native shipped to New Zealand in 1942 where he trained with the National Expeditionary Forces before deploying to Guadalcanal.

"They plunked him out in a remote village there and said rally some troops and get them ready as guerilla fighters." The story is one of many burned into the memory of Heinmiller's son, Lee. Housed with his family in the upper two floors of the former Fort Seward infirmary, Lee Lives and breathes his father's legacy. The high-ceilinged, thinly insulated rooms of the shambling four-story building are packed with treasures—Tlingit, military, family. Part art cooperative, part museum, part gallery, and part ghost mansion, Alaska Indian Arts stands as testament to a vision. In Carl Heinmiller's case, monocular.

With his distinctive eye patch and characteristic gruffness, Heinmiller exuded a sense of military authority. His Boy Scout background was vital to Fiji Commando successes, due in part to exchanging "woodcraft" tips for traditional knowledge. As he told it, Native knowledge helped him avert one disaster after another. When his first aid skills became evident, the Major earned allegiance from his commandos, grandsons of cannibals. It hardly mattered that Heinmiller sacrificed an eye and two fingers outside the battle zone, when the decorated officer returned to Washington, D.C. he looked all the part of a returning war hero. He worked in the Pentagon "turning around paper clips for the brass," when he heard about former military properties on the market. He joined a group of a dozen veterans that met to "romance about goin' to Alaska." Among the regulars were Ted Gregg, recently a Navy cartographer in the Aleutians, and Steve Homer who dreamed about starting a ferry in Southeast Alaska. The veterans' campaign to colonize Alaska gained notoriety among bureaucrats who noted Heinmiller's iron-jawed determination.

Heinmiller's wartime experiences and his experiences amongst the Fiji Commandos was what I wanted to focus most of my efforts on finding out more about. I wanted to understand something about how someone who was tasked with organizing native Guerilla bands would go about accomplishing that task; and also how they would go about teaching Commando type tactics.

The mention of Heinmiller's experience as a Boy Scout in Henry's article checked out. The earliest mention I had found of Heinmiller in the press, was a tiny article from the April 1933 issue of Boys' Life. Heinmiller had received an honorable mention for participating in a carved paper knife contest.

I contacted Henry to discuss Heinmiller. Henry suggested that I contact Heinmiller's son, Lee, to find out more about what I wanted to know. Once I had established the connection, I asked Lee about the boy scout references amongst other things. I had written a bit about the Junior Commandos and Boy Scouts during the war, in Commando Craze. There had been a letter written by Lord Mountbatten instructing boy scouts in what type of training they would need in order to become good Commandos.

Concerning his father's experience as a Boy Scout, Lee told me:

> My Dad was in Scouting for 50 years, like his Dad. He got a Golden Eagle Award in the 1990's, only given for 50 years in Scouting. Only 108 so far by then. Some were astronauts, a few Presidents, etc. He was the first Alaskan! He was the youngest Eagle Scout in Ohio when he was young, I have his Merit badge sash's, Two... 108 total if I remember correctly!

In the article "Lord Louis Mountbatten sent this letter of advice to some boys in America on How to be a good Commando" which was printed in the Daily Mail on January 9th 1943. It stated:

Boys of Northfields Minnesota, inspired by the deeds of British Commandos, decided to form themselves into a body of Junior Commandos.

Their leader wrote to Lord Louis Mountbatten, Chief of Combined Operations, and asked for advice on how to train.

Lord Louis replied by sending them notes prepared by his Vice-Chief, Major-Gen J. C. Hayden, just before the general flew to North Africa to help in staging the great Allied landing.

Here are the training instructions the American boys are now studying:

First, it is imperative to be physically fit. This needs careful training and a good deal of thought.

It is no good embarking on ambitious undertakings unless one is trained for them.

Concentrate as much as you can on working in the dark. If you can move easily, quickly, and silently over rough country under cover of darkness there will be little difficulty in doing the same by day.

Remember always the effect on the enemy of feeling that people have worked through his lines and are operating somewhere behind him, but he doesn't quite know where.

For night work, cover up everything that reflects light, such as your face, hands, and any shiny equipment.

Make sure that any equipment that might rattle or make a noise is either wrapped in cloth or tied so that it cannot swing about.

To work well at night you must be able to see well. Find out those who have good night vision and choose them to lead the way.

In all that you do, try to make sure that the enemy is kept in ignorance of where you are and how many you are.

Try to imagine all the time that there are hostile eyes trying to find you.

It is little use being careful for three-fourths of the way if during the last fourth, somebody is careless and gives everything away.

You will always find that some like to lead and others to follow. The latter are either shy or nervous of being a failure. Those who want to lead, you need not worry about, but the others want careful handling.

Your rule should be not to give responsibility only to those who are senior ones in your troop.

Give everyone the opportunity to lead, because they might have to do so in battle, owing to somebody getting wounded.

One of the tests of leadership is ability to get the best out of everyone under you. The way to do this is to make them feel that their presence is really necessary.

If you possibly can, borrow a compass or two and maps of various types. Use them to the full so that you become really quick and good at using both. In working with a compass and a map you will find that you develop what is known as "a good eye for country."

That is to say, you will become skilled in picking a route for yourself which will get you to your destination without loss of time. It will also provide you with maximum cover from view.

For instance, it is little use for a scout to come back and say, "I saw part of the enemy." He wants to be able to say where he saw them, how many were in the party, what time it was, in what direction they were moving, whether they were all on foot or had motor vehicles with them, whether they had guards with them, and did they look alert.

Never forget that a very high standard of discipline is the fundamental requirement. If your leader asks you for ideas or suggestions, then you should give them, but when your leader gives an order, obey it.

If he cannot rely on instant obedience and conscientious performance of the allotted duty, then you may be sure that the unit will be caught out in battle.

Set yourself standards to reach in every branch of your training, such as cooking, map-reading, compass work, sketching, marching, unarmed combat, shooting, and so on.

Do all you can to study mechanical subjects. Facility in being able to deal with an engine in a car or boat is one of the most useful attributes you can have.

Learn all you can about handling boats and about navigation. You should feel as much at home on the water or in the water as on land.

When you are carrying out training schemes remember that surprise is still one of the most important factors in battle. Therefore, in all that you do, try to confuse and mislead the enemy.

Practise writing short but clear messages. It is extraordinary how difficult some people find this is to do.

Practise living on rations. We get so used to going into the shop round the corner to buy something extra that we hardly realise what it means when there is no shop to go to.

Start off for a day with a certain amount of food and water for each person and see that everyone sticks to his ration.

You probably already know all about Morse and semaphore, but try to work it out to a very high standard and devise a code so that you can send short signals to each other.

Your watchword should be:

"Skill, silence, and speed." If you can work with real skill in every department and with silence and with real speed, then you stand a good chance of outwitting any opponent you are likely to meet.

There is one article from Heinmiller's time at Camp Shelby that sort of set the stage for his future endeavors in Fiji. The article written by Mickey Dover, provides us with a glimpse into Heinmiller, the Boy Scout's mindset. The article "Hunting Snakes Is Not Without Its Moments" from The Camp Shelby Reveille, August 13th 1941, stated:

Lieutenant Carl Heinmiller is quite a gent.

You may, in fact, take my word for it. He's a snake charmer from 'way back, and he conclusively proved it before my own wide and popping eyes.

The genial, blond 145th Infantry officer, who has been "filling in" as 37th Division morale officer, had been telling me tall (I thought) tales of the not-at-all gentle art of snake-catching.

His best story dealt with how he catches rattlers alive, with only a small noose and a forked stick as weapons.

"Like to come along and catch a five-footer?" he queried.

Not being exactly fond of our reptilian friends, it took me exactly one-tenth of a second to answer, "Hell, no!" Then Photographer Steve Loska pleaded the cause of art, and in almost no time at all (one hour, to be exact), the pair convinced me I should go along.

Lieutenant Heinmiller talked me out of wearing the leggings, leather shin-guards, knee-pads and football pants. All I would need would be a small forked stick, he assured me.

In the wilds of the DeSoto National forest, the lieutenant began beating the brush piles and high grass. I wasn't exactly scared. But once I looked back from twenty feet away after hearing a bunch of snapping twigs.

Snake hunting is a tedious job. After two and a half hours of tramping, and still no snake, Lieutenant Heinmiller was taking quite a razzing. The "little" stick I was carrying for protection (a young fence rail) was beginning to get quite heavy.

Then it happened!

I saw the lieutenant suddenly bend over, forked stick pointed downwards. Then a black shape emerged from the grass, looking as large as a sea serpent and heading my way!

What happened next is a little vague. After all, I don't have eyes in the back of my head. I didn't "retreat," however. A soldier in the United States army never retreats. I just made a rapid, tactical "withdrawal."

When I looked again, the snake was pinned down with the forked stick, and the triumphant catcher was slipping the rope noose around its neck.

When convinced that the situation was well in hand, and that the snake was definitely the loser of the battle, I consented to come down from my perch half-way up one of Mississippi's choice scrub pine trees for a closer look.

The catch was a sure-enough five-footer-an ugly-looking (but quite photogenic) coach whip snake. This species, according to the reptile-wise Lieutenant Heinmiller, is the most ferocious non-poisonous type in the South. No amount of persuasion succeeded in making me look close enough to see the "small, beautiful lines on his throat." But, according to the lieutenant, the lines are there. Take a look sometime. But don't talk any reporters into going along. It's bad on the blood pressure!

Carrying a "young fence rail," Mickey Dover accompanies Lieutenant Carl Heinmiller on a snake hunt. Obviously, he was of little assistance in making the catch (upper photograph), or in carrying it home.

Fiji Scouts

Now that some things had been established concerning Heinmiller's background, it was time to understand something about the people he would serve with. The article "New Zealand Fighters Outwit Yanks" from the Salt Lake Tribune, April 28th 1943 provides us with some background on the Fiji scouts. It stated:

> Suva, Fiji, April 7th. Brigadier J. G. H. Wales, commander of New Zealand forces in Fiji, believes that he has trained his jungle fighters to be the finest group of commando troops in the world and that they are ready to meet the Japanese at any time.
>
> The Fijian warriors, with their bronzed skins, deep muscled bodies and bushy black hair and clad in the regular uniform of the New

Zealand army, have been studying commando tactics for more than a year.

Wales' efforts to convince American authorities at Fiji that the jungle fighters through heredity and training are better qualified to drive the Japanese from their south Pacific defenses than any troops now in the field caused embarrassment to some American troops.

Wales proposed that his commando troops attack an American camp during the night and mark an "X" on all men "killed" and on all equipment destroyed.

American troops doubled the guard. The Americans thought the night passed peacefully, but when morning came they found that many of their number had been "killed" and much of their equipment wrecked by "Xs".

"It sounds incredible," Wales said, "but it is really quite simple. They were born and raised in the jungles. We have merely taken their abilities and developed them to fit into the pattern of modern warfare.

"Their ability to move about in the darkness is remarkable and their woodcraft is in reality a sixth sense. Never once in maneuvers have the Fijians succumbed to an ambush."

Every commando trooper is a volunteer selected by the chief of his village. The majority of the commissioned and noncommissioned officers are Fijians. The senior officers are new Zealanders chosen by Wales for unusual abilities in jungle fighting.

In the battle for the southeastern Solomons, where these men would have been fighting in country suitable for their type of jungle warfare, only a handful were used, and those late in the campaign, but they made such an impression that American officers requested reinforcements. The battle for Guadalcanal ended, however, before they could be used.

Captain C. W. H. Tripp, New Zealand commander of the Fijians, took one battalion on a five-day maneuver across the island of Vita Levu with full equipment. They lugged supplies over jungle, climbed mountains and slid down canyons. At the end of five days they had traversed 100 miles, and only one man dropped out through exhaustion.

But the Fijians are dissatisfied with maneuvers, obstacle courses, rifle practice and judo instruction. They want to kill Japs.

In the process of trying to figure out exactly how Heinmiller fit into the overall story of the Fijian Commandos, I had to backtrack a bit, to the time period prior to the arrival of the Americans in Fiji.

There are only a few sources concerning the Fiji Guerrillas. The main one is the book "Pacific Commandos New Zealanders and Fijians in Action" by Colin R. Larsen. That book is a history of the Southern Independent Commando and First Commando Fiji Guerrillas. The second book is "Among those Present" which was the official story of the Pacific Islands at War, prepared for the Colonial Office by the Central Office of Information. It was published in London in 1946 by His Majesty's Stationery Office.

Both books are important in documenting the history of that time period, however I had been informed that there were inaccuracies in the Pacific Commandos book.

My search for information about the training and organization of these Fijian Commando units, led me to the National Army Museum Te Mata Toa in New Zealand. I was told that they had one additional book in their archives titled "The History of the Fiji Military Forces 1939-1945" which had been compiled from the official records and diaries by Lieutenant R. A. Howlett, in 1946 and published by Whitcombe & Tombs. The book has the history of The Commando, Fiji Guerilla units and each unit has a chapter dedicated to it in the book. They were:

1. First Commando, Fiji Guerillas.
2. Second Commando, Fiji Guerillas.
3. Northern Independent Commando, Fiji Guerillas.
4. Southern Independent Commando, Fiji Guerillas.
5. Eastern Independent Commando, Fiji Guerillas.

Although the book is a history of the forces in Fiji, there is very little mention of the actual training which was undertaken by those soldiers. New Zealand contributed in the defence of Fiji in the earlier stages of war including the training of the Commando units until the American's arrival in July 1942. During that time period the Fijian Defence Force including the Commando battalions came under the United States Pacific Area Command. Colin R. Larsen's book stated that the "First Commando Fiji Guerrillas was organised, trained and led into action by forty four New Zealanders."

There is a New Zealand Army Training Manual referred to as a Military Training Pamphlet (M.T.P.) from 1942 which is titled "Military Training Pamphlet No. 52. Forest, Bush, and Jungle warfare against a Modern Enemy. The pamphlet originated from the British Army. It was published by the War Office and reprinted in New Zealand under the authority of H. M. Stationery Office.

Pamphlet No. 52 contains a section concerning the use of local volunteers and guerilla forces. It stated:

1. *Local Volunteers.*   Locally raised troops should not all be used merely as second-line infantry to guard vulnerable installations and for tasks of secondary importance. Their chief assets will be that they will have the necessary training to work with the regular army and that they will have a greatly superior knowledge of the country, inhabitants, and language. Full use should be made of them to act in close co-operation with the army and to provide an essential link between the army and local inhabitants.

A proportion should be formed into local intelligence units, from which attachments should be made to each regular company or equivalent unit on the scale of one officer and up to ten other ranks. The duties of other ranks would be to accompany sub-units and patrols, and to assist in the collection of information from local inhabitants. Similar attachments should be made to battalion and formation headquarters. With the latter of duties of volunteer officers would include the collection of supplies and transport from local sources. If necessary, local intelligence units should be employed on an area basis for attachment to regular units and formations operating in their area. For obvious reasons, local personnel are of less value when employed outside areas of which they have an intimate knowledge.

It is important that local volunteers should include as many planters, forest officers, and officials, as possible whose work will be suspended in the event of local operations; that they should receive special training in map reading, jungle navigation, and intelligence work to meet military requirements; and that they should be suitably equipped to carry out their tasks.

2. *Guerilla Forces.*   In many likely theatres of operations, especially in the dominions and colonies, the local inhabitants are friendly to the Allied cause—e.g., the patriots of Abyssinia. Their characteristics should be studied and used to advantage. The

attachment of specially selected officers and N.C.O.s for the purposes of organizing the inhabitants, helping in their administration, and providing liaison between the inhabitants and the field army will be of value. These officers need not necessarily have an extensive knowledge of the country, but should be chosen for their personality, power of leadership, and endurance. They will be required to live the life of the inhabitants, and their tasks will be facilitated if they are allotted personnel such as forest officers, planters, local volunteers etc., who know the ways of the country and may themselves be known to the inhabitants.

Where the inhabitants can be employed in fighting they should be used only in the areas which they know. Their tasks, whether on the flanks of the enemy or behind his lines, will be many and various. Their chief limitations will be that they must be allowed to fight in their own time and by their own methods, and that too much reliance must not be placed on their close co-operation in any particular phase of an operation. Consequently, they should be employed chiefly in harassing the enemy and in causing him to make large detachments for the protection of his installations and lines of communication.

In trying to understand what type of training had been received by the Fijians, I checked an additional source. The Salt Lake Tribute article had mentioned a Captain C. W. H. Tripp, New Zealand commander of the Fijians. The museum had also mentioned Major Charles Tripp, a New Zealand officer who had been in command of the Southern Commandos. It turned out that his son Dick Tripp had recently written a short book about his father titled "The Hero from Nithdale Station: the remarkable true life story of Major Charles W. H. Tripp". It seemed like the next logical step, to check out what Dick Tripp wrote concerning his father's wartime experience and the training of the Commandos.

In April 1942 when the Western, Eastern, and Southern Commandos were being set up, Tripp had been placed in command of the Southern ones.

According to Larsen:

> Charles Tripp was a tall, raw-boned man over forty, of the pioneering type. He was affectionately known as the 'Boss' because of his dominant personality and steadfast character. A successful farmer in civilian life, he used practical, common sense ideas in the development of the Commandos. He had a theory that if he placed absolute confidence in the men under his command, the men would do their utmost to live up to the reputation he gave them. Few failed to respond to his leadership.

Concerning Charles Tripp's military background Dick Tripp wrote:

> My father's leadership qualities really came to the fore during his time with the Commandos in the Pacific. He felt it necessary to resist the Japanese and wanted to play his part. In the first year of the war, 1939, he had tried to join the Expeditionary Force, but being 38 and having a family of three, he was over the limit for overseas service (unless a senior officer). As an alternative, he joined the Southland Regiment. After training in Addington, Burnham, Forbury and Trentham, he was sent to Fiji as a lieutenant. I was nine at the time and living at Orari Gorge, and I remember going out to the Five Hills and looking (as expected, unsuccessfully) for a bayonet that one of Father's unit had lost in manoevres on the property. Father's initial job in Fiji was a desk one, as Staff Captain of the 8th Brigade, which didn't appeal to him. He took six months to growl his way out of it, though when he was later asked to set up the Commandos, he found that what he had learned in Army administration was most useful.

Dick Tripp went on to write about his father, that while Charles had been in command of the Southern Commandos:

> The Fijians gave him the respect equal to that due to their high-ranking Chiefs. Some platoons had no contact with the others, except by messengers, but the Fijians always knew by 'bush telegraph' when Father was on his way. When he paid a visit, there would be Fijians from work parties in the bush popping up along the track and every village had a 100% turnout to give a welcome. As he passed by, women would be seen dipping a knee and whispering "tangane"—strong man! Discipline was always handled speedily and fairly, which enhanced his mana with both races. Father became firm friends with the paramount Chief, Ratu Sukuna, who was a man in the same mould, with a law degree from Oxford, and who showed a particular interest in the Commando activities. With his ability to meet people of all ranks as equals, Father used his contacts well to further his military knowledge.
>
> The unit began with about 40 New Zealanders, who provided the officers and sergeants, and 200 Fijians. Later they were joined by some Tongans and Solomon Islanders. The initial idea was that they were to be stationed at various points in the bush around Fiji to delay any Japanese landing until larger forces could arrive. By this time, early in 1941, the Japanese had reached the Solomons and it was generally expected that Fiji would be next in line. When the Commandos eventually joined the Americans in the Solomons, their role was primarily a scouting one, gathering information behind Japanese lines to keep the Americans informed of enemy movements. Father was promoted to captain, and as it was only a small unit of about 300 it wasn't until later in the campaign that he was promoted to major. Someone once told me that if he had been in the Middle East he would have been a general. The Commandos explored their respective areas of some

very rugged 200sq. miles, knew every track, river and hill and sorted out places to set ambushes and places for reserves of food supplies and ammunition. The New Zealanders taught the Fijians the use of weapons and military discipline, and the Fijians showed their skills in bushcraft, which were to be so vital later on.

There were a lot of gems in Dick Tripp's book about his father and the type of training the Fijians under his command had received; but it was obvious that I needed to try and understand something of how Commando type training took hold in New Zealand in the first place. My assumption was that the New Zealanders learned their commando tactics from the Australians who had in turn learned them from the British. I came to that conclusion because of the Military Training Pamphlet.

I asked Dick Tripp about his father's experience training the Fijian Commandos and whether his father had ever mentioned Heinmiller. Tripp told me he couldn't be of much help, that he had never heard the name. He let me know about some of the sources he had used for his book, again the main one being Larsen's book. Tripp also mentioned that his father told him that the book had a few inaccuracies.

One source Tripp suggested I contact was a war historian from Dunedin University, Dr. Aaron Fox, who had been familiar with this history and who knew Charles Tripp. When I contacted Dr. Fox, he told me about some of the New Zealanders who trained at Wilsons Promontory and how that had been the missing link I had been looking for.

I had initially thought that the New Zealand instructors to the Fijians had something to do with Z Special Unit, which had been a joint Allied special forces raiding/commando unit, which had been organized in June 1942. Z Force contained several British SOE officers who had escaped from Singapore, and they formed the nucleus of the Inter-Allied Services Department (ISD) which was based in Melbourne.

The problem with pinning it on Z Special Unit was the timing. According to the museum, the only training that occurred of New Zealand and Australian forces together, had been 'Z' Special Unit and the two independent companies which had formed in New Zealand and trained in Australia in 1941. Those companies were disbanded when they returned to New Zealand.

Because of timing, Z Force was out, and the people who had trained the Fijians had already been operating in 1941. But what about the two independent companies?

A pamphlet prepared by the Military Intelligence Service of the United States War Department on August 9th 1942, titled "British Commandos" stated the following:

> The Australian and New Zealand Armies have several units which are the equivalent of commandos but are designated as independent companies, organized on a platoon instead of a troop basis. The total strength of each company is 267 officers and enlisted men. The primary purpose of the independent companies is to educate remote and undefended communities to cooperate in striking back at any enemy that might land on Australia, New Zealand, and other nearby islands of the British Empire. These companies will also be used in the warfare of the southwest Pacific for manning new bases and for reconnoitering. Eventually they will also operate against the enemy in his own as well as in friendly territory.
>
> In general, the same high standards are required for personnel in the independent units as are demanded of the British commando members. Trained soldiers, single and without dependents, between 20 and 40 years of age, are selected. They must be of good physique and health and have courage, determination, intelligence, and individuality; and they must be amenable to strict

discipline. Other requirements are unassailable loyalty and reliability.

As in Great Britain, the independent companies receive special training at an infantry training center that was organized for this purpose. The basic course of instruction takes 6 weeks, but this is followed by combined training with units of the Royal Australian Navy and the Royal Australian Air Force in places suitable for amphibious air operations.

According to the Dr. Fox, the Fiji Guerillas were raised in Fiji to operate as left behind parties, similar to the commando units which had been trained in Britian in 1940 to operate after a German invasion of the UK, or the independent companies which had been formed in Australia in 1941.

A number of the New Zealand 'thousand pounders' had trained with Freddie Spencer Chapman, Mad Mike/Dynamite Mike Calvert and their team at Wilson's Promontory in Victoria went on the serve with the New Zealand forces in the Pacific, where they assisted with the formation and training of the three local commandos of the Fiji Guerillas when these were formed in 1942.

Aside from Charles Tripp's experiences and what he had brought to the table, it seemed that Commando type training made its main entrance into Fiji via the individuals who had trained at Wilson's Promontory in Victoria. But what exactly was Wilson's Promontory? Now there was another angle that I had to look further into.

I wondered how influential had those instructors been to the Fijians? Did the Commando type training the Fijians had received ultimately even matter in the scheme of things, did the Fijians become more efficient warriors because of such training? Or were they already warriors in their own right?

Wilson's Promontory

It was not my intention to become an expert on Australian or New Zealand military history overnight. I simply wanted to understand what type of training the Fijian's had received. It was relevant to also understanding Heinmiller's story. I wanted to find out about what training he may have also received during his time in Fiji. In order to understand that I first had to understand what Commando type training the New Zealanders had received.

According to the book "A History of Wilsons Promontory National Park, Victoria, Australia" published in May 2009 by the Victorian National Parks Association; Terry Synan wrote about the war years and the commando training that occurred there:

> With WW2 came the proposal from London for Australia and New Zealand to train shock troops, or commandos. Wilsons Promontory, the chosen location for this project, became, as a consequence, a high security 'Top Secret' military area for much of the war period. Relatively isolated, mostly surrounded by sea and with an easily secured isthmus linking it to the mainland, Wilsons Promontory seemed ideally placed and away from prying eyes. The Prom also greatly appealed because. It was mostly unsettled National Park containing a rich variety of topographical features and vegetation cover. Accordingly, a considerable range of commando training environments was available – mountains, plains, seascapes, sand dunes, mud flats, swamps, rivers, eucalypt forests, coastal scrub and open grasslands. Access to the area had just been upgraded with a new tourist road to Darby River which linked that area to railheads at Fish Creek and Foster.
>
> Humbling defeats in 1940 suffered by the British in Norway and at Dunkirk at the hands of well-organised German forces, and the capitulation of France, left London's military strategists with no

land army in Western Europe opposing the Nazi menace. Their thoughts turned to using commando units in order to carry out fast-moving sabotage and intelligence missions. They were also concerned that Nazi, Fascist and Japanese fifth-column cells were active in various countries. As a consequence, Military Mission 104 was dispatched to New Zealand and Australia to advise on military intelligence and to set up an Independent Company Training Centre at Wilsons Promontory.

Called No 7 Infantry Training Centre, it had a Headquarters Camp at the Darby River.

Synan continued:

The Military Mission was led by Lieut. Colonel J C Mawhood, who served in the Australian Army during WW1 but had later gained both Indian army and intelligence experience, including some association with M15. He had with him a team of four expert soldiers and a shipment of the latest explosives and infantry weapons available in Britian. His team also included Captain Freddie Spencer Chapman, fieldcraft; Captain Michael Calvert (Mad Mike), engineers and explosives; Warrant Officer Frank Misselbrook, signals and wireless telegraphy; and Warrant Officer Peter Stafford, weapons training.

On completing their Australian – New Zealand training assignment, the four soldier specialists were posted in India and South-east Asia to fight the Japanese war. Calvert became famous first as a daring assistant to the legendary Major-General Orde Wingate in Burma, and later during the Malayan emergency, where he became pivotal in developing modern SAS-style forces. He and Chapman left indelible impressions on the New Zealand and early Australian Independent Companies trained under their direction. Command of No 7 Infantry Training Centre went initially to Major W.J.R. Scott DSO, one of Australia's most intriguing military personalities of the two world wars and the inter-war period. He played an important role with the secret armies of the 1930s. Scott handed command to Major Stuart Love, also a much-decorated WW1 soldier, in May 1941.

For the purpose of this book we don't need to delve into exactly who those individuals were. We are primarily concerned with what training the New Zealanders would have received at Wilson's Promontory .

Synan wrote:

> During 1941 and 1942 eight Australian and two New Zealand Independent Companies trained at Wilsons Promontory. A company comprised of 273 soldiers. It possessed a higher proportion of officers than regular army units — a Major commanding, five Captains and eleven Lieutenants. Its sub-structure consisted of three platoons, each of 60 men commanded by a Captain. Platoons contained three sections each with a Lieutenant in charge. Independent Companies also had medical staff, engineers or sappers, a transport section, a signal section and a wide range of skills in those selected to join them.
>
> Intended to operate independently of larger army groups, they carried a wider assortment of weapons including pistols, rifles, light machine guns, submachine guns, mortars, grenades and signal pistols. All members had to have completed basic training prior to recruitment and were expected to display initiative, a spirt of adventure, and superior military skills. Recruits had to be young and exceptionally fit physically. Other Army commanders were directed by Headquarters to send forth the names of only their best soldiers.

Each Independent Company undertook its commando training in two parts. First the officers and NCOs received six weeks of intensive training from instructional staff. In turn the officer cadre trained the ordinary ranks at No 1 and No 2 Camps for another intensive six weeks. Once this was completed the Independent Companies were formed from the soldiers who stayed the course. Training involved a strict timetable of lectures, field exercises, physical endurance tests, air-army co-operation exercises and amphibious naval exercises. A typical training day could include fieldcraft experience, demolitions, a hill climb and swim, physical exercises and weapons training. The day's program commenced at 8.00 am, finishing at 8.30 pm. Night lectures or a night march which included wading the Darby River in battle order might follow. A map-reading exercise would be combined with a cross-country treasure hunt or a battle exercise between opposing Australian and New Zealand Troops. Exercises were undertaken in full battle dress with full packs using live ammunition and simulating war conditions. Men were taught how to blow up buildings, bridges, communications facilities and army vehicles as well as how to use field radios and co-ordinate activities to meet up with pre-arranged air drops of food and ammunition. Camouflage was studied, as was ambush, these being backed up with lectures on commando tactics and infiltration techniques.

No 7 Infantry Training Centre was formally established in January 1941. In February the training of the Officer Cadre and NCOs commenced for the 2/1st Independent Company along with No 1 New Zealand Special Company. The 2/1st Independent Company was formed at Wilsons Promontory in May 1941 when training finished. On 7 July, it began the move to Sydney and on 12 July it left on the *Zealandia* for Rabaul and the islands north of New Guinea where, as part of 'Lark Force', it added to Australia's forward defence strategy. New Zealand No 1 Special Company did reach the war location Australian companies initially expected to go to – North Africa and the Middle East. Sadly, however, they never fought as a unit but were split up by General Fryberg around various other New Zealand units. Similarly, No 2 New Zealand Special Company never served as a unit, although some of its members did join and train commando units in the Pacific fighting the Japanese. It seems the Hush Hush Companies, as the New Zealanders called them, were too hot to handle for that country's military and political leaders, and as a consequence great military opportunity was lost to the allies.

Dr. Fox explained it this way, he said that once the threat to New Zealand and the South Pacific in general had eased, New Zealand's military priority remained the Middle East; in exchange for the thousands of US troops who garrisoned New Zealand and then fought in the South Pacific.

The troops that had trained as independent commandos were therefore absorbed into other units. Many of them converted to armored units, operating M4 Sherman tanks in Italy.

According to the book "Among Those Present", concerning the training the Fijians received, it stated:

> It was the immediate threat of a Japanese invasion of Fiji (a threat which happily never materialized) that gave the Fijians their long-awaited opportunity to serve overseas. In the course of an informal discussion on ways and means of defending Fiji, Major (now Lieut.-Colonel) Ratu Sukuna, a senior Chief who had fought with the French Foreign Legion in 1914, and Major "Nixie" Caldwell, M.C., a District Commissioner, hit upon the idea of forming a small number of "Commando" units. They quickly interested the military authorities in the project and the Commandos sprang into being. At the outset their intended role was purely defensive—to harry Japanese invasion forces and to counter infiltration tactics. The New Zealanders who were

appointed to train the Commandos found them apt pupils and soon discovered that they themselves had something to learn from the Fijian about the art of concealment. On one occasion, as part of their training, the Fijians were required to carry out a night attack on a camp of European troops. No bullets were to be used, but the Fijians were given pieces of chalk with which to make crosses on any objects the vicinity of which they managed to reach unobserved and which they could therefore claim to have "destroyed." The night wore on with no sign of the Fijians, and the Europeans congratulated themselves on having escaped attack. But when morning came they were mortified to find the entire camp liberally adorned with white crosses. To establish beyond cavil the extent of the Fijian's success, there was a clearly distinguishable cross on the trouser-seat of the Sergeant of the Guard!

The author of Among Those Present continued:

With this material to work on, the New Zealanders produced a band of guerrilla fighters which would have made residence in Fiji uncomfortable for any invader. Yet the Commandos, when they were attested, were perhaps the rawest recruits ever to don the King's uniform. They came, not from the regular battalions of the Fiji Infantry Regiment, but straight from their villages. They had never before handled any weapon more complicated than an axe or a cane-knife; and they could speak no English, so that early instruction had to be imparted painstakingly through interpreters. At first acquaintance, they stood in great awe of the bullet, not because of its power to inflict injury, but because its flight was invisible. This initial nervousness, however, soon vanished and before long they were carrying out manoeuvres unperturbed by live ammunition bursting round them. These and other difficulties experienced in the first stages of training were more than offset by the fact that the Fijians entered upon their military career already endowed with qualities which made them good soldiers. Their physique was excellent and they lost no time in mastering all the devices of unarmed combat. The course of training was tough, as all Commando courses are, but the Fijians were tougher; and they cheerfully survived many an exhausting march over the worst terrain that the rocky, forest-clad island of Viti Levu could provide.

This is very much in line with what Dick Tripp described of his father's instruction to the Fijian Commandos. It's also important to note that initially the Fijians were being trained for stay-behind operations. In his book Dick Tripp wrote:

Fitness was a top priority. In training, they would often go until they were exhausted in order to maintain maximum fitness. Dad was impressed with the journey one of his men made right around the main island of Fiji. This meant crossing rivers and going through some of the densest bush and mountainous parts of the island. He told me of one occasion, when in the Solomons, they had to escort a senior American officer some distance through the bush. He was not at all fit. When he wondered how they were going to get their supplies to their destination, he was amazed when Father told him they would be carrying them on their backs. They had to carry most of his equipment, and he perspired so much in the heat that every so often they had to stop and boil the billy to give him a cup of tea. Generally speaking, the Japanese were better fighters in the bush than the Americans, but none of them were as well trained as the Commandos. During their time in Fiji, the unit regularly took on groups of Americans to give them training. One aspect of their training was to be able to move silently in the bush. Father told me that it became so natural to move silently that he often wondered how they did it.

The Fijians were particularly good in the bush and had great eyesight. On one occasion in the Solomons, Dad was walking in front of a Fijian and they started to cross a stream on a log. The Fijian suddenly pulled him back. He had spotted someone at some distance. It took Father a while to see the man as just the side of his face was showing from behind a tree. They stalked him and found it was an American who had slipped out of camp to write a letter home. They sent him back!

Dick Tripp told another version of the X marks the spot story. I discovered there had been so many different variations of that story. Tripp wrote:

On one occasion during their training in Fiji, they decided to set up a mock attack on an American camp. The Americans had taken over the defence of Fiji in July 1942. They were told they would be attacked during the night and so were well prepared. The Fijians went right through the camp during the night. In the morning, one American who was on guard duty found a chalk cross on his water bottle that had been strapped to his waist. Father was not personally involved in the exercise and was talking to an officer in the camp in a tent at one point. When they turned around they noticed a piece of cardboard on the ground on which was written 'Time Bomb'. Not one Fijian was spotted.

Commandos From Oz

Members of an Independent Company, about to set off on a training exercise. Wilson's Promontory, Victoria January 1/4/1942.

In order to better understand what type of Commando training occurred at Wilson's Promontory we can gain some knowledge of that by taking a look at an eleven page document located in an Australian archive. It provides some insight into what subjects the Australian military thought Commandos who were going to be fighting in a jungle environment should know. It also outlined the role of an independent company.

In 1942 a Lieutenant Colonel George Matheson's No. 3 Independent Company, while garrisoning in New Caledonia as part of Robin Force utilized this document to instruct and train American troops in guerrilla warfare. Matheson was subsequently seconded to the American forces.

For his service on Guadalcanal in late 1942 he was awarded a United States Distinguished Service Cross, but was later killed on Bougainville on January 30th 1944.

The document titled "Notes On Commando Training" stated the following:

PRINCIPLES OF GUERILLA WARFARE

1. Select for attack targets vital to the enemy. Exploit his weak points, attack his HQ, centers of communication, supply routes, etc.
2. Force the enemy to weaken himself by taking precautions against threatened action. Make raids well behind his lines and at widely dispersed points and force him to use his man power on guard duties.
3. Do not engage in pitched battles. The object is to achieve maximum destruction with the minimum of losses, NOT to win ground.
4. Have superior information of the enemy. Never lose the initiative. Plan carefully.
5. Exploit surprise to the full. Move by night. Vary your tactics. Ambush.
6. Be cunning, ruthless, and audacious. Disguise. Use civil agents.
7. Maintain a high standard of training and discipline. Each man must be able to operate independently, but he must also be able to carry out his orders implicitly.

CONCEALMENT AND CAMOUFLAGE

1. On soft ground or in short grass place heel down first. On hard ground or in long grass place toe first. In scrub lift high and put down flat.
2. To move quietly you must move slowly.
3. The sound of talking, particularly of hissing s's, or coughing or sneezing betrays more easily than the sound of movement. Cigarette fumes are easily noticed.

4. Beware of noisy or shiny equipment. Deaden matches.
5. Advance up wind if possible. Use cover of local grounds.
6. Keep sun or moon behind you. Avoid skylines. Use shadows. Merge into broken background.
7. Make no sudden movement. If observed, freeze or drop imperceptibly, never retreat hastily.
8. Avoid isolated or conspicuous cover. Look around or through cover, not over it.
9. Hide trail by moving through water. For silence swim breast stroke. Normally take off boots but not clothes. Float equipment on log or in waterproof sheet.
10. Stop frequently to listen. Put ear to ground or knife in ground. Sound travels best uphill or across water, particularly downstream.
11. Do not carry identifiable objects.
12. Camouflage clothing and equipment. Dye is better than paint which is noisy. Camouflage boldly. Break up outlines. Use darker colors above and lighter below. Blend with dominant color of countryside. Mud and water are substitutes for dye.
13. Darken face and hands. Hide luminous watch faces.
14. Conserve your energy. Only crawl when necessary.
15. When crawling, keep head and bottom down and arms and legs flat on the ground. Trail rifle at your side or place across your elbows.
16. At night follow a path by feeling with your feet.

KEEPING DIRECTION

1. Look back frequently to remember route.
2. Study track of animals, men, and vehicles.
3. Study how to blaze a trail or to follow a blazed trail.
4. Use direction of prevailing wind. Use sound of frogs, sea, railways. Use smells – smoke, paint.
5. At night use skylines.
6. Use watch to find north from the sun. (Remember to point 12 at the sun). Find south from the stars (Extend the tail of the southern cross 4 ½ times).
7. Be proficient with compass. Know the length of your pace.

JUDGING DISTANCE

1. At 300 yds the outline of a face becomes blurred. At 600 yds the head appears as dot, and the body tapers noticeably.
2. An object will look closer than it really is if the sun is behind the observer. The object is different in color from background, or the intervening ground is flat and or an even slope.

PATROLS

1. Before setting out a patrol, commander must be given complete orders, such as: Task, time to leave and return, pass and counter-pass, prisoners and wounded. He must obtain as much information as possible, study the map and the ground if possible. He must then make his plan and pass on as much as possible to his men.
2. The choice of a route will be a decision between the best tactical route and the easiest route.
3. Time must be allowed for halts, scouting, and unforeseen delay. Remember movement is much slower at night.
4. Take as few men as is necessary to fulfill the task. Reconnaissance is often best carried out by 2 or 3 men.
5. Formation depends on the terrain. The conflicting factors are control and concealment.
6. Patrols must have an observation plan to cover all directions and including all members.
7. There must be a plan for action in the event of surprise.
8. Work scouts in pairs. Scouts are responsible for keeping contact with the patrol.
9. Have a get-away man in rear or to a flank whose duty it is to report back to his unit in the event of plans going astray.
10. Each man must know his place in the patrol and who is near him.
11. Develop a system of quiet signals – by hand clicks. If verbal messages are passed, allow time for them to reach the rear and be acknowledged. Check up by numbering from rear to front.

12. Responsibility for keeping contact is normally from front to rear. Straggling must be avoided. It may be necessary to hold rifles, hand, or clothing of man in front.
13. Stop frequently to listen. Men should automatically take cover at halts though they continue observation until otherwise ordered.
14. Do not open fire prematurely. Wait for enemy to reveal himself. Control fire. If all men fire simultaneously it will be harder for an enemy to place individuals.
15. Use surprise where possible. Use ambush in attack or defence. If surprise is not possible use automatic or rifles to cover advance of main body and to distract attention.
16. Prisoners must be handled roughly – searched, bound and gagged if not killed.
17. In making a plan never forget action to be taken immediately after objective is attained.

SENTRIES

1. The choice of a position will be a decision between security and communications.
2. Sentries' positions and the approaches to them should be concealed. They should be changed frequently.
3. A sentry must not challenge until he is nearly certain that an enemy is approaching or cannot miss the camp. Wait till he is close and speak clearly. Avoid firing. Kill with rifle butt for preference and quietly rouse men.
4. Sentries should if possible work in pairs so that one can investigate or report without post being left. Relieve alternately.
5. Sentry changing, reports, and alarms must be arranged to work smoothly and quietly, e.g. string communications.

BIVOUACS

1. Considerations in choosing a site are concealment, particularly of smoke, water, firewood, protection from weather. Avoid obvious sites, such as streams.
2. Each man must keep his belongings together in a definite place so that he can move at a moment's notice.
3. Making and breaking camp are the most vulnerable periods.
4. If a fire is to be used at all, it should be distant from the sleeping site.
5. Sentries can be augmented with booby traps.
6. A bivouac should be left without trace.

TRAVELING DISTANCES

1. Start day's journey slowly. Make pace on level or easy going. Take shorter steps up or down hill. Breathe deeply and move rhythmically. Keep men advised of next halt.
2. Keep body and clothes clean. Wearing wet clothes will have no ill effects.
3. Essential medical gear is: Needle for blisters, APC for headaches and sleeplessness. Iodine or Dettol for cuts. Oil of cloves with zinc oxide for toothache. Elastic bandage for sprains. Elastoplast for blisters or sores.
4. Hobnails are essential for rough or mountainous country. Adjust packs so that there is not undue strain on the shoulders nor constriction of the chest. Wear thick socks. Soap or powder prevents chafing.
5. Patrol leader must ensure that work and food is shared fairly particularly when going is hard.
6. Packs should be allotted equally except that scouts should travel light.
7. Each man should be a self-contained unit in arms, ammunition, rations and sleeping gear.
8. For endurance, order of importance is drink, sleep, food.
9. Sleep off the ground if possible. Sleeping bags are much better than blankets for weight but may become infested with vermin.

10. Eat and drink frequently in small quantities. Have largest meal at the beginning of the day. Immerse body in water whenever possible.
11. Sugar is important energy. Add salt to water in heat.
12. Concentrated food saves carrying unnecessary weight: sardines, honey, chocolate, raisins, oatmeal, dried fruit, candy. Hot food is only refreshing, not essential.

OBSERVATION

1. O.P.'s may be sited for general observation over all ground visible or for a special purpose such as a raid on an installation.
2. In siting O.P's avoid conspicuous and obvious places. Have covered approach. Make O.P.'s as comfortable as possible. If possible, observer should be relieved frequently as eye strain is felt after half an hour.
3. Search ground with binoculars and examine detail with telescope. Use telescope with either eye and rest one eye by covering it with hand instead of closing it. Keep binoculars and telescope clean and dry.
4. Observer's Report:

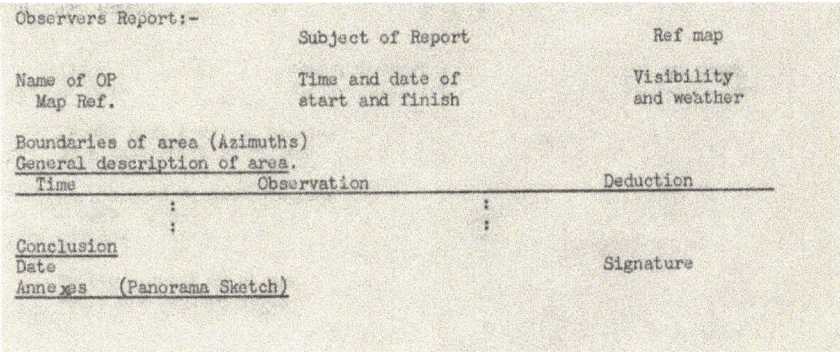

Observers Report:-		
	Subject of Report	Ref map
Name of OP Map Ref.	Time and date of start and finish	Visibility and weather
Boundaries of area (Azimuths) General description of area.		
Time	Observation	Deduction
:	:	
:	:	
Conclusion Date Annexes (Panorama Sketch)		Signature

AMBUSH

1. Choose a site where banks or vehicles are likely to bunch and where ambush is encountered suddenly.

2. Attackers should be concealed from view and from fire. They should be able to open fire at point blank range and to reach the target with grenades and incendiaries.
3. Attackers must be able to cover the whole area with fire and must be prepared for the enemy to scatter. The enemy will probably face the direction of fire making himself vulnerable from behind.
4. Ambushes must be well planned. Have a scout to give warning of approach of target and subsequently, if necessary, of reinforcements.
5. Opening and ending action must be simultaneous and clearly signaled. Be prepared to withdraw if resistance too great.
6. Remains should be looted and destroyed. Men searching dead and damaged vehicles must be covered.
7. In ambushing vehicles, tanks, or trains the convoy may be stopped by actually destroying one of them or merely by stopping one by an apparently natural block.
8. Ambush of troops is more difficult than of a convoy. However booby traps and hit and run ambushes break down morale.
9. Scouts should be allowed to pass unmolested but should be dealt with when the attack has developed.

PANORAMA SKETCHING

1. Sketches may be drawn entirely by eye or with the aid of ruler, "window", or compass.
2. Use ruler or window to measure off view horizontally and vertically. Window is board--with oblong shaped hole cut out of center and squared with cotton. Hold ruler or window so that it covers sector and always the same distance from the eye (by fixing in ground or attaching string and holding between the teeth.)
3. Square paper proportionately though no necessary equal to divisions or ruler or window. Except in mountainous country exaggerate the vertical scale.
4. Use compass to fix boundaries of sector and prominent points.
5. In drawing a sketch, after deciding sector to be included, first fix prominent points, then fill in detail.

6. Follow principles of perspective. Keep drawing simple. Every line should mean something. Draw nearer objects bolder than distant. If possible draw actual representation – otherwise use conventional signs and shading.
7. A panorama sketch should have the same notation as an observer's report. In addition, write in the azimuths of the left and right edges of the sketch. Also, outstanding points should be indicated by an arrow and a vertical line and description written along it.

FIELD SKETCHING

1. Guerilla troops must be able to read maps, sketches and air photos. They must also be proficient with a compass and at drawing field sketches. It is often essential to have an accurate sketch of a target and/or of routes to it.
2. The methods of drawing sketches are: Plane table, compass traverse, eye and memory, air photo; the following points apply to sketching in general and compass traversing in particular.
3. The first essential is to fix a framework of points correctly orientated spaced, and heighted. To save going over the ground twice, detail is filled in at the same time.
4. Points can be fixed by:
   Azimuth and distance from a known point.
   Distance from two or more known points.
   Azimuths from two or more known points.
   Eye.
5. Heights can be determined from horizontal distance and angle of slope using trigonometrical tables or formula:

$$\text{Altitude} = \frac{\text{Angle of Slope x base}}{60}$$

6. Choose scale carefully to give necessary detail and to fit on paper.
7. A sketch should show: Subject, north points, legend of unusual conventional signs used, methods of plotting, scale of yards in words, as fraction and scale line, contour intervals (if any) and method of obtaining heights, date, time, and weather, and signature.
8. A traverse is a sequence of measured distances or legs from station to station, each of which lies on a measured azimuth.
9. If possible traverse between two known points or else close on starting points. Then if there is an error of closure it can be spread over each leg of the traverse.
10. Data is usually recorded in a field book and plotted later. Preferably plot out squared or lined paper with protractor and ruler. Set out field book as follows:

Azimuth	Left	Legs (Yds)	Right	Height or slope
:	:	:	:	
:	:	:	:	

RECONNAISSANCE

1. It is usually better to observe from a fixed position than to keep constantly on the move.
2. Learn to notice detail. Negative information is often of value. Exact timings are important.
3. A reconnaissance report should show: to whom it is made out, what it is about, map references, time and date, and signature.
4. Distinguish clearly between observation and deduction. Note: What, When, Where, How, Why.
5. Information must get back to where it is wanted and IN TIME.

ORDERS

1. Note guide for sequence and wording: They are, We are, We will, You will, I will be.

2. Orders for guerilla work may often have to be given in great detail. These should be given in annexes. Note: sketches and diagrams, organization table showing what each individual man will wear, what he will carry, where he will go, what he will do.
3. Orders must be clear, complete, and concise.
4. In giving orders, do not forget: R.V. if unit scatters, what to do after a successful action, pass and counter pass, synchronised watches.

MESSAGES

1. Note sequence: To—From—Text of message—Time—
2. If possible write a message and write it clearly. Before giving a verbal message, think it out. Have messenger repeat it back correctly once or twice before setting out.

SIGNALS

1. Guerilla troops should know morse and semaphore and be able to use the radio.
2. Service signaling lamps and flags are not necessary but may be improved.
3. Semaphore is easiest learned and quickest to send in field. However, it involves exposure and cannot be used at night.
4. Morse is quickest learned by groups of like and opposite symbols.
5. For speed a prearranged code is of value.
6. Note that, particularly in close country, runners are the most reliable means of communication.

WEAPONS

1. Guerilla troops must have a complete knowledge of the use and care of their weapons, and a general understanding of

weapons in general so that they can make use of captured material.

2. They must be first class shots, from sniping to instinctive fire and they must be proficient at judging distance, recognising targets, and fire control.

3. The rifle particularly the automatic rifle is an excellent weapon. Note that a rifle can be fired with accuracy aimed instinctively from the hip. The bayonet is very valuable for close quarters though the scabbard is an encumbrance in silent movement.

4. Grenades are excellent for close fighting as in the jungle or in streets. Rifles to be used as grenade dischargers should be specifically bound to avoid damage.

5. Grenades can be used effectively by tying 4 to 6 feet above the ground and detonating by means of a string hid to the pin and either pulled by the attacker or the enemy.

6. The pistol is only useful for self-defence such as in the case of scouts or demolition parties.

7. The sub-machine gun is excellent for close quarters but remember that the ammunition has to be carried.

8. In addition to its use at long ranges for covering or distracting fire, the light machine gun is very effective aimed instinctively from the hip.

9. Heavier weapons are used by guerillas but the problem is to have a means of hiding or withdrawing in the event of counter-action.

10. Snipers should make themselves comfortable.

11. Firing at night must be instinctive or else aided by tracer ammunition, phosphorescence on sights, or illumination from flames or incendiaries.

12. The long bolo knife is good for hand to hand fighting. The knife or truncheon are best for silent elimination. Unarmed combat is an essential for self-defence.

13. Weapons can be effectively augmented by missiles improvised from explosives.

14. Silencers can eliminate noise of discharge but when bullet travels faster than sound (1080 ft per sec), when passing an object it makes a report which is not affected by the silencer.

15. Firing at a man, aim at a spot mid-way between the navel and the throat. Do not follow him with rifle but train rifle ahead and take pressure on trigger.

EXPLOSIVE CHARGES

1. An explosion is a sudden change from solid to gas with resultant tremendous expansion.
2. The rate of expansion varies:
   Instantaneous – Detonation
   Fast – Cutting Charge
   Intermediate – shattering charge
   Slow – lifting charge
   Very slow – burning.
3. A charge consists of fuse, detonator, primer, and high explosive (H.E.)
4. Means of lighting fuse are (Initiators): Match or cigarette end, fuzee, fuse igniter, percussion cap. Only slow burning (Safety) fuses may be lit with a match.
5. Some explosives will be detonated without a primer but their rate of expansion is then lower.
6. Charges may be connected by detonating fuse of H.E. (Cordtex) which requires a detonator to initiate it.
7. Fuse and detonator may be replaced by electric detonator connected by leads to batter, light mains, or exploder.

SAFETY PRECAUTIONS

1. Do not smoke near explosives. Do not use metal instruments. Keep detonators separate.
2. In practice keep away and look up. Blowing trees of ground – 300 yds, concrete or metal – 500 yds, brick – 300 to 1500 yds. Post sentries.
3. Store H.E. and detonating fuse underground but give them air. Keep incendiaries and detonators separate.

PREPARING AND LAYING CHARGES

1. Beforehand: Decide on side of charge and stores required. Inspect explosives. Test fuse. Prepare charge in portable units. Waterproof.
2. Beforehand: or at objective: Prepare length of fuse, one end square, one slanting. Crimp detonator onto fuse. Place primer in charge. But do NOT connect detonator and primer to charge.
3. At the objective:
   Lay charge.
   Place detonator with fuse into primer or charge. Secure with packing or with insulating tape.
   Strike match box against match placed against slanting end of fuse.
   Retire.
4. Electrical methods – Beforehand.
   Examine cable and see if circuit will pass through. Test exploder or battery over length of cable to be used and actually blow the number of detonators to be used.
   Prepare for an alternate method of firing.
5. Electric methods – at objective.
   Keep leads of cable away from source of current until charge is laid and personnel clear.

PLACING CHARGES

1. Essentials are:
   CONTACT with object and several parts of charge.
   TAMP wherever and as much as possible.
   LLR – Explosive follows the line of least resistance.
2. Bridges – Wood and steel. As bearers are separated, blowing one pier will bring down two spans. Bearers may also be blown but steel girders will be difficult. In blowing a pier, stagger chargers on piles and blow inwards to get fall from weight of bridge.
3. Bridges – Steel and concrete. Blowing a pier may not bring down both spans owing to reinforced concrete webbing.

Blowing bearers, place charge one-third distance of length to get fall from weight. Cut on slant. To blow abutments usually requires a lot of H.E. In blowing girders, follow same principles as for blowing bearers. It is difficult to blow a girder off a pivot because of tension. Use scissors charges on cables.

4. Bridges – Masonry. Blow at crown by digging or on underslung plank. Blow abutments with mined or borehold charges. Look for fissures.

5. Roads. Blow by means of mined charge under culvert, in retaining wall or embankment, use slow explosive. Use camouflet for rapid road erasing. Improvise with iron bar. This method is difficult in wet, sandy or rocky soil. When blowing at an embankment, place charges both horizontally and vertically. More than one charge with craters over-lapping is preferable.

6. Rails. Attack points and crossings, tunnels, bridges. In cutting rails, blow alternate joints so that one end of each rail is damaged. If possible unscrew fish plates first.

7. Go for maximum inconvenience – that will take the longest to repair.

8. Avoid unnecessary work. Look for essentials and ease of carrying out job. Use other methods if they are simpler – fire, flood, sledge hammer, saw.

CALCULATION OF CHARGES

1. Given the dimensions and composition of an object, charges can be calculated from formulae. (See Engineering Manuals)

2. Rough rules are: Untamped, H.E. cuts its own thickness of metals, 20 times its thickness of masonry, 4 times its thickness of wood, and half its thickness of concrete. However the cross-section must be increased proportionately with the thickness.

3. Blowing rails, one lb. of H.E. will cut a rail and 3 lbs. will cut both fishplate and rail if placed on the side. 3 lbs. of H.E. will cut a rail placed underneath. 10 lbs. of H.E. placed

not more than 4 inches from rail under ballast will cut the rail.

4. Placed mined charges at a depth a quarter of the proposed crater. In average ground 50 lbs. of H.E. will blow a 20 ft crater.

5. Where reconnaissance is inadequate or demolition to be hastily or inexpertly carried out, add 50 to 100% to be certain. This will apply to most guerilla operations.

PORTABLE CHARGES

1.   Wrap and tie up charges securely. Arrange so that they are easy to carry, noiseless, neutral in color, and if necessary waterproof.

2. Ensure quick fixing and interconnection and firing.

3. An average weight of explosives should not be greater than 25 to 30 bls. It is often necessary to divide charge into parts which, however, must be capable of interconnection. Note use of cordtex. PHE is useful for connecting charges over short distances or for improving contact.

4. Electric charges are difficult as portable charges owing to the weight of the initiator and the intricacy of connecting the leads.

5. If no waterproof containers are available, improvise with tires, finger stalls, insulating tape.

6. Slap type service explosives can be cut and nailed.

MISSILES, INCENDIARIES, BOOBY TRAPS

1. Missiles may be service equipment such as the hand grenade, anti-tank grenade or they may be improvised as the jam tin bomb.

2. A charge under a pile of rocks is the ill-provided guerilla's substitute for the anti-tank mine.

3. Some incendiaries are the M.L. flare, the thermite bomb, tyesules, smoke candles. However, the Molotov cocktail is effective against vehicles and fires can be started, if slowly,

with sacking soaked in petroleum or other high inflammable. Very light cartridges and tracer bullets will also act as incendiaries.

4. The time pencil enables a charge to be laid but not fired till after a given period. There are also more complicated devices, some electrically operated. Improvised methods are the alarm clock, bucket of water, etc.

5. There are mechanical devices for setting charges as booby traps. Note the simple pull, pressure, and release switches (used in conjunction with trip wire).

6. Booby traps can be used offensively or defensively. They have a great demoralizing effect. They are best used in constricted localities and in dense concentration. Variety is added by bluffing with dummies or double bluffing with dummies with live charges underneath.

7. Explosives designed against personnel must be placed to get greatest fragmentation effect. The grenade with string attached to pin and the anti-personnel (A.P.) switch are best.

SABOTAGE

1. The objects of sabotage are to cause damage to vitally important targets and to obtain the maximum harassing effect.

2. Personnel.
   Destroy HQ. Capture documents.
   Snipe or knife sentries and stragglers.
   Set fire to barracks and cinemas (Remember to remove fire extinguishers).
   Start avalanches or marching columns.
   Start rumors.

3. Supplies and utilities.
   Burn or blow up ammunition, gas, petrol, or food dumps. Put acid or disinfectant in fodder or food. Alternatively poison or bacilli. Put salt, disinfectant or paraffin in water supplies or overchlorinate them. Blow up or block sewer systems. Burn or let flow petrol or add linseed or crude oil.

4. Transport and communications.

Burn, smash, or blow up aircraft, trucks, tanks.
Run petrol engines at full speed without water or oil.
Let water out of steam engines and stoke up. Blow
cylinders or boilers. Blow up railway tracks. Jam tracks.
Cut signal wires. Block roads by blowing craters, digging
trenches, felling trees. Destroy bridges. Smash up wireless
stations. Remember to put off master switch. Cut telegraph
lines. Alter connection of wires. Burn mails or destroy with
acid.

5. Industry and Production.
    Run riot with sledge hammer but beware of electricity.
    Shoot highly skilled personnel.
    Burn warehouses.
    Throw a spanner into turbines. Pour emery filings into
    lubricators. Break power lines.
    Start bush-fires and floods.

COOPERATION WITH OTHER ARMS & SERVICE

Guerilla warfare is primarily to be fought by specialized infantry troops.
However they can be effectively supported by other arms of the army and
by the air corps and the navy. Preparation by bombardment, transport, and
supply are the chief objects of supporting units.

TRAINING

1. Training of guerilla troops should cover the subjects given
    above, but the scope is unlimited. Particular emphasis
    should be placed on patrol work and cross-country
    movement.

2. The only effective method of instruction is to conduct
    realistic exercises and field firing practices. Practice is
    everything.

MODERN WAR TRAINING IS TOUGH, STRENUOUS, AND REALISTIC

THIS war has been said to be a war of materials and equipment, of aeroplanes, tanks, motorised vehicles, and artillery, and of automatic weapons. It has developed almost entirely into a war of movement, with the blitz theory as the basis and the method of infiltration as an adjunct to turn any static position. Exploitation of the blitz weapons and tactics have paid huge dividends to the Axis Powers, while the Allies have paid dearly for their unpreparedness in equipment and their failure to realise the trends of development of warfare.

Britain, the Empire, and France entered the war still wrapped in old traditions. They had vaguely glimpsed modern developments, but their ideas and training were based on the pattern of fighting from prepared positions, as in the last war. They had not learned the lessons of the Spanish civil war, and did not learn much from Germany's devastating campaign against Poland. It took the French debacle to drive the lesson home that modern war meant movement, planes, motorised equipment, and automatic weapons, and that the day of the foot-slogging, rifle-carrying soldier, fighting from trenches, was over.

Once that lesson went home it meant complete revision of all training methods. It was shown that blitz warfare was a tough business and that tough men were needed. It demanded that even the many specialists should have a high degree of fitness, and automatically the parade - ground grind and route marches had to give way almost completely to tougher and more realistic training.

And so today the first aim in Australian military training, as in British training, is to make troops as physically fit as possible. Physical fitness has become the basis of training, because speed, endurance, and manœuvrability are the prime assets for modern soldiers. These are the qualities which guerillas, commandos, and paratroops must have. For this reason every man for these units is specially selected. Therefore the previous history of each man is sought, so that the best use can be made of him. Athletes are most favoured for these units, but country youths are almost as popular, for their knowledge of fieldcraft makes them invaluable. The call for the Army generally today is for young men, but the Army does not like them too young for these units.

Military training is no longer carried out in a leisurely way. There is a desperate urgency to use every hour to the fullest advantage. Every man is put through gruelling training in every type of combat he might use or encounter on active service. He must know the moves and the answers and be able to accomplish them better

than the enemy. He is encouraged to use all-in methods, and employ his boots, fists, or elbows if they will avail him better than weapons in overcoming opponents. Apart from his knowledge of the normal weapons of modern warfare—rifle, automatic, bayonet—he must have all the science of a boxer and tricks of a wrestler. He must also be adept in silent killing, so that sentries can be quietly removed.

All this involves considerable train-

ing and practice. First the troops are toughened with physical training, which actually remains a part of each day's routine. In unarmed combat they learn particularly efficient and unpleasant methods of countering an armed opponent. Every man also must go through the assault course daily. This involves realistic charges on enemy positions, during which they have to clear barbed-wire traps, creeks, fences, and other obstacles to reach a firing pit, while disposing of enemy posts on the way by rifle fire and the bayonet. These assaults are done in small parties, and live ammunition and respirators are used to make it even more realistic.

Every man must know how to handle explosives, for blowing up of bridges, ammunition dumps, tanks, and so on. All are trained with tommy-guns and hand grenades, and in field craft and camouflage. They are taught how to find their way unerring through wild bush country, how to cross streams, how to infiltrate, how to ambush the enemy, and how to stalk him. In this respect they must have the skill and astuteness of a Red Indian scout, the bush lore of an Australian aborigine. They must learn to move silently and unseen, and to know all the sights and sounds of the Australian bush.

Today these highly trained men are used in units of 25 to 50 men, and they might divide up into groups of 5 or 10 to accomplish various tasks,

THE SPIDER HOLE, which is invisible at a few yards, consists of a full length pit, covered with wire netting, inside which the guerilla waits armed with some type of weapon. Excavated earth is placed in waterproof sheets and removed ... to leave no new earth visible.

GUERILLAS MAKING A SURPRISE ATTACK over a roof, after having previously thrown smoke bombs to cover their advance. For this and other special work, they are provided with what they term "creeper boots," consisting of very pliable leather top boots, with heavily ribbed rubber soles.

An article from the Australasian, April 25th 1942 which described
Commando "Type" Training and the attributes that make a Commando.

83

STALKING THE STALKERS is another aspect of guerilla training. This requires the skill and astuteness of an Indian scout, and a complete understanding of bush lore. The men must move silently and unseen, and must find their way unerring in the path of the "enemy."

HOW TO POUNCE ON OPPONENTS: These fights are most realistic, and are too much like the real thing to be comfortable, even for spectators, who become alarmed at the way the guerillas manhandle each other. In the case illustrated here, the guerilla has shot the leading "enemy" stalker, and is instantaneously tackling the second.

DESTRUCTION OF A TANK: The tank is first put out of action by a mine, operated by a guerilla in a spider hole. Then, as the track is broken, making the tank helpless, they throw smoke bombs to cover their approach while the tank crew is unable to use its guns effectively. Final destruction of the tank may be carried out with a sticky bomb, stuck on the side by one of the intrepid guerillas. Either the crew is destroyed or it surrenders.

while still maintaining contact with the unit. Every man can act independently if circumstances demand it, hence resource and initiative are highly cultivated. These units are taught to travel light and to get their food from the country as they go. They include a high proportion of officers, for it might often become necessary to split a unit of 50 men up into 5 or 10 parties. These sections are then led by lieutenants, sergeants, or even corporals. It might almost be said it is developing into a section leaders' war.

This realistic training is being given now, not only to the AIF, but to the AMF, garrison battalion men, the VDC, and to other groups who might be called upon in an emergency. Methods employed by the enemy in every sphere are constantly studied and reported on. Reports come from British, American, Chinese, Russian, as well as from our own sources.

Counter tactics are then devised and applied.

Obstacles which were once regarded as impassable by troops without special equipment are now overcome. For instance, commando troops have devised a way of getting over barbed wire barricades by the skilful use of men's web equipment and using men's bodies as stepping stones. Special boots enable them to scale walls and go over buildings. As so much of modern military manœuvres takes place at night, men are trained to move, act, and keep contact with one another in the dark.

The soldiers in our armies today know that the lessons of Malaya, Java, the Philippines, the Middle East, Russia, and China have been put into practice, and it is certain that when the testing time comes—Australians will not be found wanting in the ingenuity, skill, and endurance needed to repel the enemy and drive him back in defeat. This arduous training of today might easily be the deciding factor once the Allies match their enemies in mechanised and automatic equipment.

GUERILLAS MUST STAY PUT — MOTIONLESS: Training teaches them patience, and the patience of Job is at times essential for Aussies.

WHILE THE TANK IS IN DISTRESS, a relief party is coming to its assistance, crossing a stream with weapons carried aloft.

Pacific Commandos

Six South Pacific Scouts with their New Zealand leader, July 15th 1945.
Source: Combined Arms Research Library.

I thought it might be best to quote some passages from the books Pacific Commandos, and The Pacific, in order to provide a better understanding of what the Fijians had to undergo as far as their Commando type training was concerned.

According to Larsen in his book Pacific Commandos:

> The commandos worked almost entirely with American forces, and reference is sometimes made to the work of the allied units. Comparisons with the main body of troops are unavoidable if the reader is to gain an impression of the specialized nature of the commando unit's work; but it must be borne in mind that the Americas were carrying out a different role from that of the commandos. For instance, the Americans used vast quantities of

ammunition on areas where Japanese were suspected to be: this method saved risking lives, and was sound military principle when an abundance of ammunition could be supplied. The commandos, however, could not use this method of clearing a way for an advance because they would have lost their greatest advantage—mobility—if they had carried a lot of ammunition: thus their method was to hold their fire and try to make every shot count.

In the chapter concerning why Commandos had been formed in Fiji, Larsen wrote:

December 8th, 1941, (New Zealand time) was a very significant date for the people of New Zealand, but much more for their relatives garrisoned in the Fiji Islands of the Pacific. The subsequent expansion south of the Japanese forces was the cause that led to the unusual experiences in the otherwise mundane lives of the New Zealanders mentioned in this narrative.

At the "Washington Conference in 1922, Great Britain and America agreed to the expansion of the Japanese Navy within certain limits. However, this Navy grew and grew until, in 1941, Japan had absolute supremacy in the north-west Pacific. By the early months of 1942, the Japanese had had a succession of victories (though mostly unresisted), which brought them as far south as Guadalcanal in the Solomon Islands: they had also established bases in the Gilbert Group, less than eight hours flying time from Fiji. At this period the British Navy was being kept busy in the Atlantic and Mediterranean, while the American Navy had not yet recovered from the Pearl Harbour attack.

The combination of these factors placed Fiji in a very critical position for several months while the United States was organizing her forces. Fiji possesses, among other things, two good harbours and two airfields: its geographical position put it astride the sea and air routes of all supplies transported from America to Australia and New Zealand. Thus, apart from the use Japan could make of Fiji as a base, the enemy was well aware that to deny the Allies the use of Fiji would mean disaster to New Zealand and Australian life lines.

The small number of troops garrisoned in Fiji was reinforced with all the men New Zealand could spare, or divert from her commitments in the Middle East. It also became necessary to mobilise Fijian manpower where practicable. Even with the reinforcements the Force was not large enough to maintain defensive positions at all points of the Fiji Group, so it was divided and troops stationed at each end of Viti Levu, the main island of the Group. These troops were to defend the important strategical points of Suva Harbour and Naurosi Airfield in the east, and Lautoka Harbour and Nandi Airfield in the west. The rest of the island was covered by mechanized patrols; but as there was only one road winding for three hundred miles around the island, and as visibility was restricted because of the dense bush on all sides, the position was not entirely satisfactory. The Third New Zealand Division therefore decided to set up commando units at all the most inaccessible spots between the fixed defence positions. The commandos were to oppose, with delaying action, enemy landings from sea or air, and to deny the enemy the use of the road until the main Allied forces could be brought into position.

The island was divided into three sectors—Western, Eastern, and Southern—and in April, 1942, commando companies were formed in each of these sectors.

The name "commando" was used in its older sense and applied to these units because they were independent companies, almost self-contained. They were more strictly speaking, "guerrillas," for had the Japanese actually landed in Fiji they would have adopted a harassing role; and while they were not large enough forces to prevent a landing, they would have been sharp thorns in the sides of an invading enemy.

This was ultimately what they had been trained for by the New Zealanders prior to the arrival of the Americans. They were being trained as stay-behind operatives.

Larsen's' book contains a chapter in which he discussed the history and background of Fiji. There are some very interesting tidbits of information in there but I won't recount all of it because it is not the primary focus of the book. I am primarily concerned with training the Fijian's Commandos had received. The main passage of note is the one in which Larsen described the working relationship between the New Zealanders and the Fijians:

> Ever since King Thakombau ceded his territory, the Fijians have respected the British in these islands, and they show exceptional loyalty to those in authority. They look to the white man for guidance, and they have become used to regarding the Europeans as their bosses. Before the soldiers arrived in Fiji, no white man of any standing in the community did manual labour; and when the Fijians found New Zealand soldiers working beside them on the wharves and on defence works around the coast, they could not understand the new relationship. At first the natives thought that the soldiers were of a low class, but they soon detected the difference between the soldiers sincere friendliness and the patronizing friendliness of some of the local Europeans. The New Zealand soldiers have since become so popular with the Fijians that the local residents fear that a great deal more will be expected of the white man after the war; and some fear that the soldiers have upset the traditional white man's prestige.

The white people in Suva find the tropical life very easy. Thee average man can afford native servants to wait on him, and some exalt themselves in a temporary superiority of which the Fijian is fully aware but powerless to combat. Class consciousness and colour consciousness are inevitably accentuated in such a small community, in spite of the efforts of some administrators to overcome them.

As the commandos were to work closely with the Fijians, it was necessary to break down some of the traditional barriers; this was not easy. The Fijian liked being bossed by good leaders, but the subservient kind of discipline was not the kind the commandos wished to develop; they wanted self-reliant scouts who would show initiative and volunteer information without being diffident about approaching their senior officers. The Fijians take note of every little action of the white man, and the commandos had to be most meticulous in their conduct.

Whatever the mixture of attitudes, the New Zealanders set out to train the Fijians with the utmost goodwill emanating from both races.

The chapter on Setting Up Commando Headquarters And Outposts is also relevant. Larsen stated:

Volunteers from the infantry battalions provided the New Zealand officers and non-commissioned officers for commando units. On the dry and less thickly wooded side of Viti Levu the Western Commando covered its territory on horseback: this company was mainly composed of New Zealanders with a few Fijian guide-interpreters attached. The Eastern and Southern commandos, however, worked entirely on foot, and these two units were mainly composed of Fijians who were trained by the New Zealanders in the remote villages. The mounted unit selected men of short or light build and with rough riding experience; while the Eastern and Southern units selected the strongest built New Zealanders they could find, consequently most of these were big men. Character was a very important consideration too; the commandos were to uphold the white man's prestige whilst living with the natives, and they had to carry out the work without direct supervision. Many of the NCOs had been farmers in civil life, and because of their individualism, they had a strong desire to use their initiative, to break away from the usual army routine, and to seek the freer life of the commandos in spite of the concomitant hardships of isolation. Several men who were chosen for these units had had training with a special company in Australia a year previously. The commando training of these men had included hard living combined with advanced instruction in the use of explosives, field wireless sets and other technical devices. When the special companies returned to New Zealand the idea of commando units was shelved and the men were transferred to various other formations. It was a fortunate coincidence that a few of these men were in infantry battalions in Fiji just when their special knowledge was required. The Southern Commando secured three of these men and their instructional services proved most valuable.

The mention of the training with the special company in Australia, would have been the same training which occurred at Wilsons Promontory. Larsen continued:

There exists in the minds of experienced military men, two strongly opposed views on the desirability of commando formations. The enthusiastic officers point out the advantages of selecting the most capable soldiers, giving them a great amount of independence, grouping them in such a way as to develop, and the maximum initiative within each man, and thereby creating a small mobile and formidable company which can strike the enemy where he least expects. The opposing contention is that the gain in efficiency of a small section of a force, say five per cent., does not compensate for loss of spirit and feeling of inferiority engendered in the other ninety-five per cent of the troops when their efforts are unfairly compared. Added to this objection to commando units is the relative independence that they develop, and the fear that they may get beyond the disciplinary control of the headquarters of the whole force. Each of these opposite opinions could be justified under differing circumstances, and the latter view may have been a factor in the decision made in New Zealand in 1941, to disband the special companies when they returned after a very successful period of advanced and costly training in Australia. In Fiji, however, circumstances were such that commando or guerrilla units were not only an obvious solution, but also the only solution, to the problem of covering large areas with the few men available.

In another chapter Larsen described the training of the Commandos, he wrote:

The chief item on the first week's syllabus was close order drill, and the Fijian soldiers learned the English words of command as they went through the actions. They did not learn the literal meanings of the words like "eyes right." Or "attention;" but by the end of the week they knew what to do when they heard the commands uttered—especially when the sergeant's tone of voice left little room for doubt.

The only flat piece of ground on which to drill the men was the village green, where every man, woman, and dog turned out to watch and giggle at the soldiers marching. This did not make things any easier for the NCO's, and the natives' childishness exasperated them at times. The first day's work was taken up in teaching the Fijians to form three straight lines, something they had never done before, and it was generally necessary to hold one man still while someone else placed the next man in position.

The Fijians were disappointed that their uniforms were not available for the first training period, and that they had to use bamboo sticks instead of rifles in their arms drill. The NCOs lent their rifles to the Fijians who took turns in cleaning and oiling them and thus learning the parts. By the time half a dozen of them had worked on a rifle it would pass the inspection of the most fastidious R.S.M. The Fijians wanted to play at soldiering, and they resented having to build themselves bures to live in during the training week. Nevertheless, they were quick to learn anything that captured their interest: for instance, they could lob a grenade accurately to a distance of forty or fifty yards (the average New Zealander throws accurately thirty odd yards). There was certainly no need to teach them stalking or bush-craft; in fact the New Zealanders learned a lot about bush-craft by watching the Fijians.

Although the New Zealanders had been in Fiji for many months before the commando units were formed, they had little knowledge of the native people. The infantry battalions were mostly confined to the Suva Peninsula, and the troops were rarely permitted to travel outside the defence area unless on duty. It was also a standing order that New Zealand soldiers must not fraternize with the Fijians in Suva. The commando NCOs, therefore, set out to train the Fijians with little or no knowledge of the native temperament.

The New Zealanders had to use orthodox training methods at first; then, as they learned the Fijian language and the Fijian point of view, they altered their methods of instruction to suit the conditions. The OC studied the history of the Fijians, and learned that the Fijians, in their warlike days, excelled in the art of ambush: he also learned that the Fijians were not so brave and bold when they got out of their natural environment, the jungle. Therefore the New Zealanders, realizing the Fijian's limitations, concentrated on developing their natural ability, with the object of using them mainly as scouts. A small amount of parade-ground drill was necessary to make the Fijians realise that they were working together as a team.

In that same chapter Larsen wrote:

The New Zealanders were very enthusiastic about the possibilities of the commando units. Each sergeant made an "appreciation" of his platoon area, and no one was prepared to accept that the reefs or the mangrove swamps were completely effective natural barriers to a determined invading force. They tested out the swamps by travelling through them themselves, and found that although it was a disagreeable business, it was possible to get through any swam by using the breathing roots of the mangroves as stepping stones. The NCOs read anything on Japanese tactics that they could obtain: reports on the endurance of the Japanese in Malaya stated that the enemy had waded through the waist-deep mud of the rice fields, and he had marched thirty miles in a day over rough country. The New Zealand commandos found that, with determination, they too could do these things—and more. Knife throwing was practiced very keenly, and on one occasion an NCO accidently received half an inch of cold steel in his ribs. Nevertheless, it was proved that the successful use of the knives was not limited to orientals.

I will discuss knife fighting tactics and how they are applicable to Commando type training in a later chapter. Larsen closed out the chapter regarding the early training of the Commandos by stating:

The OC formulated a flexible system for the commandos to work to in the case of an invasion. This system was based on the fact that the whole coast line was vulnerable to a greater or lesser degree at different points, and plans were laid so that no matter where the enemy landed the commandos would be harassing him within a few hours. As knowledge of the area increased in the succeeding months, the inter-communication of the platoons was reduced from a few days to a few hours.

In the article "Evolution Of A Fiji Commando" written for the Pacific Islands Monthly, March 1944, journalist Harold Cooper summed up the training experience of the Commandos in this way:

Commandos are made, not born, even in Fiji. Not so many months ago the Fijian men who won such a reputation on Guadalcanal were living quietly in remote villages and had never handled any weapon more complicated than an axe or a cane knife.

When they reported to their New Zealand instructors they were perhaps the rawest recruits ever to don the King's uniform. They could speak no English, and the New Zealanders no Fijian, so that early instruction had to be imparted painstakingly through interpreters.

The Fijians at first stood in some awe of the bullet, not because of its power to inflict injury, but because its flight was invisible. This initial nervousness, however, soon vanished and before long they were carrying out manoeuvres unperturbed by live ammunition bursting round them.

Their physique was excellent and they lost no time mastering all the devices of unarmed combat. The course of training was tough, but the Fijians were tougher and they cheerfully survived many an exhausting trek over the worst terrain these rocky, forest-clad islands can provide.

The second quality which gave the Fijian recruit the hallmark of the fine soldier was his sense of discipline. From birth he had been taught to respect his Chiefs and obey the reasonable orders of his seniors in the village community; and he readily adapted himself to the severe routine of army life.

But all the instructors are agreed that the Fijian's outstanding quality was his unbounded zest for soldiering. From the hour of enlistment his one desire was to learn how to fight and to learn so thoroughly that the opportunity to practice his skill in actual combat could not be long denied him.

Even before he was allowed to use ammunition he was completely absorbed in his rifle and would spend hours practicing the modest preliminary art of holding and aiming. By way of relaxation he joined with his comrades in devising mekes (or ceremonial dances) in which the rifle was the chief state property and which gaily dramatized the successes to be achieved in future engagements with the enemy. It is scarcely surprising that in the end this enthusiast became (as many a Japanese on Guadalcanal had the misfortune to discover) a formidable marksman.

These Fijians were hand-picked men, selected from many volunteers for the honour of representing their various villages, and were the pride and envy of other islanders. Their enormous prestige sometimes hampered training, for wherever they appeared they were welcomed and feted as heroes. This popularity was a source of acute embarrassment during periods when the Commandos were out "on a stunt" with strict orders to "live on the country" and eat only wild food. The villagers would try to load them as usual with produce from their gardens and the officer in charge would find it difficult to explain that for once this generosity was entirely misplaced.

The Fijian has made a tremendous hit with his American ally. In the transport on their way to the Solomons the Commandos kept the crew and their fellow-passengers entertained with native songs to the accompaniment of the guitar. From the moment they landed on the beach at Guadalcanal they struck up a firm friendship with the Marines, hundreds of whom crowded round to welcome them as the first British Colonial reinforcements.

Provision had been made in the training curriculum for lectures to the Fijians on the origins of the war and the cause for which they would be fighting. But no such education was necessary. The Fijians knew the Japanese was on his way south and they wanted to turn him back before he could reach their own islands.

After they had observed him at close quarters on Guadalcanal they grew to loathe him for the bestial manner in which he lived and fought. They saw Japanese encampments which presented spectacles of appalling squalor, with unburied corpses left to rot beside tents still occupied by living soldiers. They were filled with indignation and incredulity that this unclean and degenerate creature should dream of becoming master of the world.

The Fijian is a devout Christian. When the Commandos were not on Sunday patrols they could be seen in Guadalcanal's little thatched churches joining in worship with their comrades of the Solomons Scouts. Those who decry Britain's Colonial record might ponder this picture of the former cannibal and the former head-hunter kneeling together to give thanks for a new way of life which they, in common with millions of their fellows throughout the Empire, have found worth fighting and worth dying for.

In Oliver A. Gillespie's book The Pacific, he discussed what occurred with the Fijians once the Americans took over from New Zealand. Gillespie wrote:

> Although, under the principle of unity of command, responsibility for the military security of both Fiji and Tonga was vested in the United States from 1942, New Zealand continued to provide essential equipment, supplies, and personnel for both the Fijian and Tongan forces, the majority, of course, going to the Crown Colony. When 3 Division left Fiji, New Zealand also agreed to the American request for the retention of certain units and men, principally coast and anti-aircraft artillery, until their relief by American units later in the year or early in 1943. Colonel J.G.C. Wales was gazette in his new appointment as Commandant of the Fiji Defence Force and Commander 2 NZEF Pacific Section on 18 July, at which date there were 1500 New Zealanders in Fiji, including 1035 with artillery units.

Gilespie continued:

> Under the Americans Fiji became a separate island command, commanded by Major-General C. F. Thompson, and all Fiji forces came under him for operations. American artillery ultimately took over the coastal batteries at Vunda, Momi, Bilo, and Suva from the combined New Zealand and Fijian gunners, leaving only the Flagstaff Hill batter to the Fiji command. As the Americans withdrew in February 1943 they handed back the Suva and Bilo batteries, and 1 Heavy Fiji Regiment was created to control them, with Lieutenant-Colonel P.M.B. Barclay in command of the fixed coastal defences.

> The Fijian Infantry Brigade came into being with the idea of sending a force overseas to play a more active part in the war, and this no doubt affected the commitment of units to the battle in the

Solomons. At a meeting of the Council of Chiefs in September 1942, they were informed by the Governor that further calls would be made for men and materials on the Fijian community. The Council agreed but expressed the wish that a detachment of Fijians should be sent overseas. Recruiting among the villages was stimulated with this as the objective, since years of garrison duty in Fiji led to ultimate boredom. Although at this date New Zealand was hard-pressed to provide sufficient men to bring 3 Division to full strength, she fulfilled the Fijian request for further key personnel—first for 58 officers and 214 noncommissioned officers, most of whom reached the Colony at the end of the year, and a further 45 officers in January 1943. Increased supplies of equipment were also sent from New Zealand, which was not always kept as fully informed of the activities of the brigade as was consistent with calls for aid. This was remarked by Puttick in March 1943, in his comment on a signal from Fiji asking for further supplies and equipment because of the immediate prospect of one battalion and one commando unit leaving for the battle area. Puttick emphasized that New Zealand had not been consulted about any departure of troops from Fiji and that there was a danger that New Zealand might be compelled, through the pressure of events, to contribute resources in replacing men and equipment without having had any voice in the prior arrangements. This emphasized, also, the difficulties of commanding a small force within the framework of a large command. Wales was responsible to the Americans for operations, to New Zealand for supplies and some of his personnel replacements and to the Governor of Fiji for the satisfactory employment of Fijian ground forces. However, the brigade was never committed as a formation. Negotiations to incorporate it in 3 Division foundered when the Governor, Sir Philip Mitchell, who succeeded Luke in 1942, refused to allow the commitment of single battalions at different places.

In a message to the New Zealand Government during these negotiations he explained that he would have to explain to the Fiji Legislative Council why the Colony had gone to great pains and expense to raise, train, and equip a brigade, only to break it up unused and scrap its ancillary services. The whole trend of the discussions between Governments and commanders which followed proposals to use the brigade with 3 Division, suggested a desire by the American command to use the Fijians as scouts and small patrols in the jungle and this they eventually did. Two battalions, the 1st and the 3rd, and two units of commandos served in the Solomons under American command but never under their own brigade command, and the ultimate dispatch of these units to the battle area suggested a political desire to keep faith with the promises made earlier to the Fijian Council of Chiefs.

In reorganizing the Fiji forces Wales disbanded the commandos, which emerged as new units organised into guerrilla groups. By 31 December 1942 his force had increased to 6519 all ranks. Peak strength was reached in August 1943, when the number increased to 8513, of whom 808 were New Zealanders. Changes of command, both of staff and units, were frequent, and there was a constant flow of returning sick and replacements passing between New Zealand and the Colony as climate and conditions weeded out those not physically fitted for such arduous tasks.

Wales insisted on hard training and placed emphasis on individuality and initiative in leadership. Indeed, one of the exercises he organised became memorable as a training exploit and indicated the excellent standard of physical endurance achieved by all members of his force. This required each battalion to march 100 miles in five days over the most rugged country and made exhausting demands on the men, who were required to climb a cliff face, cross rivers while harassed by commandos, and traverse broken jungle tracks rising to more than 1000 feet. In

February, the hottest time of the year in Fiji, 1 Battalion completed the exercise with the loss of only one man. Only a few months previously many of those men had been brought from distant villages, knowing neither the feel of boots on their feet nor the sight of rifles and accoutrements of war.

Source: Paterson Evening News, May 10 1943.

Source: Quad City Times, March 18th 1945.

Source: The Southwest Wave, April 19ᵗʰ 1945.

101

Source: Marine Corps photo. Caption: When the Marine beachhead was established on Bougainville, largest of the Solomon islands, part of the Fiji Regiment participating in the engagement set up an outpost at Ibu, barely ten miles from the heart of the Japanese forces at Numa Numa, while on this sixty-day foray into enemy territory, these fearless jungle fighters killed upwards of four hundred Japs, with a loss of one man. Supplies were parachuted to the Fijians and cub planes used for artillery spotting made a daily flight to the garrison, landing on a miniature strip hacked out of the jungle by the scouting party. After months of harassing and ambushing the enemy, the patrol as recalled to the Torokina base when it was definitely established that the Japanese could never evacuate their trapped thousands of troops from the island.

Private John Seduaua is typical of the gay, fearless Fijian scout, serious one minute and laughing the next. Like most of his companions he has been in the Army since Britain declared war on Germany. When on patrol in the "bush", a soft olive-drab cap will replace the metal helmet because it makes too much noise rubbing against vines and branches in the jungle.

Carl Heinmiller and the Commandos

Carl Heinmiller's photo. Source: the Pictorial History Thirty-Seventh Division Camp Shelby 1940-1941.

When I had gotten in contact with Lee Heinmiller, we discussed his father's experiences in Fiji. Lee still lives in the same town in Alaska that his father built up after the war. He told me:

> My dad was sent to New Zealand right after the War broke out in 1941, he was already an officer in the Ohio National Guard, so they made him active Army and sent him to NZ. After three weeks, the NZ expeditionary troops went to Fiji (five guys, my Dad and two NZ and two other US soldiers, I think).
>
> Dropped them in a couple different villages with orders to "raise up some troops" sorta. Three groups of Commandos, Eastern Independents, Western Independents, and I can't remember what the middle group was called. My Dad was the Commander of the

Eastern group. He said they were natural jungle fighters, subsistence specialists, generations of warriors with traditions of killing their enemies. Men only ate major muscles...good parts, with special forks, smashed captured heads on a special stone in their village... women didn't eat or touch the enemy flesh. Kinda like eating the heart of your enemies!!

Needless to say, long before The British came to Fiji...don't know when that started but Fiji didn't get free until 1972!

Heard details from him a lot. The Top brass didn't believe that Black troops (Fijian especially) could be reliable soldiers, which my Dad thought was just the Racist attitude of the military at the time! A Captain named C.W. Tripp... high graded the three groups of Commandos for the first action in the South Pacific, was extremely successful... I think that was to Guadalcanal... my Dad and his group were sent next and they were there raiding and running for three weeks before the Marines landed (to save the Day!!!). I have my Dad's Signal Corp map with pencil marks and compass directions (like in Boy Scouts) of the island around Mundo Airfield!! Many stories from then.

Only a few books written about the Commandos...

One from Fiji, one form England, and one by a guy from the Commandos who retired to Hollywood FL. I have one of them, some of it matches up with parts of the diaries!!

From Heinmiller's diaries Lee was able to pin down his father's service dates. They were as follows:

Heinmiller was inducted into the Ohio National Guard, 145th Infantry, 37th Division, in October 1940 as a 2nd Lieutenant. In April of 1941 he was a 1st Lieutenant and stationed at Camp Shelby, Mississippi. From January

1942 until April or May of that same year he had been at the Indiantown Gap Military Reservation when he departed to New Zealand for three weeks.

He departed from New Zealand to Fiji on June the 2nd 1942 on the ship Uruguay where he was stationed with the Eastern Independent Commandos.

In Early 1942 he was assigned to Company "F" as Commander and in April 1943 he was sent to Guadalcanal. That was where he was cited for the Legion of Merit for removal of booby traps in the area.

He was then present for the assault on Rendova in early July of 1943. After that Heinmiller was reassigned to the Fiji Scouts in New Georgia. He was wounded there and sent to the hospital on Guadalcanal.

It was really great to be able to hear Lee's recollections of his father. Because Lee had mentioned it, I thought it would be important to understand something about General Beightler and his divison. For that I referred to an article on the website Ohio History Connection. I got the answers I was looking for regarding who Beightler was, from an article titled "The Pacific: General Beightler and the Buckeye Divison" written by J Haas and posted on May 17th 2010.

The article starts off by mentioning the miniseries The Pacific, which had premiered in the United States on March 14th, 2010. It stated:

> Recently the HBO Network aired the multi part series The Pacific, about World War II Marine combat in the Pacific Theater of Operations. It has been compared to the series Band of Brothers about the US Airborne forces in Europe during World War II. Both were based on specific historical units and the real soldiers and Marines of those units. This has brought new interest and insight to American forces and especially Marine combat

operations in the Pacific during World War II. But to be fair the Marines were not the only American forces fighting in the Pacific during World War II. Ohio had its own National Guard division, the 37th Infantry Division, the Buckeye division, fighting in the same Pacific theater of operations. Major General Robert Beighter commanded the 37th from its call up in 1940 till its final combat operations in the Philippines in 1945.

The article referenced another article which had originally appeared in the Ohio Historical Society publication, Preview, in 1996. It continued:

The history of the Thirty-seventh Ohio National Guard Infantry Division dates form July 17, 1918, when the unit received its official authorization and designation from the Federal government several months after America's entry into World War I. The story of the division during World War II begins in 1940, shortly after Adolf Hitlers conquest of Western Europe in the spring and summer of that year. President Roosevelt and Congress decided it was time to organize (and reorganize) America's national defense establishment, which at the time was in a sorry state of repair. On September 26, 1940, Ohio Governor John W. Bricker received a telegram from the secretary of war ordering the Thirty-seventh into Federal service effective October 15, 1940. The Thirty-seventh first received the name "Buckeye Divison" because its constituent battalions and regiments were Ohio National Guard units.

The first Buckeye Division troops left Ohio for Camp Shelby, Mississippi, on October 16, 1940, and the rest of the Thirty-seventh followed a few days later. On arrival the troops had to build much of the camp themselves before they could even begin training exercises. About nine thousand soldiers went to Camp Shelby from Ohio, and in the succeeding months they were joined by ten thousand selectees sent from the state to bring the division

106

to full strength. Intense training and maneuvers followed throughout much of 1941. In December 1941 after the United States entered the war, the Buckeye Division stood by for transport to the Philippine Islands. But it became apparent that the Philippines could not be defended, much less reinforced; and the Thirty-seventh was sent to Indiantown Gap, Pennsylvania, where it soon received orders for the South Pacific, setting sail from San Francisco on May 26 1942, bound for New Zealand and the Fiji Islands. On board four ships were the bulk of the division's chief combat units — the 145th and 148th Infantry regiments and the 135th, 136th, and 140th Field Artillery battalions. Major General Robert S. Beightler, a Marysville, Ohio, native and a descendent of naval hero Oliver Hazard Perry, led the men of the Buckeye Division.

The Thirty-seventh trained on Fiji and several other South Pacific islands until July 1943, when the Buckeye troops saw their first action during combat operations on New Georgia in the Solomon Islands. The Thirty-seventh went into the line to relieve the Forty-third Infantry Division, which was about to disintegrate as an effective force, and then proceeded to pummel the Japanese army until the middle of August, a running battle that cost the division 206 killed and 928 wounded. Although its casualties were high, the Buckeye Division's long period of training (as well as Beightler's policy of expending materiel rather than men) had paid off during the dense jungle fighting on New Georgia — as they would in later campaigns.

An article "Famous U.S. Army Divisions" which appeared in the Fredericksburg Standard on October 10th 1945 discussed the 37th Infantry Division and provided some more interesting details:

The Buckeye Division, which had its nucleus in the Ohio National Guard, has battle traditions from Montfaucon in France in 1918, through the bloody jungles of the South Pacific to the blazing walls of Manila and finally into the hills of Northern Luzon in the closing days of the war to crash the Jap positions around Baguio and Baleta Pass. It has a record of hand-to-hand fighting and heavy casualties but it invariably took an immense enemy toll and won its objectives. Columns of its 148th Regiment seized the notorious Bilibid prison in Manila and liberated 2,000 American internees.

The Division was inducted into Federal service in October 1940, and trained at Camp Shelby, Miss., and Camp Clairborne, La. It sailed for the Southwest Pacific in May, 1942, its components being the 129th, the 145th and 148th Infantry Regiments and the 6th, 135th, 140th and 136th Field Artillery Battalions. Training was continued while the Division fortified the Fiji Islands and after at Guadalcanal the Buckeyes went on with their training while harried by Jap aerial attacks. Elements of the 37th entered combat on New Georgia Island in June, 1943. The entire Division was committed to the Munda campaign. With the I Marine Corps units of the 37th landed on Bougainville, and on November 13, 1943, the remainder of the Division entered the conflict. It held the Bougainville perimeter until moving to the Philippines. On January 9, 1945, the 37th, a part of the Sixth Army Task Force, landed on the beaches of Lingayen Gulf. Infantry spearheads raced inland and after savage fighting with Jap suicide defenders Clark Field and Fort Stotsenberg air strip were captured. The drive continued to Manila and thence into the hills in the north.

Distinguished unit citations were awarded as follows: Companies E and F, 148th Infantry; Company F, 129th Infantry, Headquarters Company, 129th Infantry; Headquarters Company, 148th Infantry and Company F, 145th Infantry. Pvt. Rodger W. Young. Of Clyde, O., hero of the popular song "Rodger Young", was awarded the Medal of Honor for his heroic action on New Georgia where he gave his life to save the withdrawal of his platoon. Another Medal of Honor winner, Pfc. Frank J. Etrarca, of Cleveland, O., likewise made the supreme sacrifice to save a wounded comrade.

Throughout its service the 37th has been commanded by Maj. Gen. Robert S. Beightler, who enlisted in the Ohio National Guard as a private in 1911. He won a commission in 1914 and served with the Division on the Mexican border and in France in 1917-18. He re-entered the Federal service in October, 1940.

The Buckeye shoulder patch is a brilliant red circle on a circular background of white. It was adopted from the design of the Ohio state flag. Troopers refer to their Division insignia as the "fried egg" patch.

A thesis paper "The Battling Buckeyes of the 37th Infantry Division" by Tyler R. Webb stated:

The 37th Infantry Division was originally supposed to be part of a force to relieve U.S. forces in the Philippines. This plan was quickly discarded because it was simply impractical based on the situation – just as War Plan Orange designers feared. Rumors surged in the division that they were to be sent to Ireland. Instead, the Joint Chiefs of Staff decided the 37th Infantry Division would fight its battles in the Pacific after the Arcadia Conference in early January 1942. Japan was rapidly progressing southward, capturing the Solomon Islands and enhancing the threat to New Zealand and Australia. The 147th Infantry Regiment was detached from the 37th Infantry Division and sent to Tonga, an island on the southeastern coast of Fiji.

Thus the recently triangularized 37th Infantry Division, as of January 16, was left with only two infantry regiments. It was not until after the division's combat on New Georgia that it received a replacement, the 129th Infantry Regiment. Nevertheless, the Buckeyes departed on May 26, 1942, from San Francisco for Fiji as part of Task Force 6429.

The Joint Chiefs of Staff deemed Fiji a point at which the Japanese advance must be halted. If Fiji fell then American ability to retaliate and effectively ship supplies and troops to Australia and New Zealand would have been greatly compromised. The main island in Fiji, Viti Levu, was where most of the division resided in 1942. The elements of the division that landed on New Zealand assisted in training the New Zealand Home Units, guarded important areas, and manned defensive positions. The occupation of Fiji was more intensive because the island lacked a significant defensive infrastructure. In the event of Japanese attack the division was ordered to hold Fiji at all costs.

Beightler used the ten months on Fiji and New Zealand to conduct training in Pacific conditions focused on combating Japanese tactics. Fiji had a diverse geography with features ranging from mangrove swamps to rainforests, harboring all of the many discomforts of the tropical battlefields to come. Additionally, the division spent significant time interacting with Fiji natives, who provided the soldiers with lessons of jungle survival and a bond to Fijians who helped them fight in the Solomon Islands campaign. Fijians served in many capacities with the 37th Infantry Division throughout Operation Cartwheel, the Solomon's campaign. However, the training on Fiji did not provide a skilled foe to provide the GIs with actual combat experience. The division history recalls that "there were no Japs (sic) on Fiji, and no large American cemeteries where the 37th bade goodbye to its buddies."

The next stop for the 37th Infantry Division was Guadalcanal, which had been seized after a fierce campaign that began on August 7, 1942. Although the Japanese ground forces on

Guadalcanal had been defeated, the war was closer now than ever to the Buckeyes. This reality became evident on their first night ashore, when five Japanese planes bombarded Henderson Airfield. The danger was minimal, no casualties were suffered, but the NCOs had to jokingly tell their men digging their foxholes too deep that "one more shovelful and you're AWOL."

Beightler combated the disparity in experience through constant training whenever possible prior to the division's first combat action in New Georgia. The close proximity to combat operations meant that there was now an incredible amount of supplies available to the 37th. Beightler utilized the immense amount of shells to endlessly drill his artillery battalions. He also focused training on small unit tactics, landing operations, and beachhead establishment. Just as on Fiji, the 37th Infantry Division on Guadalcanal did not contact Japanese forces and thus remained an untested division. This was about to change.

Putting the focus back on Heinmiller and his experience amongst the Fijians. According to Lee his father told him the Fijians had military training to some degree, however there were various groups developed as the Commandos. Most of those being developed were from remote villages. Lee said:

> My Dad was the Commander of the Eastern Independents. The first troops that got sent out were "high graded" and went to fight first... when the Army wasn't convinced that Native/Black soldiers were capable of doing anything but cooking and other support work. That was why they did the "Commando Test Action" in Suva before they sent them out!! My Dad's group were the ones that snuck in, marked the X's on everything and disappeared in the dark!! Proving their skill and effectiveness!!

As noted previously the initial training of the Fijians was to prepare them to operate behind Japanese lines in Viti Levu. They had already been well-versed in bushcraft on their home soil so it's unlikely Heinmiller the boy scout would have contributed anything in that regard. But perhaps he had been helpful in other ways.

My understanding is that the military upper brass still needed some more convincing of their effectiveness as Scouts. Heinmiller in perhaps what could best be described as a liaison role was one individual who became involved in their vetting process. He appeared to have been in the right time and place in order to be able to help them expand their operations. Heinmiller had asked to be embedded with them in order to gain some of their essential knowledge. One good turn deserved another.

Heinmiller's Legion of Merit citation reads:

> The President of the United States of America, authorized by Act of Congress, 20 July 1942, takes pleasure in presenting the Legion of Merit to Captain (Infantry) Carl W. Heinmiller (ASN:0-381754), United States Army, for exceptionally meritorious conduct in the performance of outstanding services in the South Pacific Area from 11 September 1942 to 29 May 29 1943, while serving with the 145th Infantry Regiment, 37th Infantry Division. To further his military knowledge Captain Heinmiller requested and was assigned duty with an organization of natives experienced in jungle craft and warfare. Under the extremely adverse conditions of the jungle, and by living the life of a native, he gained a wealth of knowledge which he later imparted to members of his command. Following this achievement Captain Heinmiller devoted his own time to the study, construction, and perfection of booby traps. As a result, selected men of his organization have become proficient in detecting, disarming, and destroying enemy booby traps. As a further immeasurably aid to combat efficiency. Captain Heinmiller devised a pack for carrying light machine guns

silently through the jungle. Finally, during the period May 24 to 29, this officer volunteered to clear an area known to contain numerous uncharted anti-tank mines and booby traps. Without regard to his personal safety, and cognizant of the hazards involved in the task, he personally searched for, found, and disarmed the traps, making the area safe for occupancy. The singularly distinctive accomplishments of Captain Heinmiller and his dedicated contributions in the service of his country reflect the highest credit upon himself and the United States Army.

The citation puts Heinmiller's story into the correct perspective. It matches the known timings for the Fijian and US Army Forces on Fiji, and the development first of anti-Japanese training for the defense of Fiji, and then for offensive operations in the Solomons.

Despite Heinmiller not offering the Fijians anything in terms of woodcraft survival skills, or as the New Zealanders called it, bushcraft; the opposite was true, they taught him a great deal about Jungle fighting. It did appear that he had some knowledge to offer some of them in return, however, as we will see in another chapter.

37TH DIV. TROOPS BLAST JAP OCCUPIED PILLBOX.   U S Army Photo 167-16.

Charles Tripp

At this point I knew why Carl Heinmiller had been stationed in Fiji. I also knew the importance of Fiji as a strategic location and why Fijians were being trained to be guerrillas there. I needed to delve a little bit deeper in order to understand who had been responsible for training them to be stay-behind operatives and Commandos.

Wilson's Promontory had been the logical starting off point for discovering what I wanted to know regarding what the New Zealanders had been attempting to pass on. But Tripp had not trained there along with the other New Zealanders who would also become instructors to the Fijian Commandos.

Once the Americans had taken over Fiji, what was their involvement in training? Heinmiller had made it sound as if he had improved upon the training that had initially been given to the Fijians by the New Zealanders. In some ways it sounded as if all these "Commandos" were building the plane while they were flying the plane. They were improving their training methods in the field and pooling their knowledge.

When I mentioned that to Dr. Fox, he told me that it was his understanding that the American army troops were taught by the South Pacific Scouts, rather than vice versa. The South Pacific Scouts was the US Military term for the Fiji Guerillas or Fiji Commandos as the Americans did not like to use the term Guerillas. The Americans were there to learn jungle fighting tactics.

According to Dr. Fox, it the Fijians, began their training at home with their New Zealand officers in Fiji, and then perfected their scouting techniques later in the Solomons.

For example they figured out simple things such as cutting open ammunition boots so that they can drain in jungle conditions, not using the British steel helmet in the jungle, focusing on silent movement and minimal shooting – shoot low, and drop the enemy.

Tripp and his team had determined US or Australian weapons were better suited to jungle scouting – first the M-03 Springfield, but then the Australian Owen Gun. Tripp found that the US M1 carbine jammed on him at the worst possible moment. They also favoured the US camouflaged uniforms – the zoot suits.

I asked Dr. Fox about the stuff I usually like to research, I asked if unarmed combat methods had been taught and if so what did their training consist of? I also wanted to know if that training had been similar to the training of the Commandos in Scotland. In addition to that, I also wanted to know if any of the New Zealanders had actually trained in Scotland.

He told me that Larsen had described the training regime in Fiji in some detail. He was the unit intelligence Officer. As previously noted, some of the New Zealand NCOs, had trained with Spencer Chapman and Calvert in Australia. Their training was specifically for commando or left behind parties. Chapman detailed his experiences in his book The Jungle is Neutral. They were the original commando experts in Australasia. Any training the New Zealanders had given would have mimicked the training they had received there.

Dr. Fox had not been aware of any New Zealand personnel or Fiji Guerillas who had been graduates of any Commando school in Scotland. He told me bushcraft and commonsense, plus trial and error covered most of the curriculum in Fiji. Charlie Tripp's formative experiences in the New Zealand bush had also prepared him for training Fijians on scouting work in the jungle.

The Guerillas were meant to operate quietly and quickly in the jungle. As with the SAS in Italy, 1 Commando incurred casualties mainly when involved in larger scale operations such as Vella Lavella and Munda airfield.

While there really wasn't any need for the Fairbairn and Sykes style of street fighting, in terms of their unarmed combat training, Dr. Fox did point out that Larsen mentioned knife throwing in his book, and that an NCO had gotten stuck with a knife during training.

Regarding Heinmiller, it seemed as if he did not have much active involvement in the training of the Fiji Commandos. For the most part they had already been trained by the New Zealanders prior to his arrival. Larsen had mentioned that six Americans were attached to the Southern Commando to learn the art of jungle warfare, and they trained for six weeks. Fresh US troops were then attached every six weeks after that. So it was likelier therefore that the Americans were there learning from the Fijians and their New Zealand officers rather than the other way around.

Dr. Fox's told me that that it looked like Heinmiller had been Eastern Independent Commando and then 2 Commando, Fiji Guerillas, under the command of Phil Ellis. It was his opinion that it would be incorrect to state that Heinmiller was the CO of either of those Commandos. Charlie Tripp took 1 Commando into action in the Solomons, while Phil Ellis and 2 Commando went to Bougainville.

Regarding unarmed combat training specifically, which is usually my area of interest, Dr. Fox mentioned that Tripp once encountered two Japanese in the jungle. One grabbed him about the waist in what he described as a ju jitsu hold after his M1 carbine had jammed, pinning his arms to his side. The second Japanese laid his rifle across his comrade's back and fired. The under-powered round was deflected by a cigarette case. Tripp then stabbed or shot the first Japanese with his 1911A1, and then killed the second one. This story is recounted again from another source toward the end of this chapter.

Having consulted Larsen's book I noticed that training in unarmed defence tactics had been mentioned a few times. Dick Tripp had also mentioned it in his own book. Additionally, there was the article that had mentioned that the Fijians had grown bored of learning Judo. Because of those sources I knew that unarmed combat was indeed being taught to them even if it was ultimately not something which had been utilized much in the field. However, the use of the knife in combat does appear to have figured quite prominently in many of the sources.

Dick Tripp, wrote in his book concerning one incident:

> After the American Navy's victory in the Battle of Coral Sea (May 1942), which was a turning point of the Pacific war, Fiji gradually faded into the background. This meant that the Commandos had no immediate objective for training and they began to slacken off a little. Father desperately tried to get his men into action. Eventually, Sir Philip Mitchell, Governor of Fiji, who had taken a

great interest in the Commandos, persuaded the Commander of the South Pacific to try out a sample force. At the beginning of December, a Special Party of 30 Commandos was selected from the Souther and Eastern units and sent to Guadalcanal under the command of David Williams. The Americans at this point were holding a ten-mile beachhead that extended two miles inland and encompassed the Henderson airfield. The job given the Commandos was to patrol beyond the perimeter and provide the Americans with information as to Japanese movements.

Frank Williams was the youngest member of the Commandos, joining up when only twenty-one. He told me that Father felt a special responsibility to look out for him. Frank was included in this initial Special Party and told me of one event in which he was involved. He and four Fijians were leading an American infantry company in the bush, and Frank and two of the Fijians were well out in front, acting as scouts. They suddenly stopped as they sensed that there were Japanese ahead. Father once told me that the Japanese had a distinctive smell and that you could sometimes sense their presence for that reason. However, that may not have been so in this case. There were three Japanese officers hiding behind a large Banyan tree and the scouts noticed that the ground had been trampled around the tree. The Japanese carried swords—this was customary for their officers. If the patrol had continued, they may have had their heads chopped off. A battle started around the tree, which had large roots. A grenade landed at Frank's feet but fortunately there was a root between it and him. He told me he lay flat and put his hands over his head. A Japanese poked his head up to take a shot at him, but one of the Fijians, who had been wounded in his left forefinger but was still holding his gun at his hip, got in first and blew his head off. Frank decided to jump clear of the tree and rely on accurate shooting, which he did, but his gun misfired. A bullet grazed his forearm, but he got back behind the tree. He reloaded and tried again and this time shot a

Japanese who was charging at him with his sabre. Frank tried throwing a grenade, but they were on a slope, and it rolled down the hill. The last Japanese finally took off down the hill. When he was about 20 yards away, both Fijians fired. It was found on inspection that both bullets had entered his head an inch apart. Though Frank had a few minor splinters from the grenade, he insisted on staying with his Fijians until they returned three days later with a great deal of information. Frank never fired another shot in action. There were opportunities to ambush Japanese, but the scouts' job was to gather information without the enemy discovering their presence. Frank was later given the Silver Star by the Americans. Of the six Silver Stars awarded to New Zealanders during World War Two, three were given to the Commandos.

It's important to look at the timing of things. Dates are always important in setting a historical record straight. Heinmiller mentioned in his article that he had arrived at an outpost of the Eastern Independent Commandos at Viti Levu, in July of 1942. Dick Tripp had noted, that was around the time when the Americans had taken over. Larsen wrote in his book:

> In April, 1942, Charles Tripp, then a lieutenant, was given command of Southern Independent Commando which was at first known as Eight Brigade Commando. Charles and his second in command, David Williams, accompanied senior officers, who went out to the villages on the southern coast and, with the assistance of the District Officer, Mr R. H. Lester, and the native chiefs, recruited two hundred Fijians. The natives were to train on a territorial basis of one week in each month, for which they were to be paid one pound. They were also to receive two khaki shirts and two pairs of khaki shorts.

Larsen also mentioned:

This history covers the commandos who served under Major C.W.H. Tripp, during 1942 and 1943, first in the Southern Commando and then in First Commando Fiji Guerrillas. The members of Eastern Commando who later joined the southern unit to form First Commando, carried out similar activities to those which will be described in the first half of this book.

Heinmiller had also pointed out in his article that he had been stationed at an outpost of the Eastern Independent Commandos. So because of that we are able to pinpoint exactly where he had been stationed on the island at that time in comparison to Tripp.

Larsen wrote:

On 18th July, 1942, the American Forces took over the defence of Fiji, and the Third New Zealand Division returned to the Dominion. But the American Commander asked for the retention of several New Zealand units, among which, were the commandos, until the United States troops became familiar with the Fiji territory. It was a bitter disappointment to the commandos, for, apart from their longing to see New Zealand once again, they wanted to go wherever their comrades in the Third Division would go after their stay in New Zealand. No one at this time could foresee the, Third Division's going to New Caledonia; otherwise garrison duty in Fiji might have appeared the lesser of the two evils. The greatest loss to the commando units, however, was the support of senior officers of Third Divisional Headquarters and Eighth Brigade Headquarters. These officers, who had been enthusiastic about the commandos from the beginning, had been in a position to make strong claims on equipment for the commando units as soon as the equipment became available in New Zealand.

Later the Americans were so impressed by the work of the commando units that they caused them to remain in Fiji indefinitely. The commandos became part of the Fiji Brigade Group which included the local Fiji Military Force under the command of Brigadier J. G. C Wales, M.C. Because they were using British weapons, New Zealand was still responsible for the maintenance of equipment, but the commandos came under the operational control of 37 United States Division.

That was Heinmiller's outfit and the rest of the chapter lines up with what Heinmiller discussed in an article he wrote discussing their lack of skill in marksmanship and how he helped to correct that issue. That article which Hienmiller wrote for American Rifleman will be presented in the next chapter.

Larsen also mentioned the story of another American, Johnny Cox, who was an excellent marksman. He wrote:

Six Americans were attached to the Southern Commando to learn the art of jungle warfare. These men were selected from the most physically fit NCOs the Americans had, and they trained with the commandos for six weeks. After the first group returned to their units the American commanders commented on the transformation of the men, and they continued to send fresh groups out to train with the commandos every six weeks.

One of the Americans who worked with the commandos was Lieutenant Johnny Cox. Johnny had an outstanding personality and an infectious Southern drawl. He became very popular through his wit and skill in handling weapons, and the New Zealanders were disappointed when he had to return to his unit. Johnny was one of the best pistol shots in his Division. One day the commando sergeant-major thought he would try Johnny out and he tossed his hat in the air, saying: "Have a shot at that!" From twenty yards Johnny put two holes in the hat before it hit the ground—much to the consternation of the sergeant-major. The New Zealanders in the commandos were all first class shots but they were not up to this standard. It was always regretted that as Lieutenant Ben Masefield, New Zealand's best, was in Tonga at this time, a match could not be arranged between these two crack shots.

It seemed that there might have been some room for improvement in the training of the Fijian's marksmanship skills. Larsen wrote:

> On 14th November the unit received one hundred Springfield rifles; ten were allotted to each platoon immediately. This equipment was a milestone in the training of the Fijians as range practice could now be carried out in an efficient manner and marksmanship increased at a surprising rate. In the initial states of training the Fijians had the chance of firing only five rounds each training week, and they could not get beyond the stage of being frightened of the weapon: whilst aiming at the target some would sweat for five minutes before they could be induced to squeeze the trigger, with the result that their shots went wild. The native's nervous tension worried the NCOs, and some of the New Zealanders would have lost faith in the Fijian's ability to become soldiers had they not shown remarkable abilities in other directions.

That lack of skill in marksmanship would ultimately be improved upon by their instructors, and luckily that did not take-away from their usefulness in other ways. Most notably their skills in undetected movement, concealment and ambush which was why they had been selected for stay-behind operations and Commando training. We also have to remember that the initial batch of Fijian Commandos trained by Tripp had already been high graded, and had already proved their worthiness in combat.

In 1943 the New Zealand newspaper the Evening Post contained a story "Fijians In War" which was published on the 5th of November. That story again described the close quarters combat incident which occurred between Tripp and the Japanese. Like the chalk story, there are multiple reports of that incident. The article stated:

> The extraordinary contribution the Fijian people have made to the war in the Pacific was described by Brigadier J. G. C. Wales, M.C., N.Z.S.C., till recently commandant of the Fijian military forces. Brigadier Wales has been succeeded by Brigadier Dittmer, M.B.E., D.S.O., M.C., N.Z.S.A., who formerly commanded the 28th Maori Battalion in the Middle East.
>
> Brigadier Wales went to Fiji when the resident forces organised as a defensive force consisted of one battalion. When he left the force had been reconstituted as an offensive formation trained in amphibious operations and jungle warfare to play an active part in the field against the Japanese. The field force is now of considerable strength, the majority of its soldiers being native Fijians, some of the others being resident Europeans, and the remainder New Zealanders.
>
> On top of the field force there is the coastal defence artillery formation, in which Fijians have eagerly enlisted, and on top of this force there are two labour battalions, organised on an Army basis and numbering more than 2000 in strength, who have set such a standard of work loading and unloading ships that they are commonly regarded as being the fastest wharf workers in the Pacific. There are a number of Fijian commissioned officers, so far up to captain in rank, in the field force.
>
> There are two guerrilla or commando formations. As early as last December a section of one of these commandos was sent to Guadalcanal, more or less as an experiment, to see whether they would be useful in action against the Japanese. The section—

actually about a platoon in strength, with New Zealand officers— was employed as scouts right up to the successful conclusion of the Guadalcanal campaign. Their native talents, among which their almost magical bushcraft, keenness of sight, and excellence at snap-shooting and cheerful endurance stand out predominantly, were so successfully employed that they killed a large number of Japanese and notably fulfilled all their assignments without loss to themselves.

More recently the commando for which this section was part has been employed in the attacks on New Georgia and Vella Lavella. It was in action from the beginning of July till the end of September with only one rest of ten days. It was customarily used as a patrol screen for the American forces, and was so extraordinarily successful that two American officers of high rank wrote special letters to the Governor of Fiji paying an extremely high tribute to the value of its work and the manner in which it was performed. In three months of action the commando's casualties numbered about one-fifth of its strength, including ten killed and one missing.

The commanding officer is Major Charles Tripp member of a well known Canterbury family. Major Tripp was specially mentioned in one of the American letters. Among other things it told how once Major Tripp was confronted by two Japanese, one of whom thrust his rifle into Major Tripp's chest and pulled the trigger. The bullet was deflected by a clip of cartridges for the New Zealander's automatic rifle and caused only a slight wound. Major Tripp killed both Japanese with his pistol.

In addition to the commando, a battalion has also been in the Solomons for some time carrying out an essential but so far only protective duty. The rest of the field force is anxiously awaiting the day when it can go into the forward areas.

The October 1943 issue of Pacific Islands Monthly contained an article "Fijians Led by New Zealanders" which again discussed Tripp's encounters with the Japanese. It stated:

> In Fiji, the New Zealanders augmented their forces, available for the defence of Fiji, by drawing from the Fiji Defence Battalion. This battalion was composed of sturdy islanders, accustomed to the rigors of jungle life. The New Zealanders began the task of whipping the untrained but willing, Fijians into a well-disciplined army unit.
>
> Then somebody conceived the plan of training the New Zealanders in jungle tactics, using the Fijians as instructors. This Pygmalion set-up worked admirably.
>
> By the time the course was over, the New Zealanders were adept in jungle lore. One of the graduates of this Commando course was Major C. W. H. Tripp, of Canterbury, NZ. Another was Capt. David E. Williams, of Hawkes Bay.
>
> In January, 1943, after US Army and Marine units had taken Guadalcanal, a small detachment of these South Pacific Scouts, consisting of NZ officers and noncoms., with Fijians, were sent to the Solomons to aid in the final push.
>
> The patrol reached Guadalcanal in time to participate in the final clean-up of the Japs. Capt. Williams headed this party and American naval boats landed them far behind the Jap lines, in the Visale area. Coming upon the surprised Japanese from the rear, the small patrol played hell with the enemy defences, destroying guns, infiltrating into Jap positions at night, and paving the way by demoralization for the American drive along the coast.

To Captain Williams and his South Pacific Scouts was assigned the honour of leading the first contingent of Allied troops to invade the Japanese-occupied Russell Islands. They met with almost no opposition.

The Scouts landed with the first troops to hit the Japanese garrisons in New Georgia, and they have since been used with combat forces moving into strange areas, and for learning the location and plans of the enemy.

"Perhaps the luckiest day of my life," remarked Major Tripp, after an affair in New Georgia, "occurred about a fortnight ago. I was leading a patrol into Jap territory at night—at best a risky business—when a Jap jumped me from a foxhole. He held me around the waist, while another shot at me. One of the bullets ripped down through the pocket of my jungle suit, and through a notebook which I carry, without scratching me."

"Then," the major continued, "about half an hour later two rifles and a machine-gun opened up at me from less than 10 feet away as I was walking down the trail. They missed me completely. Earlier that day I had had a hand grenade go off not 10 feet from me, which miraculously did no damage."

What the major neglected to tell was that the Jap had jumped him from the foxhole and the Jap who put the bullet through his notebook were both dead—by the major's hand—and that after being fired upon by the two rifles and machine-gun he had flopped down on the ground in front of that withering fire and expended all the ammunition his carbine carried at the three Japs; and after the ammunition was gone he had thrown the carbine and a few choice New Zealand expletives in the direction of the enemy ambush.

On one occasion the Scouts were assigned to lead a regiment into a bivouac area, close to the front lines. A group of them—including Major Tripp—had all but completed the task when the Japs concentrated 90-millimeter mortar fire on the column of troops.

Tripp and his Scouts, who were out in front clearing the way, were cut off completely from the main body, and had to get out of the trap in groups of two and three. The major made it alone. Three of the Scouts did not come out of that ambush, but there were at least 30 Japs who did not get out, either.
Since getting into actual operations, the Scouts have had few losses.

The Fijians possess the happy—or unhappy—faculty of being able to smell out the Japs. Happy, because it enables them to watch while sleeping; unhappy, because the Jap smell is definitely dissimilar to Chanel Number Five. The New Zealanders are also able to recognize the Jap odour, and they tell me that several Americans can do it also. Major Tripp says that when the Japs ambushed him from the foxhole, he was able to smell the Jap odour on his jungle suit, where the Nip had grabbed him, for a week afterward.

Another newspaper contained another variation of that story. The article "Scouts' Jungle Daring" from November 23rd 1943 stated:

The Allied forces in the jungles of New Guinea would have little chance against the Japanese without the men who are the eyes and ears of the attacking units, writes Osmar White, correspondent of the Sydney "Daily Telegraph" in the Solomons.

Feats of almost unbelievable daring are being carried out behind enemy lines each night and sometimes by day.

Here is a typical exploit:

Captain Charles Tripp, of Geraldine, New Zealand, who was in charge of the first commando of Fijian guerrillas, penetrated the Japanese lines on the night of July 12 to spot and plot strongpoints for the artillery. After some hours' travelling, he discovered that a Japanese unit had closed behind him, and he was trapped between them and a hilly strongpoint where machineguns and mortars were placed. He crept off into the jungle. Tripp found himself in the middle of a large Japanese group which encircled him, firing rifles and machineguns. He had lost touch with his patrol and decided to do the unexpected thing—to make directly back through the middle of the Japanese encampment. He almost fell into a Japanese machinegun pit. He tried to shoot the crew, but his rifle jammed, so he hurled it at the amazed Japanese.

He killed one of them with his pistol and ran off and hid till nightfall under a hollow log.

Tripp said: "I spent the time praying for rain, but it was brilliant moonlight. I was right in the middle of a Japanese bivouac. Our artillery shelled it. I could hear the shells coming but wasn't too worried. The Japanese knew I was there and threw grenades at me, but missed. I kept on the move and found myself near a Japanese in a foxhole. I waited till he went to sleep, and again moved. Then two more Japanese in a foxhole saw me. One of them leapt out and seized me by the shirt while the other tried to shoot me with his rifle. The bullet glanced off my cartridge clip and hit the cigarette lighter in my breast pocket glancing down and nicking my wrist. The powder scorched my chest. I shot both Japanese with my pistol and ran off. I realized the only way to get out was to pretend that I was a Japanese. I stood upright and walked among the foxholes, making as much noise as possible. Several times I trod on men, and they cursed me, but none fired and no one challenged me. I could see them cooking food under their shelters on little spirit lamps. Once clear of the bivouac areas the rest was simple. I came home the next morning."

Tripp immediately returned into the enemy country.

Gillespie provided the following account in his book concerning the Guerrillas:

The first Fijian force to undertake service in the Solomons was a special party of 23 guerrillas, commanded by Captain D. E. Williams, which was drawn from the Southern and Eastern Independent commando units formed as part of 3 Division and retained in Fiji after the division's departure. Williams and Lieutenant D. Chambers as his second-in-command and Sergeants S. I. Heckler, L. V. Jackson, F. E. Williams, R. H. Morrison, and M. V. Kells as section leaders. They reached Guadalcanal via the New Hebrides and disembarked at Lunga Beach on 23 December1942. The Japanese garrison was then still fighting desperately along the Matanikau River-Koli Point line, and the American command employed the Fijians to probe the wooded country behind the Japanese garrison. The first patrol, led by Heckler on Christmas Day, was uneventful, but on 28 December a second small patrol led by Sergeant Williams, acting as scouts for 182 US Infantry Regiment, wiped out a Japanese patrol at short range, and without loss or injury, on the left bank of the Lunga River.

This little action was fought out with grenades, rifles, and revolvers on sloping ground round the massive, tangled roots of a banyan tree, and was characteristic of swift individual action and thought which spelled victory in a type of warfare these men were fighting for the first time. As the remnants of the Japanese force fell back before the Americans towards Cape Esperance throughout January and February, patrols from William's small but resolute force moved ahead of the advance, producing vital intelligence and creating havoc among the Japanese, whose morale was born of desperation. Their work was of such value that Major-General Alexander M. Patch, island commander of Guadalcanal, asked for more Fijian troops similarly trained for patrol work in densely wooded country.

The guerrillas wore camouflaged American jungle suits, the green and blotched material of which was difficult to detect among the tangled growth. New Zealand army boots were preferred to the soft rubber-soled jungle boot, and had a longer life. Arms were varied and consisted of Owen guns, rifles, revolvers and hand grenades, and the men all carried sufficient rations to last them for at least five days. Because mobility was of the first importance, these guerrillas carried as little personal gear as possible, consequently they suffered in some places from the unmerciful attention of mosquitoes. Patrols sometimes worked only a hundred yards apart but were unaware of the existence of each other. Malaria, control of which was not strictly administered until later, played havoc with this special party during its brief but intense period of activity, and when the Guadalcanal campaign ended every member of it returned to Fiji with the exception of Captain Williams and Heckler, who transferred to units which followed them into the combat zone. Before departing, however, they trained a group of Solomon Islanders under Major M. Clemens, a member of the civilian administration, who moved forward from island to island with the advancing troops, both American and New Zealand.

The American request for more Fiji guerrilla troops was met by the dispatch of two further units—1 Commando Fiji Guerrillas and 1 Battalion, Fiji Brigade Group, both of which landed on Guadalcanal on 19 April. Tripp commanded the guerrilla unit, which the American command designated South Sea Scouts. It was made up of 39 New Zealand officers and non-commissioned officers selected from the Southern and Eastern Independent Commandos, and 135 Fijians from the same units, organised into a headquarters of 24 all ranks and two companies of 75 all ranks, each commanded by a lieutenants. Each company was broken into three platoons, each of three sections, with a New Zealand sergeant in charge of each platoon and New Zealand corporals as section commanders. Twenty-eight Tongans, commanded by Lieutenant B. Masefield, increased the strength of Tripp's unit to 203 before it went into action on New Georgia. Further training was carried out on Guadalcanal to accustom all ranks to the new territory in which they were to fight. During this time two hundred Solomon Islanders were absorbed into the unit, and changes made in its organization so that each platoon became a patrol, commanded by a New Zealand sergeant with a New Zealand corporal as his second-in-command. A unit patrol under Lieutenant P.M. Harper reconnoitered the island of San Cristobal, but apart from obtaining valuable experience in the jungle no Japanese were encountered there.

Regarding Tripp and his Commando operations, Gillespie later wrote:

In planning his attack on Munda, Griswold gave his force ten days in which to capture the airfield, but it was not finally captured for 35 days, during which three divisions of American troops were committed to action. The Corps commander wished to employ both 1 Commando and 1 Battalion as scouts, but this scheme was abandoned because of Taylor's objection to committing his battalion piecemeal instead of as a whole unit. The scouting work therefore fell to the commandos under Tripp, and the battalion remained in the rear on the island of Florida until the following October.

The first task allotted to Tripp's unit was the clearance of islands in the Rovianna Lagoon. This was little more than an exercise. Patrols were then allotted to units of 43 Division, one with 169 Regiment on the right flank and others with 172 Regiment, both of which worked as combat teams. Fighting was confused and uncertain in the early stages of the costly struggle for Munda airfield, as the division moved forward only a few hundred yards a day, clearing out nests of Japanese strongpoints and avoiding ambushes. On one occasion, when an American battalion ran out of food, it was supplied by the commandos, who transported rations and ammunition in native canoes up the Bariki River. Malaria and war nerves, brought on by close fighting under dense overhead cover, rapidly reduced the American strength.

Led by New Zealanders, the commando patrols acquitted themselves fearlessly in their first clashes with the enemy along the Munda and Lambeti trails, which led towards the airfield. Their information enabled American artillery to be used with reasonable precision on any strongpoints encountered along the jungle trails. Masefield, a most able leader, was the first New Zealand casualty among the commandos. He spent some days with four of his Tongans in enemy territory, reaching the Bairoko Trail and moving along it to the outskirts of the Munda airfield. He was unfortunately killed while patrolling ahead of the Americans, caught in their artillery barrage. Two of the Tongans were wounded by splinters from the shell which killed their leader. On 12 July, while patrolling about 100 yards ahead of an American platoon of 172 Regiment, Tripp and 23 of his men were cut off when the Japanese opened fire on the platoon. They had run against a defended enemy bivouac area, with several patrols established in the thick undergrowth. In the confused fighting which took place as the Fijian patrols tried to regain regimental headquarters, they were ordered to break into small groups and made their way to the rear under cover of darkness. Most of them eventually regained the main force the following day after personal adventures involving narrow escapes. Tripp, with some Tongans, encountered a patrol strongpoint. In a personal encounter he shot a Japanese, and was himself saved from injury when a cigarette lighter and cartridge clip deflected an enemy bullet, the force of which felled him. Before he regained his feet he accounted for another Japanese whose companions were firing at the fleeing Tongans. He then hid in the undergrowth. Under cover of darkness he made his way back to the American regiment, investigating enemy positions on the way.

In August 1944 The first presentation in the South Island of American decorations awarded to New Zealand officers serving with the United States forces in the South Pacific took place at Burnham Military Camp. The Silver Star, awarded for gallantry in action, was presented to Major Tripp and Captain Williams by Colonel J. H. Nakivell, the military attache at the United States Legation in Wellington, on behalf of the United States Government. The awards were made for gallantry in the Solomons, where they had led forces of the Fijian guerrillas.

The citation to the award of the Silver Star to Major Tripp said that it was made for gallantry in action on New Georgia during the period July 6-13, 1943, when he was serving with the First Battalion, South Pacific Scouts. It also noted that information obtained by his courageous efforts contributed in a large measure to the success of military operations against the enemy.

The citation to Captain Williams award said that it was made for gallantry in action while leading patrols of native scouts on numerous dangerous missions in the Marovovo sector at Guadalcanal from January 1st to February 1st, 1943.

In closing out this chapter there is one more thing I wanted to mention about Tripp. Dr. Fox told me that Charlie Tripp trained the Fijians under his command to shoot low and drop the enemy, it was advice which he himself had received from an old American gunslinger when Tripp stopped over in the US while traveling between New Zealand and England (shoot low, shoot for shit was the advice, the idea being that you dropped your opponent and gave yourself the opportunity to think what to do next). Tripp had to discipline two of his Fijian troops when they both took snap shots at a Japanese soldier from either side of a tree and both shots hit the enemy's head. Fine shooting, but not what they had been taught to do. Colonel Weston had also mentioned learning the same thing in his book:

> For us, survival required the quickness of an Old West gunfighter. We would instinctively drop to the dirt at the first crack of rifle and machine gun fire.

It's interesting to point out that a document, Report No. 123 Historical Officer Canadian Military Headquarters, which concerned Battle Drill Training of troops, dated August 31st 1944, states the following in one section:

> If full preparedness for war is to be achieved it is essential that all ranks should be able to use their weapon with confidence and without fuss. They should be "weapon conscious" and bring their weapons into play as spontaneously as the cowboy of Zane Grey's novels used his six-shooter in the past and the modern gangster uses his Tommy Gun in New York today.

Tripp's story is also interesting and ironic in a way because we have an American who passed on some vital knowledge to a New Zealander who passed it on to the Fijians who later passed on their own vital knowledge to the Americans!

Pay it forward you never know when it might get paid back.

Hip-level, quick-firing position by which Marines fire within a split second is demonstrated with pistol, submachine gun and rifle. Source: The Atlanta Constitution, September 15th, 1943.

Colonel J. H. Nankivell, Military Attache at the United States Legation in Wellington, with Major C. W. H. Tripp (left) and Captain D. E. Williams (right).

Heinmiller's Article in American Rifleman

Most of the newspaper articles about Carl Heinmiller were written toward the end of the war. A lot were also written postwar. I was able to locate one article Major Carl W. Heinmiller wrote for American Rifleman for their October 1946 issue. Heinmiller described events which occurred during the war in his own words. In that article titled "Fiji Scouts, Marksmen" he wrote:

> One of the neglected chapters of World War II is the extent to which natives were used in jungle warfare. Although many of them were employed as guides and labor troops, there were many others who excelled as guerrillas and raiders. In the early stages of the Pacific war, I was assigned to the organization and training of the famed Fiji Scouts. Known in official records as the South

Pacific Scout Company and the Fiji Defense Regiment, the boys made a great record as commandos and scouts.

After struggling through the jungles for several days in July of 1942, I finally arrived at an outpost of the Eastern Independent Commandos at Viti Levu, in the Fiji Islands. My job was to form about 400 natives of the surrounding country into guerrilla bands, in the event that the Japs should attack. When I arrived, they looked like a pretty sad outfit as far as equipment was concerned. Clothing was not a major issue, but the men did want something to make them look like soldiers—and weapons were limited to Enfield .303 rifles that had to be converted to .22 caliber. When I arrived, I brought with me three tommy guns, two Garands, and a Browning Automatic Rifle. That was all we had.

I spent a few days observing the training of the Fijian troops and was so astounded at their jungle craft and ability to move in that mass of twisted green, that I did not notice too carefully the teaching of the New Zealanders in preliminary marksmanship. The natives were the absolute masters of the bush. The Fijian is a man of tremendous physical stature. I had expected him to be rather short, but a six-footer was the usual size. The muscular development was superior to any people that I had ever seen. Being fuzzy-haired, they could be seen at rare times as they moved, but in battle they cut their hair close to their head. I was enthralled with the idea of a soundless weapon, as the men could hide so well that it was impossible to see them. Having been a bug on archery, I baffled the village with some simple feats. I tried concealing myself and shooting from that position, believing that the natives would not be able to find me. They found me so easily that I was amazed. It was not long before I became confident that a Fijian could find you by smell alone. If we could have had smokeless and flashless powder, we would have never have been observed.

137

The first day on the range was novel indeed. We walked out to a convenient hillside that was steep enough, to assure us that nothing more than a goat, and good one, could be up there. I explained what was needed to my First Section Chief, Joni Roko, a beautifully built native of about six foot three. He rattled off the orders in Fijian and the boys went to work with cane knives and machetes. In a short time they had all the undergrowth cleared over a thirty-yard range. The night before we had made up some six-inch targets on eight-by-ten paper and set them up on any material available.

The instruction began with the New Zealanders' giving the Fijians a handful of .22's and telling them to shoot. I wasn't quite sure whether these men had any preliminary marksmanship training or not. Knowing that "face" was all-important for the first few days, I gave in to an ANZAC Sergeant to save any embarrassment that might be caused by too big a change or repetition. The first ten men went to the firing line. The Enfields were single shot and I was quite surprised to see one round go into the gun and the other four rounds into the mouths of the natives! The order to commence firing was given.

I'll never forget the positions that were assumed. Of the seventy men in the Veria detachment, each position was different. The stock of the rifle found its resting place everywhere from the crotch of the elbow to the base of the throat. Most of the natives wanted to rest the gun on something so that they could keep both hands around the stock. Their powerful hands would wrap around the stock and trigger guard till it looked like an overlapping grip that a golfer would use. Some of the men would sight with the right eye, some with the left, and many with both.

I questioned the New Zealander on the styles that were allowed and he jauntily replied that it didn't make any difference, the natives were poor shots anyway, but better with a knife. After the first order had fired, the men went forward to check their scores. Squeals of delight pierced the air and the men jabbered excitedly about their shooting. Thinking that they may have shot fairly well, I went forward to see what had been done. Not a shot had hit the six-inch circle but the pleasure was due to the fact that all men had hit the paper at least once.

I called all the men around and spent the next ten minutes trying to get one point across. To shoot well, it was necessary to take a proper position. It didn't take long to see that the men were skeptical. The Fijian is rarely affected by talk. Action is what he respects. The time for action had arrived. A demonstration was needed to impress these boys.

My American sergeants were all rated as experts with the rifle, so we took positions on the line and fired a group of five shots each. The bullseye was of good size and the distance small. Each of us managed to hit it. For a moment it seemed that we had failed, but when the men clustered around the targets they were astounded by shooting that any three-months rookie from a training center could have done. Wanting to impress them more, I told one of my men, Sergeant Adams, that I wanted him to shoot a can off my hand at fifteen yards. The can was of good size, but Adams was rather upset as he had never done anything like it before. The act went off as planned but we did not repeat it as the bullet hit the lower portion of the can. But the mission was accomplished.

The Fijians' interest was increased tenfold. They were anxious to be able to shoot correctly. We spent long hours on correct positions, breathing, and trigger pull. Finally, the men were allowed to fire again. The improvement was terrific. The natives were like boys on Christmas Day. We finished up the day's shooting and I again impressed upon them the importance of good shooting. It was time to call it a day and I told the Kewie Sergeant to take over and I went back to camp.

Upon arrival, I heard some .22 firing and wondered what was going on. It wasn't long before I found out. The Fijians had tried shooting a can from one of the group's hand and it was hit off center. The can flew up and cut the cheek of the holder. That stopped the can shooting trick.

Two of the commando detachments were under New Zealand officers, and they had full charge of all training. I made several suggestions on marksmanship but they were shrugged off. The troops of these detachments had the same "ways" of shooting that my detachment had.

After insistent requisitions were sent in, we finally were given an allowance for the tommy guns. The Fijian Defense Command was trying to keep most of the .45 ammunition for its own use as they had received .45 automatics. There were some bitter words spilled over this deal, but in the end I got my allowance.

The training of the Fiji Commandos was scheduled on six days out of each month. I had four detachments to train, and used the same training program for each group, which made it easy to set up the schedule. When I arrived back at Veria, my base detachment was ready for the second phase of training, which included the tommy gun. I was quite surprised when I found the group had assembled the day before and wanted to start shooting early.

Once again we went out to the "ranger." In a month's time, the vegetation had completely grown up again. After clearing the land, we lashed some crude crosses of one-inch stock together and struck them in the ground. We then cut banana leaves and tied them to the crosses and used them for silhouette targets.

We gave the usual preliminary instructions. I called Joni Roko out and gave him a tommy gun to shoot. The troubles began all over again. I could not keep any of them from shutting their eyes after the first shot. That first shot would hit the target, and the rest of the burst would plow into the ground. We tried every trick we knew, but it was no use. I was so disgusted that I told them to get the .22 Enfields. I turned the range over to one of my sergeants, and tried to figure out what to do.

Sergeants Adams and Cannon of my staff came over and I said, "I can't understand it. This gun kicks less than an M1."

"But these men have fired only .22's," Sergeant Cannon said.

That fact had slipped my mind entirely. I said, "Well, that's true, but there's very little kick to this baby. I can fire this thing off of my chin!"

A skeptical look passed across Adams' and Cannon's faces, as they exchanged looks.

"I'd like to see that done, myself," said Sergeant Adams.

"Me, too," added Cannon.

I had seen the trick done several times, but had never done it. I began to wonder just how tough it would be. I knew that the Cutts Compensator would keep it from rising too much. I then noticed that Joni Roko was listening intently. That was the deciding factor. It has to be done.

As soon as the .22 firing was over, we called the men into a circle and told them the story of how easy it was to fire a submachine gun. Expressionless faces turned my way. They had tried this stuttering weapon and were afraid. I explained that there wasn't anything to be afraid of, that it was easy to fire, that you could hold it on your chin and shoot it. The Fiji boys rolled their eyes and jabbered like monkeys in a fire. I loaded a gun and put it on single shot, and after much squirming around, I managed to get the gun on my chin and still be able to look through the sight. It was necessary to turn my head on an angle to do this, but I managed it.

I fired one shot. Much to the surprise of all, including myself, I did not fall down. By puffing out my lower lip I was able to take up most of the shock. I fired a few more shots and then told the men I would fire it on automatic. The men were motionless. My own sergeants were slightly stunned by the action. I turned the gun on automatic and fired a burst. We went forward to look at the target and found that most of the shots had scored on the banana leaf. That was all we needed. The firing improved by leaps and bounds. By teaching the men to shoot in short bursts, they were able to keep their eyes open.

The most amazing demonstration occurred when we ran the men through a course in sniping. We set up several courses in the jungle. One of them extended down a trail for 100 yards. I had ten setups that, when sprung, would throw up a silhouette target. I used natural material for the trips and the natives spotted them and stepped over them. The only thing that would work was black thread attached to an electrical trip. The smallest amount of pressure tripped the trap. To make it more realistic, I added a one-second Primacord fuse with a small charge. That gave the "stalker" time to fire first.

We ran ten men down the trail without making any suggestions. Each man did exactly the same thing. As they tripped the wire and the target flew up, they immediately dove off the trail to shoot first. I was very disturbed about my "failure" for a time, but soon discovered that, for the natives, those tactics were perfect. As soon as a native hit the bush, he would continue to move like a pheasant until he could get a shot at the target without being exposed.

Another sniping course was from trees. This proved very interesting, but upset me again due to the unorthodox styles that were developed. The men were allowed to set up an ambush in the trees and the target carriers moved up to a given point and set up their targets. This given point was within fifteen or twenty yards of the "hidden" snipers. After the targets were set up, the "carriers" moved beyond and out of range. A whistle signal was given and the men opened fire. Some of the styles were very funny. Some of the men would peek out and shoot and then disappear. Many would take the rifle with one hand and shoot it in the general direction of the target. Once again, the men slipped and slow movement was stressed. It was an improvement but the men still held their weapons in varied positions.

After several weeks of training the men developed new styles again. In all positions they were able to shoot well, so thought it was perfectly all right. We made no attempt to correct them this time, but stopped all target practice till we were able to beg, borrow, or steal enough .30 caliber ammunition for a few rounds per man. I found that a P-39 had cracked up in the jungle, and took a trip out to the site of the wreck. After six hours of digging, we uncovered about a thousand rounds of .30 caliber ammunition, and were able to salvage a little under 400 rounds.

With our tongues in our cheeks we told the troops that we would fire the .30 caliber. The Fijians took the news calmly, believing that there would not be any difference in the Enfield .22 and the M1. We asked for volunteers for the first five rifles, which were all we could muster. Almost all of the men stepped up. The guns were loaded and instructions repeated in the same words that were used for the preliminary firing.

"Men, remember how you are supposed to hold this gun. Hold it right and you can hit the target. Hold it wrong and it will shoot badly." Joni Roko interpreted the words, which had to be as simple as possible.

The first volley was fired almost as one shot. Slapstick comedy never saw anything like the reaction. Each man had been holding his rifle in his own particular pose. Each one dropped his gun like it was red-hot, jumped to his feet and grabbed a part of his arm, face, or shoulder.

Once again we called out the first five. They were a sorry-looking bunch. Two split lips, one puffed eye, a badly swollen collar bone and a bruised biceps. They were such a meek looking bunch that we could hardly keep a straight face, but told them that we would fire five rounds apiece and show them it could be done if the rifle were held properly. The Fiji boys swarmed around us and made a thorough inspection to see if we had smashed lips and yes. Once again the idea was effective, but it was a long time before they could shoot without flinching considerably.

A short while after that, my division, the 37th, was alerted to leave Fiji and move to Guadalcanal. A few days after the operation into New Georgia, I was called back to the scouts. It was with great anticipation that I went, and with enthusiasm that I was received. Our training paid off. As the records show, the Fiji scouts harassed the Japs night and day. We fired very few rounds, but killed a great number of Nips. It was rarely necessary to fire more than once at a Jap. The few losses that the Fijians had were due to artillery and mortar fire. We never lost a man on patrol work. The men were able to get very close before they fired, and they did an excellent job.

Many times the scouts would fire one-handed. Naturally, they were not very accurate but they were moving all the time to a hiding place. If those natives had been brought up with guns instead of knives, they would undoubtedly have been expert marksman. With flashless and smokeless powder, they would never have been found. As it was, with only a moderate amount of training, and moderate equipment, they distinguished themselves in one chapter of the long battle to down the Jap invaders.

Chalk Marks the Spot

In his book, Larsen described the events that occurred once the Americans had arrived on the scene in Fiji. Once again we are told about the chalk incident. Since it was recounted in so many places, it was obviously an important incident that occurred which equally impressed the American and New Zealanders who had been stationed there.

Larsen wrote:

> The New Zealanders could now make themselves understood in the Fijian language which was not difficult to learn. The Fijians increased their knowledge of English too, and relationships could not have been better. Training was becoming more advanced and the Fijians were especially clever at stalking. Night raids were conducted against American forces camped along the main road. The Americas were often told the time of a raid to within a few hours, yet the commandos could creep past their extra guards and place dummy time-bombs anywhere they pleased; getting out again without being observed—once a Fijian left a chalk cross on the water-bottle worn by the sergeant of the guard. For one raid the platoon commander at Mau blackened his face with shoe polish; some of the Fijians, not realizing their existing natural camouflage, did likewise.
>
> The sergeant at Ngaloa practiced amphibious operations with his little launch. The launch held only half a dozen men, so he towed the rest of his platoon in canoes strung out behind him. In this way he made night raids on Serau Platoon, ten miles along the coast. Although the method appeared crude, the enthusiasm created and the experience gained, was valuable, and the OC encountered the other coastal platoons to use their initiative in a similar way. To get fuel for this little launch, the Ngaloa Platoon

swopped bottles of beer with American truck drivers, who, in return, filled the empty bottles with petrol.

Am American, Mike Podrosky, was attached to the Ko-mave Platoon for a while, and he and Sid Heckler planned an ambush for the American scout car which patrolled the road regularly. The platoon placed obstacles on the road and lay in wait. What happened could not be exactly described by either party afterwards, but the car pulled up and the Americans dived for cover thinking they had encountered Japanese. They contended afterwards that the Komave Platoon was lucky it was not shot up as the ambush had been a terrific surprise. Captain Tripp apologised, on behalf of Mike and Sid, to the American commander next day, thinking that perhaps the commandos had gone too far; but the American commander was overjoyed and stated that it was the best training his men could have to keep them alert.

The commandos worked in close co-operation with the United States forces, and they guided several American battalions on cross-country marches. During these marches the commandos automatically made observations of such things as broken undergrowth and footprints, which indicated the course taken, and size of some other party in the jungle. Deductions made by the New Zealanders and Fijians amazed the Americans, yet they were elementary to the commandos and merely the result of practice. High ranking American officers recognised the value of the commando's specialised knowledge and they frequently called on Captain Tripp for advice on jungle conditions. They were also interested in the method of training adopted by the commandos; this method was to foster the desire within the individual, to explore and enjoy life in the jungle.

Sporting equipment was obtained, and the Fijians were taught boxing, for which they showed great aptitude. Inter-platoon bouts were arranged and these produced some outstanding talent. Next to Rugby football, boxing became the Fijian's favourite sport.

An article in the Morristown Gazette Mail, January 27th 1944 again demonstrated how in awe the Americans were of the Fijian Scouts. The article "Wily Fiji Scout Locates Japs" stated:

> A Fiji scout who knows his trees saved an American reconnaissance force on a recent foray in the Solomons.
>
> Inching up a river, the Americans ran into deadly mortar fire. Field glasses swept the valley but the enemy battery could not be detected.
>
> Then the Fiji scout pointed to a cluster of trees on the hillside. "It's the first time I've ever seen that kind of tree growing anywhere but beside the water," he said.
>
> Fire was concentrated on the trees and out popped a Japanese mortar crew. The Americans picked the Japs off as they scrambled up the hillside.

Another article in an African American newspaper Afro-American, May 27th of that same year "Fijians Best Jungle Fighters, Japs Learn" stated:

> Bougainville. – Once when elements of the 93rd Division were pushing east of Torokina, an advance party ran into a group of Fiji scouts. One of our group called out:
>
> "Hey Joe, how many today?" A favorite question whenever Fijians are met beyond the perimeter.

"Fifteen Joe," was the answer, one scout motioning with his bayonet. Fifteen Japs bayoneted to death.

Of the thousands of soldiers on this war-torn island, the happiest, the best liked, and perhaps the most feared by the enemy are the Fijians. Brown of skin, marvelously built, possessing a warm friendliness, these tough soldiers have won the respect of all here—and assuredly the Japanese.

In their trophy room are enemy machine guns, expensive sabers, countless small arms, pieces of heavy artillery, and the coveted Jap battle flags.

British subjects, most of these soldiers are volunteers. They represent the island's best in manhood—each regional chief having sent his best warriors. Small forces landed at Guadalcanal in April, last year, then across the channel to the Florida Islands and finally Bougainville on December 21.

Since that time the exploits of the Fijians have read something like the deeds of Sir Lancelot. Officered by New Zealanders and their own people, they first pushed through the jungles, setting up an observation post thirty-seven miles east of Empress Augusta Bay—squarely in the middle of a Jap infested area. From this point patrols were dispatched.

For two months they were alone. And not only did they wage war but carved out an airstrip.

Perhaps the first time the enemy met a soldier who knew the jungles, who fought equally as well with knife or rifle, who could live for days on jungle vegetation, who could ease through the terrain with the agility of Fussy-Wuzzies, who loved nothing better than a good scrap.

The story goes that one patrol encountered twenty Japs neatly sandwiched between two knobs. Five Fijians crawled close enough to get a complete view of what turned out to be a homey scene. Two Japs were getting haircuts, several played games, some were reading. Their laughter peeled out and turned into song.

Into this atmosphere of jolliality, five grenades were lobbed. All were killed. The Fijians silently withdrew—but only after relieving the enemy of material of military value.

There is little difference in the appearance of Fijian soldiers and our own colored troops. They too, range in color. In some is a mixture of Indian, native, and Tongan blood making the final product bronze of color with inky black hair.

As noted the Fijians became true fans of the "sweet science" and also skilled in unarmed combat much like our own troops. I will expand on this more in a later chapter. Boxing is something which any learned Combatives practitioner should have at least some fundamental knowledge in.

Without the fundamental knowledge of boxing or even wrestling, you are just going through the motions. Having that foundational knowledge provides one with the confidence that you can better handle yourself in the ring or in the field. Aside from learning unarmed combat tactics, boxing and wrestling were the primary mode for developing a recruit's ruthless fighting ability during both World Wars.

At a time period when most Eastern Martial Arts systems were relatively unknown to the West, most of the physical training instructors came from boxing or wrestling backgrounds. I've written about this in some great detail in my previous books, so it would seem that I am beating a dead horse, discussing it further, at this point.

What I will do is illustrate the importance of "competitive sports" such as boxing which had been taught alongside other subject matter relevant to Commandos. The best way to do this is to discuss a document that can be found amongst General Lucian Truscott's papers at the George C. Marshall Foundation.

During World War II, General Truscott had been instrumental in developing an American Commando unit patterned after the British Commandos. The American unit had been activated by Truscott as the 1st Ranger Battalion, and placed under the command of Major Orlando Darby.

In May 1942, Truscott had been assigned to the Allied Combined Staff under Lord Louis Mountbatten. In August of that year he was the primary U.S. observer on the Dieppe Raid.

The memo found amongst Truscott's papers is titled "Training Instructions For Advanced Detachments" and it discussed how to keep up the training regimen of the Commandos; and how to reduce their boredom while they were traveling, presumably aboard a ship.

The memo, issued by J.C. Hayden, Brigadier, Commanding Special Service Brigade, stated:

1. The following notes are issued for your guidance in making up your programs of work and recreating during the voyage.
    a. It is of the first importance that all personnel should keep as physically fit and interested as possible. This is an ideal which will not be achieved unless a genuine care and ingenuity are given to the preparation of your programs.

    b. You must remember that you are placed in independent command of your detachment of first class NCOs and men belonging to your Commando.

On you and your care and efficiency will depend the well-being of that detachment. You may, in fact you probably will, have many difficulties to overcome in keeping them up to a proper standard of efficiency and mental and physical alertness. Please do not let any trouble be too much and make sure that all ranks under your Command know in practice and not only in theory that their troubles are yours and you will take endless pains to overcome whatever the particular difficulty is.

c. Try and pick out of your detachment the private soldiers whom you consider could be made NCO's after instruction and training. Having chosen them, make it your objective to give them that training. It may be very valuable one day.

d. The following is a list of subjects to which particular attention must be paid:
  (i) Physical Training, and the study of advanced first aid.
  (ii) Unarmed combat.
  (iii) Boxing.
  (iv) T.O.E.T., and the general handling of arms, so that all men are technically proficient in all weapons, even although you may not be able to give them firing practice. Such firing practice should become possible after arrival, and I particularly am anxious that you should take every opportunity of improving weapon training standard by range practices and field firing.
  (v) Theoretical side of compass and protractor work.
  (vi) The theory of map reading.

(vii)   Elementary Astronomy. This is always a subject which might be of the utmost value, and the more officers and NCOs have a working knowledge of it, the better. The navigator and other ships officers should be asked if they would be good enough to assist by giving lectures on the subject to selected NCO's and men.

(viii)   Navigational Training, including when it is possible, the sailing of skiffs or cutters. Here again the assistance of the ships officers would be required.

(ix)   Intensive semaphore training.

(x)   Lectures on subjects of geographical, military and general interest should be arranged.

(xi)   Tactical exercises, either off the map or with the aid of a sand table, should be met for NCOs and selected men. These exercises can be made to include such points as the taking of quick decisions; the issue of verbal orders message writing and the delivery of verbal messages; orders to and handling fighting patrol; the selection of routes bringing in map references and compass bearings; the care of men in the field and the making of simple plans for sub-section or section attacks on such objectives as pill-boxes or isolated centers of resistance.

e.   Please understand that no training has much value unless it is progressive. Therefore make your program for a week or more ahead so that there is no danger of either the instruction or the attendance at it being merely spasmodic and none productive.

f.   You will not find it an easy task to keep men interested and t the top of their form, and you cannot expect to do so unless you are prepared to take unremitting pains and trouble. Please do so – it will be well worth while both from your point of view and that of those under your command.

2.   In addition to the points mentioned in para d, it is important that your detachments should be self-supporting as regards cooks, because there is always the possibility that you will be placed on shore and be required to prepare your own food. In order to enable such training to be given it is suggested that you should make suitable arrangements with the master cook on board ship you will have to be careful that the men selected for training in cooking are not merely used as fatigue men.

They had to make sure they knew how to cook so they could eat. That was kind of an important one. But again, having an optimal level of fitness, and knowing how to fight were at the top of the list. This was what the Commandos in Europe were being trained to do during their formation but what about the Australian ones?

There was a lot more to it than just knowing how to fire one's weapons, or how to utilize unarmed combat tactics to destroy the enemy, or knowing how to cook. Some of the knowledge the commandos picked up had been learned in the field, by trial and error or from people who had gone through the motions before them.

Much like the knowledge on jungle fighting passed between the Fijian scouts, the New Zealanders and the Americans. That knowledge was vital knowledge. That pooled knowledge helped them all to thrive and survive in a jungle fighting environment.

There is a New Zealand newspaper, The Ellesmere Guardian which had an article "Night Fighters" in its April 22nd 1943 issue. The war correspondent who wrote the article stated:

A day with a Commando unit in its training area was the most interesting I have ever spent on army exercises. The average Fijian guerilla fighter is a fine physical specimen, darker than a Maori because of the mixture of Polynesian and Melanesian blood, but not unlike him in his boyish enthusiasm and happy-go-lucky outlook. He speaks a little English and is the essence of disciplined politeness. He has cut his great bush head of hair so that his steel helmet will fit him, and he wears a specially designed drill battledress. In the jungle he often prefers bare feet to boots, and he is armed with cane and sheath knives, an American rifle or tommy-gun, and hand grenades. His New Zealand commissioned and non-commissioned officers were mainly selected from members of the N.Z.E.F. who were familiar with bush and rural life. But as the commanding officer of this unit, Captain C. W. H. Tripp, of Geraldine, South Canterbury, told me:

"The Fijians have taught us a great deal about living off the land and understanding the bush, but we can never hope to learn their amazing sense of danger and direction and their powers of observation. Those things are born in them."

I learned a lesson in stealth and concealment by watching a three-pronged mock attack up a swampy gully with bush on either side. Only by intense concentration from a much better position that the enemy would have had could I see anything at all of the preliminary phase. Even then the only sign of movement was the momentary waving of grass stalks a mere 20 yards away and well out of the enemy's sight. One by one the men came slithering out like snakes on their wet and muddy stomachs. Of the other two prongs of the force, working through the bush, nothing could be seen beyond what looked like an occasional flitting shadow. Then with fixed bayonets and blood-curdling yells the attackers rose and converged on their objective.

Up in the jungle, other soldiers were practicing snap shooting at hidden targets along a rough track. With a New Zealand sergeant I followed closely behind one of them and learned something about the Fijian's extraordinary powers of observation. He had never been over the course before, and had no idea of the location of the targets, which were small white boards set in the trees of the track. Yet time after time, when I could see nothing, he raised his rifle to his shoulder and fired. He saw and hit seven out of the eight targets. The explanation which the New Zealanders give to this skill is that the Fijian knows the bush so well that a strange sixth sense tells him of the presence of some unusual object. He can spot and read the tracks of animals and men where a white man sees nothing.

At night he has the eyes of a cat—or perhaps it is not so much sight as intuition. Some of the New Zealanders are developing this instinct, too. I saw more burly natives and New Zealanders throwing one another about in unarmed combat, learning to creep up on sentries and disarm assailants. Then they followed one another through a toughening combat course, ploughing through mud, scaling a high wooden fence, leaping from a 10ft. bank into a shallow stream and clambering up muddy slopes.

Before moving on to the next chapter I wanted to include one more article that contains a few quotes regarding the Fiji Scouts, and a mention of unarmed combat. The article which contains an entertaining and comedic tone, was written by Robert Lewis Taylor for the December 16th 1944 issue of The New Yorker.

In the article "The Nicest Fellows You Ever Met" Taylor who had been embedded with a photographer and the Fijians in Bougainville wrote:

> From birth, the Fijians are in and out of the jungle. They understand the tangled greenery that covers the South Pacific islands the way a New Yorker understands Times Square. Their sense are sharper than the white man's and their strength and endurance are greater. There is very little left for them to learn about the jungle. Certainly the news, a year or so ago, that they were to be "trained for jungle fighting" by the Allies must have struck them as comical, though none of them ever said so. In fact, I was recently told by a New Zealand captain stationed at the Fiji camp on Bougainsville that the men there had been unfailingly deferential and kind to their white tutors. They are a people with an extraordinary sense of humor, but they have an almost pathological aversion to hurting the feelings of a friend.
>
> However, at the end of their training, which took place in the Fijis, they allowed their sense of humor a fairly free hand. The company of white soldiers who had trained them arranged to fight a mock battle with them in the bush. After dark, each side was to try to penetrate as far as possible into the other's lines. The main idea was to see how well the new Fiji scouts had learned their lessons. It turned out that they had learned them pretty well. During the night some of the white scouts worked thirty or forty feet into the Fiji lines, and figured they had the battle won, since they hadn't caught and Fijians behind *their* lines. When they came to check up at daylight, it developed that most of the Fijians had apparently spent the night in the white headquarters. They had chalked large crosses on the tents and the furniture and had left one of the most distinct crosses on the seat of the commanding officer's trousers, which he had thrown over a chair around 4 A.M.

After that mock battle it was felt that the Fijians were ready for the jungle. They were shipped up to Bougainville, several hundred strong, and introduced to the Japanese.

In another segment of the article, Taylor provided an excellent description of how the Fijians operated in the bush in their jungle war against the Japanese:

I was quartered in a Quonset hut with an American Army photographer who had just had a singular and nerve racking experience. He had been out in the bush for two weeks with a party of Fijians, having put in a request to take some motion pictures behind the enemy lines.

Someone, he said almost bitterly, had taken him up on it. He had lost about twenty-five pounds and figured that he had aged somewhere between ten and fifteen years. It was not that the Fijians treated him badly. On the contrary, they had been most solicitous, in their own way. But the photographer had nevertheless found the pace quite trying. His escorts carried all his photographic gear, but most of the time he had to run to stay with them. And he was always getting tangled in creepers and vines and tripping up.

"They didn't seem to use any paths," he told me. "They kept disappearing into walls of stuff that a snake couldn't have got through with a bush knife."

The disappearing was, in fact, one of the worst aspects of the trip, and the photographer couldn't explain it. "They must have been pulling my leg," he said over and over to me. "And yet, why would they? They were the nicest, fellows you ever met. I don't understand it. We would be going along, me hardly daring to breathe—we'd run across two Jap patrols the first hour out—and

158

all of a sudden I'd look around and I'd be alone, completely damned horribly alone, not a sign of them anywhere, no leaf stirring, no sound, nothing. I'd just stand there, thinking, 'O.K., sniper, let's have it, I'm right out in front of you and no place to go. Let's have it.' And then in a minute, all of those big black guys would be around again, and pretty soon my heart would start back up and things were all right. I don't know where they went and I don't know where they came from, but most of all I don't know why they did it. They *must* have been pulling my leg." He really seemed very concerned about it.

On the second day, the photographer said, the Fijians spotted a group of Japs in a clearing in a valley below them. He explained to them in some excitement that he wanted to take pictures, and started fitting a telescopic lens to his camera. The Fiji corporal in charge of the group gave an amiable nod; then he and his men disappeared again. It was ten minutes before the photographer was ready to shoot. When he got set up and had a look at the clearing, there were no Japs in sight. The Fijians reappeared shortly. "Where'd they go, fellows?" the photographer kept asking. "What about the patrol?"

His questions seemed to amuse the scouts. "They laughed and laughed," he said to me. "Some of them slapped their knees. I began to get the general idea. There had been some misunderstanding. The Jap patrol had quit patrolling—for good."

The Fijians, the photographer told me, carried no food. They ate herbs and roots and wild fruits and vegetables. Sometimes they cooked their meal, squatting over a quick, small fire, and sometimes they didn't. The photographer lived on some field rations he had started out with, and when they gave out he tried the Fiji diet, but it disagreed with him. Their sleeping habits distressed him, too. Several times they made camp in what seemed to the photographer the middle of the most populous Jap territory. He would roll up in a blanket, feeling exposed and uneasy, and perhaps a couple of hours later he would wake up and look around. The Fijians would be missing. "Not one left," he told me. "All gone—God knows where and God knows why. And me surrounded by the Japanese South Pacific Army. It was great."

On none of these occasions did he see any of them return. They were always on hand early in the morning, though, always fresh and ready to move. In camp the Fiji scouts wear khaki clothing similar to that of other jungle troops, but they cached it soon after they left on this trip and proceeded almost naked. They had their own methods of camouflage, the photographer said a little ruefully, adding, "Not that they had been getting in my was as it was." By a skillful use of berry juices and miscellaneous greenery, they were able to surpass their customary efforts to become one with the jungle. They usually did this, I gathered, when they were going to be operating within a few feet of the enemy.

The photographer took a lot of pictures of Japs in action during the two weeks. The Fijians wove back and forth behind the Jap front, counting the troops, noting what kind of equipment they had and how it was brought in, and in general taking inventory. It was the photographer's impression that his colleagues were spending their mysterious nights visiting the Jap camps. In view of what we learned from various sources later, the visits must have been lively.

The Fijians had side arms, but the photographer never saw any of them fire one. The scouts apparently depended on the knives and small hardwood bludgeons they carried. Also, he thought, they must frequently have used only their hands at close quarters.

"You know," he told me, "I think everybody down here feels grateful to the Fijis. Soldiers watching them come in from a mission seem to be saying to themselves, 'Fine. Nice work, boys. We wouldn't be down here if it weren't for those nasty little Japs, and a lot more of us would be alive today. We don't know what you've been up to, and we're not especially bloodthirsty, but we hope there's quite a little group of ex-supermen lying around somewhere nearby. They got better than they deserved. A nice clean death in the dark is too damn good for them.'"

READY FOR ANYTHING in the jungle is Corp. Peni Setuate, carefully cleaning his rifle before his shelter in this official Marine Corps photo. He fights with Marine and Army units on Bougainville Island.

This page's photo and the next two pages, Source: The Pittsburgh Press, August 7th 1944.

Comparing Two Unarmed Combat Systems

In the third chapter of the Marine Corps manual Jungle Warfare FMFRP 12-9, "The Nature Of Jungle Warfare", it states:

> There are no "Blitz" campaigns in the jungle. The conditions that limit the operation of self-propelled artillery, tank destroyers, weapons and troop carriers and the tracked and wheeled vehicles that have played such an important part in other theaters of war are apparent.

> The pattern of jungle fighting is one of many small combats in which groups, squads, parts of squads, automatic weapons teams, and platoons strive to eject the enemy from his positions. The small units are armed with rifles, bayonets, carbines, hand grenades, flame throwers, automatic rifles, light machine guns, light mortars, antitank grenades, "bazookas", pistols, shot guns, knives, sub-machine guns, and demolitions. These are all weapons carried on the backs of the men who fight with them.

But what happened when they lost access to any of those weapons?

Going forward this is where I shift gears somewhat and discuss my other area of interest and the subject matter I usually tend to write about, unarmed combat systems of the era and the instructors who taught them.

We can recall the Carl Heinmiller article in the Birmingham News from 1945 that stated he was a "knife and dirty fighting expert". I decided it would be important to include a chapter discussing what those claims meant in some further detail.

When I asked Lee about his father's background he told me:

I had a few bouts, by accident with my Dad, when I jumped out to scare him, on his "Blind side"… swept my feet and I was on my way to the ground before he could catch me!! Only made that mistake a couple times in my early teens!!.

Although we cannot confirm exactly what unarmed combat system Heinmiller would been exposed to which made him an expert; or even where he might have learned it, we can do a survey of what was being taught during the era.

The most sensible place to start would be to take a look at what the Commando troops were being taught in Scotland in 1940 and then do a comparison of that to one of the courses we know of from the Pacific theater. We have to remember though that Heinmiller would have initially undergone basic training so it's quite possible he could have learned these tactics when he had been stationed in Ohio.

Amongst General Lucien Truscott's files is a document titled "Unarmed Combat – Notes by W.E. Fairbairn and E.A. Sykes, Inverailort, July 1940. Revised November 1940." I will discuss who Lucien Truscott was and why he is relevant to the discussion later. For now we will take a look at the document.

The document is interesting because it condensed the unarmed combat training a Commando recruit in Scotland had to undergo, to four lessons.

It's also notable because the end of the document pointed out that the techniques could be practiced and learned on both sides of the body, they were ambidextrous. It also noted that the student should pick and choose to master ten to fifteen techniques if they don't have enough time for the whole four lessons.

A fellow researcher and author, Bill Humphries noted:

I think it was a case in those early days of the war of Fairbairn and Sykes having to quickly put together a course to teach the Commandos. So they (in particular Fairbairn) relied on what he knew best and put a lot of his prewar Defendu in there. Sykes seems to have early on realized things needed to be streamlined and some things dropped all together which is what he did with his own system. Even Fairbairn seems to have eventually realized this as he gained more experience instructing during wartime and no doubt based on reports from people who had been in the field, and modified his instruction during the OSS years.

The early syllabus used by Fairbairn and Sykes is also excellent to compare with the syllabus Sykes developed for the SOE after Fairbairn went to the U.S. and comparing the two will show that Sykes didn't agree with many of the things being taught either and eliminated them from his syllabus.

From viewing the following document one can make the observation that Fairbairn attempted to include police tactics in the training, perhaps for restraining prisoners. However, Commandos were primarily involved in hit and run operations and that portion of the training therefore seemed unnecessary.

Author's Note: The Commando unarmed combat course taught by Fairbairn and Sykes in 1940 is presented on the following pages.

UNARMED COMBAT.

Notes by W.E. Fairbairn and E.A. Sykes, Inverailort, July 1940. Revised November 1940.

For progressive lessons, the sequence to be adhered to as closely as possible.

1st. LESSON.

Chin Jab.
Blows with the edge of the hand. x
Rock- crushed blow. x
Breaking from wrist hold.
     "   "   Bear-hug (arms pinioned) front.
     "   "   "   - (arms free)   "
     "   "   "   - (arms pinioned) rear.
     "   "   "   - (arms free)   "
     "   - Throat hold, one hand or both.
Wrist and elbow hold from rear, with chin jab and/or arm lock.
Bent arm hold.
Hand-shake combined with use of knife.

2nd. LESSON.

Knot for tying up an opponent.
Hand-cuff hold.
Hand-cuff hold for shorter opponent.
Tying up an opponent.
Arm and neck hold.
Arm and neck hold followed by throw. x
Arm and neck hold on the ground.
Disarming if held up with a pistol from front.
    "   -   -   -   "   -   -   - rear.
Disarming a third party.
Revision of thumb hold.

3rd. LESSON.

Chin jab against two opponents simultaneously.
Prevention against being lifted.
Japanese strangle from rear. x
    "   "   - front. x
Sentry hold. x
Head hold.
Wrist throw.
    "   "   with leg lock, on the ground.
Revision of previous lesson.

4th. LESSON.

Police hold (come along hold) correct and incorrect.
Use of match box.
Safety razor blade in peak of cap (to shew what may be expected)
Hip throw.
Use of short umbrella or cane.
Use of baton or thong.
Arm throw (reverse of hand-cuff hold). x
Searching a prisoner without help from others.
Arm held over table.
Wrist and neck attack, combined with use of knee.
Chrome hold.
Revision of previous lessons.
Grapevine. x

Continued - Sheet 42.

165

NOTES

To avoid accidents in practice, great care must be used with all holds. throws, blows and counters starred thus : x. The "Japanese strangle" with the "edge of the hand" blow, and the "arm throw" require extreme care.

On no account should the Chinese " rock crusher " be practised over the heart.

For simplicity of instruction these four lessons have been arranged for use on th right hand, but they are all equally applicable to the left hand, and should be practised with both.

If time is limited it is obviously impossible to acquire a thorough know-ledge of the whole contents of the four lessons. Everyone should master the "thumb hold" but, apart from that , individuals with limited time are advised to concen-trate on the mastery of ten or fifteen of the most important practises. Individual needs or preferences may govern the choice.

Author's Note: For comparison purposes I have included an unarmed combat course as it was taught to Special Operations Australia otherwise known as the Services Reconnaissance Department. I do not have a course which represents exactly what was taught at Wilson's Promontory. This course appeared in Volume Four of the SOA's training Syllabi.

INTRODUCTORY LECTURE

OBJECT OF TRAINING

To get men fit and capable of handling any posn. Also, to make them efficient in the art of silent killing.

1. PT is used for the conditioning in the early stages of the training, and for maintaining condition at the later stages. The value of being fit has been borne out by every medical report of this war. Every person leaving here is entitled to be fit, even if he has no heavy physical work on his future programme, as a fit man has a co-ordination of brains and body.

2. Fighting without arms is as old as man himself, and the earliest records report of sporting contests among men. Later, the Greek, Roman and Indian styles of wrestling were evolved up to the stage of modern "allin" wrestling and boxing matches. A band of Chinese monks whose religion forbade the use of weapons, developed the art of self defence to a high degree early in the written History of the World. In the 12th century, the Japanese copied this system and called it Ju-Jitsu (the gentle art) Being a small statured race, they paid special attention to the phase of using an opponent's weight against himself.

   Later in the last century, the USA imported it and called it among other names, Judo. They in turn paid special attention to the use of pressure points.

   Early in this War, the Allies evolved the system of fighting known as UAC. This sytem was drawn from all the above methods adapted is a military system of trg which has proved successful.

3. UAC therefore is an attacker's weapon at most times, and even where used in defence, the defensive move must always be followed up aggressively until the enemy is mastered. Its main uses are : Firstly, when weapons are not available; this can happen often where infiltration is used. Secondly, where the use of weapons would cause too much noise stalking a sentry.

4. Ruthlessness must be utter and complete and many "sporting" tendencies eliminated. There is no ultimate difference between shooting an enemy and biting him to death, or between tricking the enemy by false radio messages and by scooping sand into his eyes as you approach him.

5. Success will be achieved through constant, vigorous practice, allied to good physical condition.

6. DRESS -- In the early stages, unarmed combat may be practised in PT kit. Later, however, it may be performed in any type of dress; gradually working up to battle dress and eqpt.

7. INSTN

   (a) To obtain best results, the squad should not consist of more than 14 men, and must be under supervision of a qualified Instr.

   (b) Under no circumstances should men be put through Unarmed Combat trg without first being well warmed up with loosening and quickening exercises for a period of not less than five minutes.

   (c) The Instr will demonstrate each movement to the squad at high speed to show its effectiveness, then execute slowly, explaining every detail.

   (d) To practise movements, the squad will be paired off with

/ample....

ample space between pairs to prevent one pair fouling another.

(e) The Instr will put the squad through the movements very slowly until they have been thoroughly mastered, gradually working up to maximum speed. Great care must be taken that correct technique is maintained throughout.

(f) As men gain confidence and reach a higher state of efficiency, battle tests in Unarmed Combat can be introduced for periods of 10 to 12 minutes' duration, changing partners every 2 minutes.

This exercise takes the form of hand to hand combat, with men putting into effect grips and counters, already learned, and assures that each man works with various partners and gains the experience of different weight, style, etc, thus developing toughness, initiative, and the ability to make split second decisions as opportunities present themselves.

(g) Quick decision exercises should be practised in the form of ambushes, surprise attacks, etc, eg, the noiseless capture of the last man of a patrol moving along jungle trails. This will foster a sense of alertness, and develops in men the ability to react instinctively.

(h) It is only by constant practice in actual hand to hand combat that men can be brought to that state of toughness and efficiency required of a capable Unarmed Combat man.

8. At finishing stages, one man can be attacked by several men consecutively, each applying a different grip. This has been found to quicken the classes' reactions.

-----

4. (a) Break down all fours(3) (i) Bump head into his armpit; pull the arm back and knock his body forward. As he falls, secure hammerlock.
(ii) Secure his far ankle, hump his body forward and pull his feet into his buttocks for an ankle ride.
(iii) Reach both hands over to opponent's head and force it sideways away from you. When as far over as possible, pull it back towards you diagonally.

(b) Arm Rolls, all posns Demonstrate arm rolls and their application from all posns.

(c) Pick up and slam from behind and counter Seize opponent around hips and quickly lift him in swinging motion to slam him down in any posn.

Counter lift by placing your foot back inside his leg to hook his foot.

5. (a) Leg dive and back heel trip Grasp opponents left leg with both hands and pull under armpit. Place heel of own left foot behind his right heel and trip backwards to ground. Apply stepover toehold and break leg, or ruthless tactics.

(b) Double wristlocks and throw Take double wristlock and sit back to pull opponent forward. If he rolls, follow over and secure head scissors.

(c) Counter double and reverse wristlocks Pull held arm fwd across own body to break double wristlock. Push arm up and fwd to break reverse wristlock.

(d) Counter Hammerlock(2) (i) Drop body fwd and downward to straighten arm. Swing back and punch in testicles.
(ii) Somersault fwd.

6. (a) Forward headlock and throw (or jolt) Secure fwd headlock and claim his forearm. Sit back and roll him over. Follow on over and body-press him whilst retaining grip of his chin for a neck twist.
From fwd headlock lift forearm in hand into his throat; throw him back on to his spine.

(b) Counter Grip by hair or clothing front Interlock fingers of both hands and clamp down on opponent's hands or hand. Swing body smartly bringing opponent to knees, kick in face.

(c) Counter grip by hair or clothing from behind Quickly pivot on either foot to swing around and chop opp with edge of hand.

6. (d) Application of Nelson   Demonstrate and apply ¼. ½. ¾ and
                                full Nelsons.

7. (a) How to tumble and how   Right shoulder, left shoulder,
       to kick   forward and reverse. Kick with
                                outside of foot up to knee height.

8. (a) Hip throw   Take opponent's right shoulder
                                with left hand and his left hip with
                                your right hand and step in
                                behind his right hip and hip throw
                                him on to his back.

   (b) Working out under   Bridge in under opponent and turn
       opponent   inwards.

   (c) Counter daddy attack (2) (i) Opponent striking with his
                                right hand. Ward off blow with
                                right forearm, at same time keep
                                upper part of body to left.Apply
                                reverse wristlock and throw
                                opponent backwards breaking arm.
                                (ii)Opponent striking with his
                                right hand. Ward off blow with
                                left forearm. Encircle his right
                                arm with own left arm, place right
                                hand on his face and place own
                                left hand on own right wrist and
                                throw. Kick in"nuts if possible.

   (d) Stomach throw   Grasp opponent by clothing at
                                shoulders, quickly sit down at same
                                time placing one foot in pit of
                                his stomach; as he comes over
                                straighten leg and throw him
                                somersault. Retain grip and follow
                                up by kneeling across him and
                                apply strangle.

   (e) Counter to Strangle on   Opponent has you down on back
       ground   kneeling astride applying strangle
                                with fingers and thumbs. Grasp his
                                left wrist with own left hand, and
                                with quick movement strike his left
                                elbow with own right hand. Twist
                                body to left and throw opponent
                                over to own.

9. (a) Counter fwd headlock   In one co-ordinated movement,grasp
                                opponents wrist and crutch, jump
                                fwd thrusting one leg between
                                opponent and throw self backwards.
                                Trap his off leg with own and apply
                                goose neck on his wrist,or dump.

   (b) Step under wrist,trip   Grasp either of opponent's wrists
       and throw   with both hands, retaining grip.
                                Quickly step under his arm and apply
                                hammerlock. Place foot in front of
                                opponent and trip fwd on face
                                retaining hammerlock. Break arm.

   (c) Counter to kick in   Jump aside with a sweeping motion;
       testicles   place hands under opponent's heel,
                                force upwards throwing him on his
                                back. Follow up with kick in test's.
                                (ii)Pivot on one foot and stamp the
                                outside of your otherfoot on to his
                                shin.

9. (d) Side headlock & hip throw — In one co-ordinated movement, pivot on left foot, take a side headlock and throw opponent over right hip.

10. (a) Counter grasped around waist from behind arm; free (2) pinned(1) — (i) Reach down quickly between own legs, seize one of his legs and jerk off feet.
(ii) Move slightly to one side and chop testicles with heel of palm.
(iii) Twist hip smartly outward, apply double wristlock and throw.

(b) Japanese side headlock and throw — Take side headlock, clasping wrist of arm placed around opponent's head. Apply pressure with bone of forearm across side of opponent's face, between jawbone and temple region. Sit out pulling opponent to ground face down, and force opponents head back.

(c) Counter to side headlock Standing(1) Lying(1) — (i) Opponent applies headlock with right arm. Quickly drop on right knee, place your left hand on his left shoulder, right hand behind his right knee. Throw opponent across own left knee and apply cradle hold.
(ii) Place hand or fingers under opponent's nose and force his head back. Apply head scissors.

(d) Breaking grip of wrists — Reach over opponent's wrist and grasp own fist. Wrench upwards against opponent's thumbs.
BREAKING GRIP FROM WRIST WHEN BOTH ARE GRASPED: Lean fwd smartly and jerk upward against opponent's thumbs.

11. (a) Counter knife thrusts(2) — (i) Fend off thrust with left forearm and swing outside his body. Pull him through with right hand and chop back with your left.
(ii) As opponent strikes, ward off knife arm with own forearm, step in and drive knee into testicles or kick kneecap.

(b) Flying mare and counter — Grasp opponent's wrist with both hands. If grasping his right wrist, do a right about turn, placing his arm across your own left shoulder, palm uppermost. Pull down and throw him over ownshoulder breaking his arm.
(ii)Counter:As opponent places your arm on his shoulder, place your other hand in the small of his back and push firmly. This will throw opponent off balance and prevent throw.

(c) Counters to strangle from front(2) — (i) Strangles applied with fingers and thumbs from front: In one movement, pivot on left foot, swing right arm across and against opp's left wrist and forearm, and chop back against and across his face.

/(ii)

171

(ii) Stretch one arm upward between his arms and other arm outside. Clasp own hands and jerk downward at elbow region. Drive between his arms with hands wedged and kick in testicles.

| 11. | (d) Rugby tackle | Opponent approaching from front. Dive for his legs just below knees, encircling legs completely with arms and throw to ground. Opponent approaching from rear. Dive for opponent's legs behind knees, encircle with arms and throw to ground. |

| 12. | (a) Counter grasped around waist from front; arm free(1), pinned(2) | (i) Place left hand in small of opponent's back, right hand under opponent's chin or nose, drive knee into testicles and force back. (ii) Knee in testicles. Stamp on insteps, butt opponent in face. |

| | (b) Strangle from near standing(i)&sitting(ii) | Creep up on opponent in co-ordinated movement, place forearm of right arm across throat, grasping own right wrist with own left hand. Place right knee in small of opponent's back and drag him backwards to gd. Retain grip and apply pressure with forearm, pressing opponent's head fwd by pressure applied with own chest. |

| | (c) Neck twist break & throw | Place palm of left hand under opponent's chin with fingers extended over right hand at back of his head. With quick twisting backward movement, breaking his neck. |

| | (d) Cross Arm Strangle(standing) and counter | Cross own wrists at opponent's throat, placing the hands inside his collar with the thumbs outermost. Apply pressure with a squeezing action and twist opp sideways to gd. COUNTER: Should opponent's right arm be uppermost, place own right hand under his right elbow, place own left hand behind own right hand and lever his elbow over to own right side breaking grip. |

| 13. | (a) Leg trips(2) | (i) In one co-ordinated movement, grasp opponent's clothing region of belt with left hand, grasp his upper right arm with own right hand. Turn right, drop on to right knee with left foot extended outside opponent's left ankle. With quick pulling twisting action, throw him across own left leg to the ground. Should opponent have no clothes on, grasp his left arm at wrist with both hands and throw as above. (ii) Tripping opponent who is rushing into attack when lying on ground. As he moves in, hook own foot behind the heel of his nearest foot and strike sharply in region of kneecap with other foot. |

13.	(b) Arm and shoulder throw	Grasp opponent's right wrist with both hands, pull towards you, pivot on left foot to your left, place his right arm across your right shoulder, pull down on opponent's arm, thrust back with own buttocks and throw him over shoulder.
	(c) Counter to strangle from rear	(i) Take opp upper arm and apply an arm and shoulder throw. (ii) If unable to do (i), twist under the shoulder holding you and work under his armpit and apply hammerlock.
14.	(a) Strangling a sentry	Quietly creep up on opponent and in one co-ordinated movement, place left hand across throat of opponent grasping collar; place right hand a over his mouth and nose. Kick rifle away with right foot, jump and drag him backwards to the ground landing on left knee with right leg extended to maintain balance. Apply strangle by pulling clothing to left and chin and head to the right.
	(b) Forward headlock and jawbreaker	Pull opponent into forward headlock, placing right forearm across his jaw. Place own left hand on his right shoulder; Grasp own left wrist with own right hand, apply pressure upward and break jaw or neck.
	(c) Come-alongs (4)	(i) Secure hammerlock and force opp forward. At same time, pull his head back. (ii) Lock opp's elbow between your elbow and body and gooseneck his wrist with both hands. (iii) Grasp opponent's right wrist with own right hand and pull fwd. Place own left arm over front of opponent's upper arm and place left hand on own wrist. Apply pressure by forcing down with own right hand and levering up with own forearm against his elbow joint. (iv) Approach from behind on left side of opponent; pass right hand under opp's armpit, and grasp his left hand raising his forearm until his elbow fits into the bend of your own elbow. Apply gooseneck to his hand and force his elbow and forearm straight back.
	(d) Tying a prisoner with a boot lace	Secure hammerlock on opp's- force him on to ground. Bring other arm back and bring his legs up into figure 4. Take bootlace and tie thumbs across each other below joint Hook foot in under the tie and leave him.

15. (a) Tying prisoner to tree without cord

Thoroughly subdue prisoner first. Prop him against tree with one leg each side. Put his right foot under his left knee in figure 4. Ram him down on to ground and leave him.

(b) Pistol disarms front (i) rear (ii)

(i) Only to be attempted when held at very close quarters; revolver held in right hand. Hold arms wide apart, swing left hand down striking revolver to one side, placing own body out of line of fire. Grasp his right wrist on top with left hand and underneath with right hand. Swing his hand and revolver upward and backwards with both hands, plus ruthless tactics. (ii) ARMS wide apart. Pivot smartly to left, swinging left elbow down striking opponent's revolver away from own body. Encircle his arm underneath with own left arm clasping own right hand. Opponent's arm is now across own neck. Apply pressure and break arm.

(c) Strangling from rear with cord, cordtex, etc. Take care to avoid INJURY. Have knot in running order to give quick release as unconsciousness or death can easily result.

Stalk opponent. Have running loop of suitable cord ready to drop over his head with one hand in one hand, and secure the loose end in other hand. As loop drops, start tightening around neck and pulling him backwards. At same time, put foot into small of his back to assist in pulling him down.

16. (a) Bayonet disarms (2)

For opponent moving at a steady pace in On Guard posn: Move towards the attacker to upset his timing, and take the initiative. As he lunges forward move your body to your right to dodge the point and parry off by gripping his rifle at the muzzle end with your left hand.
(i) Work in and parry with the left hand similar to above. Bring your feet to a balance posn, your right hand grasping the back of his head and the left hand on chin and face. With a quick twisting jerking action, throw opponent, breaking his neck.
(ii) Opponent doubling in fast "On Guard" posn : Work towards opponent as before. As he makes a lunge, pivot on ball of your right foot and carry your body to his left, at same time, bring your hand down hard on the bayonet or muzzle of the rifle to force the bayonet into the ground. The rifle will trip him and throw your opponent to the ground.

16. (b) Use of Steel Helmet   The steel helmet can be used with great effect as a weapon of offence, as well as serving its usual role as a means of protection. Even when kept on the head it can still be used to deal a vicious blow. Similarly, it can be used in the hand to deliver blows, full use being made of its sharp cutting edge.

Finally, it can be used as a shield, particularly against bayonet or dagger thrusts, or even against a the a thrown knife. The rubber lining of the steel helmet is intended as a shock absorber, which makes it all the more suitable for use as a shield

Whenever it is used in the hand, the chin strap should be wound around the wrist to avoid dropping and possibly losing the helmet. For this reason the steel helmet should never be thrown.

17-18-19-20   Recapitulation, Quickening work and all-in tests.

COUNTER TO BREAKING GRIP ON CLOTHING (6(b))

Place wrist across opponent's wrist near base of hand. Grasp own fist, clamping his hand firmly against own body. Swing quickly fwd, bring opponent to knees and follow up with kick in face.

By comparing and contrasting the 1940s Commando unarmed combat course with the Special Operations Australia document the first thing that is notable is the volume of the techniques in the Australian one.

The Australian Notes on Commando Training document from 1942 stated "The knife or truncheon are best for silent elimination. Unarmed combat is an essential for self-defence".

That is primarily what unarmed combat was taught for; either for removing sentries or for the rare instance when a commando was unable to utilize their primary or secondary weapon.

In the Objects Of Training section of Australian Special Forces document it stated that the training is "to make them efficient in the art of silent killing". It also gave credit to the Americans for importing Judo to the country which seems like a dubious claim. It is interesting because they don't give credit to either the Japanese or the British for any of the methods outlined in the document.

The document attempts to clarify the reasoning for its existence by stating:

> Fighting without arms is as old as man himself, and the earliest records report of sporting contests among men. Later, the Greek, Roman and Indian styles of wrestling were evolved up to the stage of modern "allin" wrestling and boxing matches. A band of Chinese monks whose religion forbade the use of weapons, developed the art of self defence to a high degree early in the written History of the World. In the 12th century, the Japanese copied this system and called it Ju-Jitsu (the gentle art). Being a small statured race, they paid special attention to the phase of using an opponent's weight against himself.

Later in the last century, the USA imported it and called it among other names, Judo. They in turn paid special attention to the use of pressure points.

The Services Reconnaissance Department (SRD) also known as Special Operations Australia (SOA), which authored the document, previously known as Inter-Allied Services Department (ISD), had been an Australian military intelligence and special reconnaissance unit which had been authorized by Prime Minister John Curtin in March 1942, following the outbreak of the war with Japan. The Inter-Allied Services Department had been formed on April 17th, 1942, having been given approval by General Thomas Blamey. It was modelled on the British Special Operations Executive (SOE), and was initially organized by SOE British Army officer, Lieutenant Colonel G. Egerton Mott. It was named ISD for security reasons and its existence was only known by the Prime Minister and the High Command.

SOA oversaw intelligence-gathering, reconnaissance and raiding missions in the Japanese occupied areas of New Guinea, the Dutch East Indies, Portuguese Timor, the Malayan Peninsula, British Borneo and Singapore.

Although Fairbairn would continue to keep his course of instruction brief throughout the war in comparison to some of the other WW2 era courses, it appeared that Australians were attempting to address more scenarios in which they might have to resort to hand to hand combat against the Japanese, who were assumed to be masters and superior experts in Jiu-Jitsu and other martial arts.

Some of the techniques in the SOA course were still straight out of the Fairbairn and Sykes playbook. But it seemed as if many more specific techniques had been included to address unarmed combat, jungle fighting scenarios against the Japanese.

Other "lectures" in the Syllabus besides PT and Unarmed Combat, included subjects such as a Cavern Course, Demolitions, Field Exercises, Identifications, Jungle Foods, Jungle Warfare, a Medical Course, Meteorology, Minor Tactics, Navigation, Supply Dropping and Security.

Although there was no timeline specified in Fairbairn and Syke's unarmed combat lecture we know it was somewhat flexible, they stated "If time is limited it is obviously impossible to acquire a thorough knowledge of the whole contents of the four lessons. Everyone should master the "thumb hold" but, apart from that, individuals with limited time are advised to concentrate on the mastery of ten or fifteen of the most important practices. Individual needs or preferences may govern the choice". Again, Commando operations were primarily hit and run operations, where the taking of prisoners was usually not a goal.

We can see from the SOA course that it was also a fast course but it was to be taught in 20 hours.

According to David L. Kentner in his article "World War 2 British Commando Unarmed Combat and Close Combat Training" he wrote:

> It became clear once the United States entered the war in December 1941 that the role of the Commandos would be changing and that a separate school was necessary to train future Commando recruits. This school ended up being the Commando Basic Training Centre, CBTC, at Achnacarry.
>
> It was at this point in time that William Fairbairn and Eric A Sykes ceased being personally associated with the training of the Commandos.
>
> Two things occurred shortly after the CBTC opened which are of significance in understanding what Unarmed Combat system was actually taught at Achnacarry. The first was Brigadier Haydon

convincing the Metropolitan Police to release some of its officers for Commando training. The second was the Royal Marines forming their own Commandos, and having them trained at the CBTC at Achnacarry.

One of the first police officers to arrive at Achnacarry was Stanley Bissell. The Commanding Officer at Achnacarry, Lt Col Vaughan, indicated that his first impression of Stanley Bissell caused him to immediately promote him to Staff Sergeant instructor on the Physical Training Staff at the CBTC.

Stanley Bissell was well qualified to be sergeant instructor on the Physical Training staff at Achnacarry, a position that included teaching Unarmed Combat. By the time he joined the police department in 1926 he was already a successful amateur wrestler, and went on to have a championship wrestling career while with the police department. In 1931 he was selected as a self defence instructor at Peel House Training School for police recruits, a position which he held until he joined the Commandos in June 1942. During this period he earned a Black Belt in Judo. He had also attended several courses at the British Army's School of Physical Training at Aldershot. So by the time he arrived at Achnacarry he was well qualified by any standard to be a physical training instructor there.

As to what he taught the police, one can only say that the officers he trained had to deal with many of the same toughs on the London docks that made other seaports around the world dangerous places and the men he taught had to do this regularly without the use of firearms.

One of the first tasks assigned to Stanley Bissell at Achnacarry was to evaluate the then current Unarmed Combat course being taught there. From the evidence available, this would have been the Fairbairn course taught at Lochailort. Apparently Lt Col Vaughan, who had been a member of No 4 Commando prior to being made the Commanding Officer of Commando Basic Training Centre, was dissatisfied with that course.

Stanley Bissell described what occurred at his first meeting with Lt Col Vaughan and what was done as a result of it as follows:

The CO told me that he had taken over the Commandos and that they were now Army Commandos with a new syllabus of training. He wanted me to look at the 'unarmed combat' being taught. I found this was mainly based on Fairbairn and Sykes' book of Self Defence. After reading it I decided that it was too complicated to instill the techniques of Attack and Defence into the minds of Commando recruits on a six-week training course. The CO agreed on the syllabus being changed. I then set up a six-week syllabus of what I termed 'direct attacks.' These were simple and direct and ones that could be allied with normal training. Eventually this was called 'Close Combat.' It was agreed that in the time available complicated techniques could not be taught.'

What were the techniques taught and how can they be found? Even late in life Stanley Bissell was still concerned about the Official Secrets Act. What he did state on the subject was, 'One must realise that due to war conditions, i.e. secrecy, very little was committed to paper. Photos were out.'

Not knowing exactly what techniques were taught, may or may not be important in the scheme of things. The point is that things had been taught that had been determined to be effective in their goal of dispatching the enemy.

Someone had to determine what was going to be taught. Usually it was the person who had been sitting in the chair at the time. The person tasked with the training brought their own experiences to the table. So in the case of the Australians and in particular the ones who were instructors at Wilson's Promontory, they were in an environment where they had to be engaged in Jungle Warfare. They also knew that their enemy had an established history and a culture embedded with the Martial Arts, most notably Jiu-Jitsu and Judo. So they had to come up with something effective to counter that. The best instructors for that were the people who already had backgrounds in those things.

As noted techniques that allowed one to dispatch the enemy were high on the list. There is some indication that Fairbairn later on in the war, during his time as an instructor with the OSS, put emphasis on weapons training over unarmed combat training. That evidence can be seen in his Close Combat course syllabus which was uncovered by the author and fellow Commando researcher Robert Allen Pittman.

Fairbairn's course stated:

1) The course consists of two sections – Armed and Unarmed
   Armed:
   1. Knife fighting with the Fighting Knife, Jack-Knife and Pen-Knife.
   2. Fighting with the Fair Sword.
   3. Fighting with the "Cosh" or stick.
   4. Fighting with a Newspaper, etc.

   Unarmed:
   1. Attacking Methods.
   2. Releasing Methods.
   3. Overpowering Methods.

   All these methods have been specifically selected as being the most practical for students about to take up work with this organization. Every one of these methods is practical, and has, on many occasions, stood the acid test of actual combat in the present war.

2) Although there are hundreds of different methods – (some good, some poor, some absolutely useless,) it is inadvisable in a short course to attempt to teach more than shown above. It would only result in the student being confused and not gaining any practical knowledge. Instructors will therefore confine themselves to instruction in the above methods only, and, as far as possible, present them in the order shown.

In this connection, it is inadvisable to spend too much time demonstrating disarming a man holding you up with a pistol. Instructors must be very firm with students on this point; otherwise they will spend all their time learning a purely theoretical method. (In war, your opponent does not "HOLD YOU UP" – "HE SHOOTS ON SIGHT"). Further, this method of disarming is now so widely known by practically everyone, that it is NOW of no value.

3) Instructors must, during the course, be 100% on the job. They must SELL and inspire confidence at all times, treating each student as a personal friend whom they wish to help. Every student is a volunteer with a man-sized job to perform, and it is the instructor's responsibility that everything possible that will assist him in making a success of his mission, is given cheerfully and willingly. The following was the highest praise ever received by any instructor:

"DEAR_____, IT WORKS!"

Learning to have confidence is key in this type of training and all Commando type training. According to an article "Confidence Breeds Initiative) written by Maj. H. M. Todd in the Canadian Army Training Memorandum (CATM), October 1945:

The spirit of aggressiveness is a sine qua non to the seizing and holding of the initiative in battle. "You must win that fire-fight". But to win that fight, and to win, and hold, and always to be seeking, the "first move"—the power to "call the tune"—and the feeling of superiority over one's enemy—all of which are integral parts of what we call initiative—the first requisite is conscious skill with the personal weapon.

The machine gunner who has fired his gun so much that he does it "with his eyes shut" acquires a feeling of invincibility which he expresses by seeking targets. The initiative, in other words.

The bomber who can throw a Mills bomb on to a spot one yard square every time is proud of it and looks for something more difficult to hit. The initiative.

And the sniper who can, and knows he can (and I have seen it done), kill an enemy sniper at 800 yards if he (the enemy) moves his head, looks for other heads to shoot at. The initiative, once more.

To talk of initiative to troops who know they are not trained is, at best, a waste of time and, at worst, "propaganda" which deceives nobody. In war, the initiative will always lie (a) with the side whose men think they are better trained and better armed; (b) with the side whose men are expert with their individual weapons and know it; and (c) with the side whose officers' knowing (a) and (b), are continually seeking it, and who, by their own attitude, communicate to their men a restlessness which will not let them "take root" with any mental ease or comfort.

What is notable about Fairbairn's Close Combat course is that he taught the armed portion first. He decided to put emphasis on that in the later years of the war as an instructor. During the postwar era when Fairbairn went back to teaching police tactics, he taught gun disarms once again. Everything has its time and place. But in a war it was kill or be killed so the taking of prisoners was not usually a primary concern.

There are a few documents that can help us pinpoint exactly how many hours were dedicated to the training of Commando Troop recruits in unarmed combat.

One such document, a memo from May 2nd 1942, "Training of First Special Training Unit for Period April 10, 1942 to May 2, 1942" concerned the training of United States Marines who had been attached to Commando Troop 3. The document which was written by First Lieutenant, Russell Duncan, stated:

> Corporals Duckworth and Mathews were assigned to this course. Their Report stated that the course consisted mostly of fast marches and physical conditioning. Only about eight hours of actual instruction in close combat (jujitsu and judo) were given. The remainder of the time was spent in weapon training, wall climbing, quick-firing from the hip, and bayonet practice. Their general impression was that the course undoubtedly toughened one, but it did not offer any new or outstanding ideas. The instructor in this course was very high in his praise of these two Marines…Corporal Duckworth now holds the record on the long obstacle course.

What this tells me is that we tend to make a bigger deal about that specific type of training today than what it actually was in those desperate times. It also tells me that the instructors truly believed that what they were teaching were some of the most effective techniques which could be taught in a short amount of time.

As previously noted, the Marines felt that they had already been a Commando "type" organization to begin with so they felt that the

Commandos were not bringing anything new to the table. In some senses they felt they had already received better training. One paragraph toward the end of the document substantiates this, Duncan wrote:

> From the above remarks it would appear that either one or both of two things are true, namely, that the courses were, in general, not well prepared and executed by the instructors, or else the standards of the Commando in training are not as high as those of the U.S. Marine Corps. In all fairness to the Commandos, however, it must be borne in mind that the Marine Corps personnel have made a trip from 3000 to 6000 miles, covering a period of two and a half months during all of which they have been kept keyed up with the idea that Commando troops perform amazing feats of endurance and that their tactics are well nigh perfect. It is small wonder then that they were a bit surprised, if not disappointed, to find themselves regularly outdoing the Commando soldiers in forced marches, assault courses, etc. and to see the Commando soldiers making poor use of cover, bunching during an advance, and failing to hit a four foot square target from the prone position of 100 yards range with a service rifle.

An article from the same time period as the Duncan memo can also help to pinpoint how much training a Commando may have received. It provides a further idea on timeline. The article "British to Train Every Soldier As Commando" published in the New York Herald Tribune, April 4th 1942, stated:

> 'Battle Schools' Simulate Combat Conditions to Fit Army for Offensive. Under a drastic new battle-training program, the British Army is being stepped up in efficiency and fighting methods to make very infantry soldier as physically tough and as capable of individual initiative as the famous Commandos, the British Press Service, 30 Rockefeller Plaza, said in an announcement here yesterday.

All British soldiers are now being subjected to rigorous courses in practical tactics at "battle schools" set up in every direction. For some months a parent school for the new offensive army has been developing instructors for the divisional schools. The pupils at the advanced training center are all officers but they live, work and learn as privates.

Drill routine has been changed from the academic business of parade marches, presenting arms, and formal salutes. It has become a practical drill in actual movements required of men as "combat teams" in real battle.

The men engage in actual battlefield maneuvers in a sector filled with the noise and clouded with the smoke of real bombs, real shells and real bullets.

Light tanks plunge through machine-gun fire and over holes in the earth blasted out by land mines. Casualties sometimes occur in this under-fire training.

The "battle schools" are also designed to toughen the men physically. They are moving constantly—for sixteen hours a day, not including lectures in the evening—and they move everywhere at the double quick.

The men are trained to fight all day and all night without food, moving in forced marches across the countryside. Carrying full equipment, they may cover as much as forty miles in a single day and still be more than fit to fight at the end of it.

According to Kentner:

This article on all soldiers receiving Commando training sort of sets the record straight. The regular soldier received 8 hours of unarmed training.

It's my opinion that as of 1942 both were receiving basically the same course.

Prior to 1942 is where the questions remain. In that period we have Fairbairn and Sykes at Lochailort teaching, but Lochailort was not a Commando school although there is evidence that some Commandos trained there. Also the question here is whether this training involved teaching of instructors only or also included the Other Ranks.

Each Commando had a Physical Training Instructor within its ranks. The Physical Training School had its own unarmed course during this pre-1942 time period. What of this training got to the average Commando?

It appears to me that Commando training went through three phases. Did this cause a difference in Commando unarmed training? If there was more than one system taught, then we might need to decide which one best reflects Commando training. Or would we need to agree to recognize all of them.
There are things we need to straighten out before we can really say we know what unarmed training Commandos actually received.

The Canadian Battle Drill Training document from 1944 stated:

1. This report deals with the development of modern methods of training and the evolution of Battle Drill Training with particular reference to its adoption by the Canadian Army in the United Kingdom.

2. It is necessary first to define clearly the difference between "Battle Drill" and "Battle Drill Training", as these terms are now understood. "Battle Drill", according to the manual Fieldcraft and Battle Drill, means the reduction of military tactics to bare essentials which are taught to a platoon as a team drill, with clear explanations regarding the objects to be achieved, the principles involved and the individual task of each member of the team. "Battle Drill Training", on the other hand, is more comprehensive. It consists of a high standard of weapon training, "purposeful physical training, fieldcraft, battle drills proper, battle discipline and battle inoculation".

3. Battle Drill training is founded upon the axiom that "until every soldier looks on himself as a ruthless killer, using cover with the facility of an animal, using his weapons with the practiced ease of a professional hunter and covering the ground on the move with the agility of a deer-stalker, infantry battle training will be based on false foundations" (C.M.H.Q. file 2/Battle Sch/1: Report on First G.H.Q. Battle Sch). Its object is, therefore to inculcate into a body of fighting men a system of battle discipline and team spirit, and to give every man a knowledge of certain basic "team plays" which will guide him in any operation he may undertake in battle. It has the further advantage of making the men physically fit, relieving boredom in training, and inoculating the soldier and his commander against the fear and noises of battle (C.M.H.Q. file 2/Reports/4: Precis on Battle Drill, C.T.S.).

4. Owing to the romantic aura surrounding the term "Commando", newspaper writers have occasionally referred to Battle Drill Training as "Commando Training". It should be clearly understood that Battle Drill Training is not a special type of training confined to units of the Special Service Brigade, but a form of training which all Canadian infantry men are required to undergo.

Since it appeared that soldiers and Commandos received very similar training, and some of it trickled down to the general population we can get a glimpse of what some of that training entailed from articles published at the time. One article published in The Sunday Post, on March 8th 1942 provided the general public with some knowledge of how to handle themselves if Nazis wound up in their own backyard. The article also offers us today with another glimpse of what was taught back then.

Ultimately we do not know exactly what course Heinmiller would have learned or the Fijian Scouts for that matter. But we can venture a guess based off some of the documents which were presented in this chapter.

It begs the question, was unarmed combat training so essential to what a Commando was? Did it have to be taught in order for a Commando to be classed as a Commando?

The Canadian Battle Drill document stated:

> Calisthenics have always been part of military training. They have usually consisted of half an hour's loosening-up exercises in the early morning. In March 1941, however, a pamphlet entitled Physical and Recreational Training was published which broadened considerably the scope of physical training. Chapter IX, of this pamphlet, dealing with Unarmed Combat (which had hitherto been considered as a means of defence in close quarter fighting when no weapons were available), advocated it as a form of attack. The pamphlet pointed out that war is a matter of life and death, that complete ruthlessness is necessary when personal survival is at stake. "Such brutal methods of attack as kicking, gouging they eyes, etc., though foreign and detestable to the Britisher, must be used without hesitation against the type of opponent we now have to face". The textbook covered physical training, obstacle training, cross-country running, boxing and wrestling, swimming and other sports.

While it was not absolutely essential for someone undergoing Commando type training to learn unarmed combat (it was lower on the list of priorities in comparison to things like physical fitness or fieldcraft), it was helpful in that it was a useful skill to have in case one lost access to their primary weapon. Also it had the added benefit of being a confidence booster and helped to develop the trainee's ruthless fighting ability.

Britain Training All To Be Commandos

LONDON, May 15.—"Battle culture," which to nonmilitary highbrows may seem like a contradiction in terms, is the name applied to the new training program which is making every British soldier a commando. The program teaches the co-ordinated use of head, hands and feet.

The scheme will be tried on all British troops, and when a soldier has "graduated" he will be able to run cross-country for two miles in full battle-kit in 16 minutes, sprint 200 yards and then score three out of five hits in 75 seconds in a firing test. This exercise will be followed by a 10-mile "forced hike," to be completed within two hours.

Here are some other feats which must be accomplished during the new training course:

A soldier is expected to carry a man of his own weight 200 yards in two minutes—both wearing full battle-kit.

Starting in physical training kit —shirt and shorts—the soldier will have to complete a 100-yard "alarm" race by running 20 yards, stopping to don full battle dress, then sprinting the remaining 80 yards to a finish; all within 330 seconds of starting.

Soldiers are expected to be thoroughly trained for "unarmed combat," which includes the full knowledge of how best to use fists, knees, thumbs, etc., in personal hand-to-hand fighting. Included in this training is a thorough grounding in Judo.

One of the primary feats which must be mastered is diving into a swimming pool in full battle order from a height of 20 feet. Soldiers must keep their rifles up during the swim that follows.

There follow instruction in how to overcome unexpected obstacles. One mortar team was recently seen to jump a ditch 102 inches wide, scale a six-foot wall, improvise and cross a plank bridge, then cross hurdles, trip-wires and wire-fences. Such tests are more difficult for these men than for regular infantry troops since the barrel of the mortar gun alone weighs 70 pounds—and the tests become really hard work when they include scaling a 12-foot wall, or spanning a 20-foot chasm on a horizontal rope with the 70 pound barrel slung over a man's shoulder.

An article stating every British soldier to receive Commando type training.
Source: The Atlanta Constitution May 17th, 1942.

Author's Note: On the next four pages is a course that was presented in The Sunday Post, March 8th 1942 and also a course from the Canadian Army Training Memorandum (CATM), January 1945.

If a Paratroop Lands in Your Garden

YOUR first move is quite clear cut.

Get a clear, concise message to the military, police, or warden's post without waste of a second.

After that you've got to deal with the paratroop. Here's how—

How do I make sure he's a German?

Assume you've no sight of plane with signs, shape, and colour to tell you. He's alone; six or more men would make you sure they weren't our own baled-out pilots.

Big clue is colour of his 'chute. So far as we know, it's invariably dead white. If he has dumped his overalls, he'll be in latish grey-short, loose tunic, open-neck collar with yellow patches.

Grey trousers fall over the very high boots in plus-four style. Round helmet fits tight, has a narrow, steel brim, no neck shield.

But he might be in Fifth Column guise?

Yes, in khaki perhaps. It's odds, even if he speaks fair English, his "W's" will sound like "V's." Even so, he might be a Pole.

If you are suspicious, lose no time in getting word to the authorities.

Should I hide myself until he lands?

Yes, if you spot him in time. You want the vital element of surprise on your side.

A tip. While picking cover and getting to it don't look skywards more than you need, or wave your hands about. White skin is the greatest enemy of camouflage.

Can he fire before landing?

Not with any accuracy. He is cluttered around with that overall zip-fastened up the front over weapon holsters, &c., so that he doesn't get caught up with the 'chute ropes. If he's an ace dropper, he may carry a loaded tommy gun. But so be nears earth he's not only got his attention on making the landing—he's swinging from side to side like a clock pendulum. In no shape to shoot—yet.

What height does he drop from?

That crack paratroop division which played so overwhelming a part at Crete slipped from their planes at about 300 feet. In reasonably calm conditions the paratroop comes down at the rate of 16 feet per second. Strictly, that works out at plane to earth in about 20 seconds. But a certain amount of drift and the forward momentum of plane brings actual time up to nearer 30 seconds.

If there's a bunch, how far apart do they land?

Nazis reckon in good conditions to put their men 60 to 80 yards from each other, making easy and quick the all-important linking-up into a party.

Best time to tackle the paratroop?

Moment he lands. He can unharness his 'chute in a second.

But he staggers, maybe goes sprawling. Gets to his feet a bit dazed.

Until he joins his pals, his morale's tar from high. Our boys found that in Crete. He has a revolver, but if you've a rifle you've got the range and accuracy to put him at your mercy.

Can't he be shot on the wing?

Perhaps—if you're a top-class marksman! But that swinging, dropping target wants a lot of hitting.

Miss, and you've warned him. He forgets all his other troubles, becomes the first-class defensive fighter bang on the alert.

He'll lie low, await his pals getting him out of the hole. Or, if

Edge of hand is more deadly than clenched fist. As opponent approaches, either (left) seize his left arm, jock him towards you and hit his throat, or (right) seize his right hand, push it up and back, and chop back of his neck.
See "Commando Tricks You Ought To Know," Page 13

alone, he may, with his intense training, be able to outmanoeuvre you.

Suppose I haven't a gun?

Well hid, you'd be better to wait and watch him, especially if you have expectation that military or Home Guard will soon be responding to your message.

It may happen you can get right on him the moment he lands. If fit, and you fancy the fight, in you go, to k.o. him or secure him, get his weapon from him.

Bear in mind, though, he's probably expert in unarmed combat, knows all sorts of tricks—so you'll not be too particular how and with what you hit him.

Best weapon short of bullets or bomb?

Iron bar or bludgeon can be used as you would a rifle butt.

Steel helmet can also be a winner.

Hold by the strap, swing hard at the Adam's apple or the unprotected nape of the neck.

It's all very much a case of the " quick or the dead "—so see you're quick.

He's my prisoner — What next?

Immobilise him thoroughly, whether you cover him with a weapon or tie him up

At the first possible moment thoroughly "frisk" him for any concealed weapons. He may have a small revolver in shoulder holster, or a knife strapped to the back of his leg.

Don't let him handle anything—not even that "pen" in his pocket. It may well be a tear-gas squirter.

If emptying his pockets, DON'T take away anything as a souvenir of the great moment. That small photo, paper, bit of identity disc may tell Intelligence a lot.

See he's in the hands of Intelligence soon as possible. A dazed man, like a drunk man, often blurts out the truth.

My wife's alone in the house. What's her duty?

The citizen, man or woman, has a clear right in law to protect his or her property, and a bounden duty under British law to resist an invader. That doesn't mean taking foolhardy risks—it does mean giving the fullest helping hand she can under the circumstances.

Will paratroops drop from gliders or carriers?

From carriers. They are first to land. Their job is to seize, hold, and clear areas for later arrivals. Radio men with each unit report progress back to Nazi bases. On their reports Nazi invasion command instructs rest of the armada, makes any necessary sudden switch of attacks.

A main thrust at Scotland's waistline might be switched further north to Aberdeen area—or vice versa—or strength might be suddenly thrown into an inland bridgehead secured by paratroops. It is vital to mop up paratroops quickly, not merely to contain them.

What's maximum number of troops carried by glider?

Seventeen, more commonly twelve. Hitler used some of his latest

You might get this done if you tackle him this way.

on a dark night, and difficult even when there's a moon.

And when defences get at them, experience shows they can survive a peppering, for they've no engines to catch fire, no mass of controls in which one shell or bullet-burst can bring disaster.

How many gliders and troop-carriers needed to land 100,000 men?

Nazis would allow big margin for losses. Proportion of planes would carry tanks — gliders can bring five-tonners. Such an armada would need 2000 power planes and 10,000 gliders.

Can Nazis find the power planes?

They've had a pretty bomb-proof winter to maintain weekly output of 1000 planes. Their big arms drive has given over a lot of its efforts to three and four-engined planes useful for invasion. Junkers and giant Condors would mainly be used.

How fast can Germany mass-produce gliders?

Take a comparison. Before the war one British manufacturer turned out 3000 mass-produced cars a week. Mass production of gliders need take no account of engine, wheels, and the many accessories needed for a car. For every troop-carrier made, you can turn out a hundred gliders. Allowing for big bomb damage on Mannheim, which has many glider factories, it's certain Nazis are not short of gliders.

How long would troop-carriers be in the air en route for Scotland?

Carriers tow gliders at speed of about 175 miles an hour. Coming from Norway they'd make the trip in about two hours. It's probable the big follow-up of the main armada would come from German centres. Hamburg, for instance, offers better defences and take-off facilities, and flying time to Scottish coast is only increased by one hour. Troop carriers have a flying time—at towing pace—of fully six hours.

Can fighters escort armada to Scotland and get back?

Long-range fighters, yes. Nazis have two types for this job — the ME.110 and the lesser known Focke Wulf 189. Latter has been specially built for a job like this. Extra fuel tanks, dropped off as they empty, give the F.W. a range of 1500 miles. As a fighter it's not the equal of the Spitfire by a long chalk, but it has armament for heavy strafing of ground defences.

What's likeliest time for air-borne troops to arrive?

The vanguard about midnight. Paratroops can land by moonlight. It's a more risky business for gliders. They would slow to under 20 miles an hour, switch on floodlight, and bump down.

It's riskier still for big planes. A glider needs only an oversize cabbage patch to sit down in. A heavy troop-carrier must find some spot to give a clear landing run of not less than 800 yards. But it has time to cruise until paratroop co-operation helps the landing.

craft to reinforce Rommel, and they took ten, plus equipment, apiece. Now we have a report that Nazis have built 100-men gliders. This terrific step-up presents great technical difficulties in flying.

Remember, the glider has to be airborne before it is actually taken in tow: 100 or gliders is that they gently crash land in small spaces. This hardly fits in with a craft that would be carrying 7 to 8 tons.

Anyway, with five gliders towed by each power plane, which may also have a complement of 17 men aboard, you have your hundred men and a better chance of getting them across and down safely.

Approaching Scottish coast, say, Edinburgh, at what point would gliders unhook?

Assuming they fly over at about 20,000 feet, they cast off fifty miles from the coast for the silent, surprise glide in. It's impossible to spot them

191

Commando Tricks You Ought To Know

IF, as an unarmed civilian, you had to tackle a Nazi, could you do it? Could you disarm him, throw him and tie him up helpless? Here are some hints by Commando experts you can practise with a pal. But go easy on the rough stuff or you'll have him in hospital.

Chin jab is useful for close-quarter fighting. Hit hard with heel of hand.

If opponent attacks with club, duck under his blow, open your arms. Then (centre) throw your right arm over his left shoulder, get him across your hip, give his legs a lift with your left hand, and (right) over he goes.

To silence a sentry. Creep up behind him and throw right arm round his throat. At same time apply left hand at back of his neck. Combined pressure strangles him.

Don't be scared of a revolver hold-up enough, strike revolver to side and grip his wrist with your right hand. Then grasp revolver with left hand, and with quick, downward movement wrench it from his hand.

If your opponent comes close

Even a bayonet need have no terrors. As opponent comes in, parry the bayonet to the left with your right hand, step in and grip rifle as shown, with right wrist behind opponent's left elbow and right leg in front of his left. A twist of the rifle throws him to the ground, leaving you with rifle.

Arm break for opponent who rushes at you. Grip his wrist, jerk him towards you. As he goes past, strike upper part of his arm with your shoulder.

Steel helmet makes ideal weapon of offence. Hold it by strap and smash to the face just under your opponent's own helmet.

If seized from behind, grip your steel helmet in both hands and smash it down on the enemy's hands.

No need for yards of rope to tie up an enemy length of cord, or your rifle pull-through's enough. Hold him firmly on the ground with knees bent right back and feet crossed. Tie his ankles together, then, keeping cord taut, tie his thumbs firmly

His own laces, a short

He's helpless.

Close Combat

ART·DAVIS

193

You've probably seen all these tricks before—there's nothing new in the science of fighting without weapons. The two pictures on the left show how to get out of a stranglehold. Seize your opponent's left wrist from underneath with your left hand. Feint as if to force it away. Suddenly pull instead of push, and seize his left upper arm with your right hand. Now you've broken his hold and you've got an armlock on him. He's all yours—unless he knows the counter!

To avoid a downward truncheon blow—attack immediately, slip out of the way, encircle your opponent's body with your right arm and follow up with a cross buttock throw. If he's left-handed use your left arm instead.

Disarming an opponent who is covering you with a pistol can be done in several ways. Here's one of them. Suppose he's marching you along, covering you from behind. You turn rapidly outwards towards your right side, swing your right arm down and pass your right hand over and around your assailant's pistol forearm, holding it firmly against your body with the pressure of your arm. At the same time hit him with the hard edge of your left hand on the Adam's Apple.

194

Boxing, Rugby and Training by Competition

To better illustrate some of the thought process behind why certain courses were taught to the Commandos; there was an article in the Frederick Press, November 6th 1942 (one of many of a similar nature, written during that time period) titled "Commando Tactics To Be Demonstrated – Sergeants Who Mastered These Methods In England Will Be Here Friday" which stated:

> When "Your Army," the colorful and practical demonstration that the fighting forces of the United States are the best equipped and trained of any in the world, moves into Ardmore on Nov. 9 to display its weapons and equipment, it will have with it two rangers to demonstrate the tough tactics of close combat fighting which they learned from the British commandos in England.
>
> The "Your Army" event is being brought here to arouse the interest of younger men—18 and 19 years old—in the opportunity offered them by enlisting in the service ahead of the selective service act to draft men of that age.
>
> Sgt. Howard Jarnod of Fort Wayne, Ind., and Thomas J. Moore of Salem, Ark., both 24, are now teaching commando methods of hand-to-hand fighting to soldiers in the replacement training center at Fort Sill.
>
> The Rangers, American counterparts of the commandos, have much the same type of training as their English cousins, and both Jarnod and Moore agree that there could be no better model.
>
> "Those guys are really hard," says Moore. "They're afraid of nothing in the world and they have the sheer determination and will to win, without which a soldier is nothing."

The physical side of the instruction in England is extremely strenuous. A 1700-yard obstacle course is one of the most rigorous features. Those who fall behind in the dash through it are spurred by slugs fired near their feet from the guns of instructors.

Designed to accustom the men to actual fighting, the use of live ammunition is not confined to the obstacle course. Practice beach landings are replete with whistling machine-gun tracers—slightly overheard—and the steady burst of land mines and grenades. In the words of Moore:

"You can forget to duck just once!"

Both men agree that top physical condition is the most important prerequisite for a commando. Size is a minor consideration but sharpness of senses and speedy muscular coordination are imperative, plus ruggedness, adaptability and durability.

In close combat, say the replacement center sergeants, the most effective weapon is the long stiletto-like commando knife. Second most valuable weapon is the "smatchet," a longer, broader bladed, single edged knife with a heavy hilt. The blade is used like a bolo, to slash and stab; the hilt to deliver crushing blows.

"We have had examples of how merciless the enemy can be," said Jarnod. "It's you and your opponent—not a question of knocking a man unconscious but killing him. That's the commando dictum: Kill him as quickly as possible, but be sure he's dead!"

The accent in hand-to-hand battles is on fast thinking and speed with the hands. Both Jarnod and Moore are accomplished athletes. The former was Indiana state badminton champion in 1939 and 1940 and is also an expert wrestler, fencer and boxer.

Both sergeants brought back with them from England the firm conviction that the work of the commandos is as vital to the successful prosecution of the war as that of any military organization in the fighting forces of the allies.

Although I have been unbale to pin down exactly how many hours Commando troops were exposed to the unarmed combat portion of their training, we do know from the August 9th 1942, British Commandos pamphlet which was prepared by the Military Intelligence Service of the War Department, that the Close Combat Course for instructors contained 14 periods of unarmed combat training, 55 minutes each period. It stated:

> Normally the last 6 of the 14 periods on unarmed combat were utilized to test the ability of the candidates as instructors.

It also noted:

> Saber fencing was included in order to develop good footwork and balance, quick mental reactions, and parries and attacks suitable for knife fighting.

Again it's not entirely clear how much actual unarmed combat training the Commando recruits would receive. From viewing Truscott's papers, it did not appear that it was a lot. The British Commandos pamphlet, merely stated:

> Many hours were devoted to unarmed combat, involving ju jitsu, wrestling, and general brawling tactics. This training improved the individual's self-confidence and developed a keen desire to fight.

The pamphlet does state the instructors also received one period of Boxing during the total 95 periods.

From Truscott's papers it again appeared that boxing and competitive sports played a larger role in terms of getting the troops ready to meet the enemy.

Amongst Truscott's papers one section of the "Special Service Brigade Training Instructions" in the Physical Fitness portion of The General Objects of Training stated:

> Boxing is to be encouraged in every way, and arrangements must be made to take advantage of any local facilities that may exist in Military or Naval Gymnasia, or in those belonging to Schools or Public Bodies in the vicinity of the unit.

> Similarly Football, both Association and Rugby, must not be forgotten.

It then states in a section "Training by Competition"

> Battalion Commanders must bear in mind the uses of competitive training. It is a form of teaching which, if not overdone, can be most valuable.

> The following are subjects which lend themselves particularly to competitive arrangements.
> (a) Boatwork of all kinds, i.e. Boat pulling: speed and silence in embarking, landing, and gaining a selected objective inshore. There will also be many occasions on which, in order to avoid engine noise, boats will have to be paddled silently into the beach. A competition can very easily be arranged round such an exercise.
> (b) Forces marches over difficult country, whenever possible ending in a field firing practice.
> (c) Night marches by compass.
> (d) Climbing.

     (e) Map reading, competitions for junior leaders and runners.

     (f) Football, boxing, P.T,. and Fencing.

All this lines up with what Orlando Darby stated in his book We Led The Way:

> Borrowing from some of the ancient Scottish games, log exercises became ritual in our training. A group of men carrying a six-inch log on their shoulders tossed it about in an attempt to keep it off the ground.

> There was boxing and close-in fighting. There was no particular emphasis on jujitsu, though the men were given a few good usable holds that each could be expected to remember and utilize when needed.

> Famous, and cursed by the Rangers, were the speed marches at the Commando Depot. Starting out with three-mile hikes, the training worked up to courses of five, seven, ten, twelve, and sixteen-mile speed marches. On these we had to average better than four miles an hour over varied terrain, carrying full equipment. As we progressed in our physical training, we were sent on longer speed marches.

I had already mentioned the quote from Larsen's book about the Fijian's love of boxing, I wondered if Heinmiller utilized it as a training method also.

An article in the Anniston Star, December 2nd 1945, with the title "Major Heinmiller To Leave Fort Today For Washington" stated the following:

Maj. Carl W. Heinmiller, Fort McClellan's IRTC special service officer, leaves today for a new assignment in Washington with headquarters of the Army Ground Forces.

Maj. Charles W. Armstrong, former special service officer for the 75th Infantry Division has arrived at Fort McClellan to take over Major Heinmiller's work.

Major Armstrong who saw action in France and Germany, is from Knoxville, Tenn. His wife and 13-year-old daughter are expected to join him here.

In a statement, Major Armstrong congratulated Major Heinmiller for his work at Fort McClellan, building up an athletic and recreation program to include boxing matches five nights a week, regimental football and baseball teams, an increase in the number of dances and other varied recreational activities. Under Heinmiller's guidance, an all-post baseball team, the Fort McClellan All-Stars, and a football team, the Riflemen, were organized to play outside tennis.

Overseas, Major Heinmiller fought with the 37th Infantry Division on Bougainiville, and organized and led the famed Fiji Scouts, a group of guerrilla warriors in the early stages of the war in the Pacific. He wears the Purple Heart and was awarded the Legion of Merit for outstanding service.

Although this article is well after Heinmiller's time in Fiji it demonstrated that he recognized the importance and value of competitive sports like the Instructors of the Commandos as well as the men stationed in Fiji. We know that the Commandos in Scotland saw the importance of boxing in terms of building the men's confidence but the Royal Marines Commandos included those techniques in their training regimen as well.

A boxing handbook issued at Fort Lee, Virginia stated the following in its foreword:

> Boxing, popularly described as the manly art of self-defense, is recognized for its quality of developing true sportsmanship in a man as well as keeping him in fine physical trim and developing coordination, power and speed of senses. Subscribing to the policy adopted by the war Department, the Special Services Section of the Quartermaster Replacement Training Center of Camp Lee, Virginia is offering boxing instruction to the trainees and soldiers stationed here as one of the chief components of its athletic program. Conditioning and teaching of the game's finer points are supervised by a staff of instructors.

> Corporal Billy Conn, and Sergeant Hank Nowak, baseball pitching star, posed for the pictures illustrating the correct stances and positions for the boxer. Experts have described training for the squared ring as the psychological and physical conditioning of an individual preparing for intense nerval and muscular reaction...that it implies discipline of the mind and power and endurance of the body...it means skill...It is all these things working together in harmony. It is not too difficult to understand how far such training would go toward making a good soldier.

In its introduction it stated the following:

> Boxing is a highly scientific sport. Prior to the days of the Marquis of Queensberry, father of boxing, men stood toe to toe and slugged it out. Brute force, with no rules, prevailed. Modern boxing is an entirely different story. The powerhouse slugger, more often than not, is bested and outpointed by the heady, scientific boxer.

In recognizing the value of the sport, the Army has mapped a program to develop the soldier's instincts for fair play as well as aggressiveness and body and mind coordination. All rules of boxing must be followed, rules that cover behavior outside the ring as well as inside.

Thousands of soldiers have been made fit for combat and other arduous duties required of the service man through the training program connected with the sport. The lack of spirit that marked the ordinary daily exercises was no longer a problem with the introduction of the boxing program.

The enthusiasm displayed at the camp's Golden Gloves and other amateur tournaments is the best indication of the game's popularity with the soldiers. Both the participants and the fans have benefitted by the idea, if their behavior at these boxing shows is a criterion.

It then stated that competition is the backbone of all sports and describes the boxer:

The successful boxer must have good vision, a good mind and a healthy body. Above all, he must learn to take instruction and follow to the letter the advice of his handlers.

The physical condition of a boxer's legs probably is more important than the strength of his arms. Ability to deliver a "haymaker," naturally, is quite an asset, but without proper footwork, the fighter soon finds himself in trouble. Poise, confidence and competence in solving his opponent's style, breaking through his defense are very important.
Combine these with a good sense of timing and proper conditioning and you have the ideal boxer.

Heinmiller had enough experience with the instruction of competitive sports that he was able to build an entire athletic program at Fort McClellan, which included boxing matches. I asked Lee about his father's athletic background. He said:

> He worked for the City of Cleveland as a director of Parks and Rec in the summers, and was the equipment manager for a pro football team that had summer practice where he worked. Not the Cleveland Browns, but the Rams or somebody. I only found out that after he was dead, from a Scout in the group that he took to The National Jamboree in 1939(?).
>
> He coached boxing and refereeing too. Mostly Black boxers I think, he was impressed with their strength and skills. I think that's part of why he did so well with the Fijian and Tlingit…he was not racist!!!

An article in the Anniston Star, on August 13th a few months prior to his departure, titled "Fort M'Clellan Boxers Itching For Action" stated:

> Infantrymen at Fort McClellan can't wait until they get overseas— they're looking for a fight right now.
>
> According to Maj. Carl W. Heinmiller, Special Service officer at the Infantry Replacement Training Center, the men of Fort McClellan's boxing team now rate themselves good enough to take on all-comers.
>
> "They offer to fight anybody at any weight from anywhere if it's a reasonable traveling distance from the Fort. Also, they're looking for return bouts here in our big amphitheater," stated the Major, adding that inquiries should be addressed to him at Special Service office, IRTC, Fort McClellan, Ala.

One final testament to the usefulness of boxing in a jungle-fighting environment, comes from an article in the Vernon Daily Record, January 20th 1943. That article "Boxing Is Helpful To U.S. Marines" stated:

> The difference between a boxing glove and a bayonet is apparent to even the most casual observer, but take it from Col. Harvey Miller, the Marines who know their beak-busting have found it an especially healthy habit in places like Guadalcanal.
>
> The boys are "learning like never before," says Colonel Miller, that a practical knowledge of boxing is important stuff, and the reason is as simple as sitting down. This is it:
>
> "In the ring, the correct side-step means only the difference between scoring a knock-down or being knocked down. In the jungle the same side-step instinctively performed—without boxing gloves but plus—bayonets—may mean the difference between life and death. That's a big difference."
>
> "There's no loser's end in the jungle league," Colonel Miller adds for the special benefit of the Jacobs beach-combers who might like their theory knocked down to the simple terms of the trade. "The motto is 'kill or be killed'."
>
> Colonel Miller, more widely known as Heinie Miller, the permanent secretary and former president of the National Boxing Association, urges boxing to recognize its duty and concentrate on encouraging and teaching youngsters the sport as a means of self-defense in the "jungle hand-to-hand league."
>
> "This war with Tojo," he goes on, "proved quickly that on Tojo's side of the Pacific, at least, boxing and its kindred mayhem— wrestling, jui jitsu and judo—are far more important than they were in 1917-1918. Tojo elects to fight that way chiefly because

he is absolutely lousy with infantry weapons at any range over 150 yards.

"And the fellow who doesn't know what it's all about in a close fight to the death is as much out of place as the lad who enters the ring knowing nothing about infighting. What's more, he has picked a tough spot to learn.

"So it is boxing's duty to graduate above the plane that sees only business and gate receipts. Boxing right now is a whole lot more important than it ever was as either a sport or business."

One other thing worth mentioning, was the Fijian's love of rugby. According to Phil Matthews, a fellow researcher, the rugger tackle in the manuals was called that as it was a known thing amongst all social classes in the Empire.

The 1942 pamphlet B.R. 621 Close Combat For Use In Royal Navy & Royal Marines stated the following.

Regarding how to utilize The boxing punch:

The ordinary boxing punch aimed at the throat, the groin, the pit of the stomach or the kidneys. Don't use it at the chin—the chin jab is far more effective.

And a mention of Rugby in the paragraph in section 3, regarding how to attack a man from behind when you are unarmed:

If you wish to take your opponent unawares, your approach must depend on the nature of the ground. You can only creep up slowly and silently over soft earth or sand—over gravel or debris you will have to make a rush for it and rely on getting at your opponent before he has time to turn.

As soon as you are close behind him, quickly swing one arm around his neck, bringing the forearm sharply against his throat. As soon as your arm contacts his throat, strike a knee blow at his back with the *opposite* knee (i.e. left arm, right knee), at the same time clap your free hand over his mouth. This will cause him to fall backwards and you can then attack him with any kicks or blows previously described.

If your enemy should start to turn before you are close enough to attack him in the above manner, the only thing to do is to dive for his knee and tackle him low as in Rugby football. Launch yourself at the back or side of his legs aiming to hit him with your shoulder about six inches above the knees. Turn your head slightly to one side and, as your shoulder strikes, fling your arms round his legs and hold them firmly. He is bound to come down and you can then pounce on him and apply blows or kicks.

In another section of the pamphlet it mentioned that if an unarmed enemy comes at you and then thinks better of it and turns to run:

Jump after him and apply the Rugger tackle described in 3(a) above.

Source: The Tackle In Rugby Football, The Windsor Magazine, 1922.

Boxing Handbook approved by the Virginia Boxing & Wrestling
Commission, March 9th 1943, for troops stationed at Camp Lee.

Heinmiller (top left) the boxing referee and coach at Fort McClellan.

208

Fieldcraft

Amongst Lucien Truscott's files and documents located in other archives we can gain further knowledge about what exactly it meant to be a Commando.

One such document "Commando Training", outlined some of the important subjects a Commando should learn, besides weapons and unarmed combat training.

The document is notable because it discussed the difficulty in having a uniform system of training for all the different Commando units. The author of the document stated:

> It is difficult to lay down a definite policy for training Commandos until two fundamental questions have been finally settled. First, what is the primary role of a Commando? Secondly, what is to be its organization?

> In the comparatively short time during which I have been connected with these units which have been described in terms as contradictory as "an undisciplined rabble" and "The Famous British Commandos" (the former by a War Office general, the latter by the German General staff) they have varied in size between Battalions over 1,000 strong, with no less than 72 officers, to units of 19 and 356 O.Rs (other ranks).

The author then described the diversity of specialists ranging from the Parachutist to the Folbotist, and they have been called upon to carry out tasks as markedly different as a coastal raid by 50 men, to a 3-day rearguard action covering the withdrawal of regular infantry.

The document stated:

The problem of their future training is therefore not easily solved, and much of what follows will appear platitudinous to the regular solider, the more so since I have always contended that 80% of Commando training should be conducted upon the normally accepted lines, there being little to add to the curriculum of the modern infantryman.

Two outstanding features cannot, however, be over-stressed. The development of the offensive spirit, and the importance of training at night.

So we see that Commandos were more or less determined to be the same as regular infantryman, or at least their training should have been. Or the opposite was true, regular soldiers should have had the same training as the Commandos. If it was good for some it was good for all.

The author of the document also stressed the importance of developing the offensive spirit and training at night. Another very important thing for a Commando to have was self-confidence and the ability to think and act independently. We will see this discussed again in the next chapter concerning an individual who knew Heinmiller, and who underwent this type of training, Colonel Logan Weston.

The document stated:

> The next attribute required is self-confidence. The individual must be made to develop a sense of self-efficiency, and must be early broken of the habit of relying on the "normal channel of communications". He must be taught that he must not expect his rations to be delivered under the supervision of kindly C.Q.M.S., nor can he always look for guidance to an officer or N.C.O., but must be prepared to act alone and on his own initiative.

Mindest is key, but also key is the importance of being able to act independently and on one's own self-initiative. The Fijian Commandos would have not only been able to fend for themselves in the bush, but they also would have been able to do so for long periods of time, on their own if they needed to. They had that type of training from a young age.

A section of the document on Fieldcraft and the use of Concealment is also notable because the Fijian Commandos had been well versed in this and had been masters of their own environment. It stated:

> Field-craft and the art of the hunter are the next to be developed and the would-be Commando expert must learn to see without being seen. He must receive training in the use of ground, in concealment and camouflage and in the use of the stalking glass, but he must bear in mind that these are only a means to an end, and are the methods by which he will achieve his objective, get to grips with the enemy and eventually make good his escape.

> It is quite remarkable how long it took us to drum some of these lessons into the modern youths recruited from the large towns. They were at first reluctant to look further ahead than the length of the average block of houses, appeared never to have observed such natural phenomena as the phases of the moon, and were quite incapable of selecting concealed positions from which other definite objects could be observed: but they trained quickly, and, in my opinion eventually made the best soldiers as they were less perturbed by the noise of battle then their normally quieter country neighbors.

A few sections down is situated the Weapon training, P.T.; miscellaneous subjects section, which stated:

> During this period, much of the time was still allotted to Weapon Training (including training in the use of enemy weapons) and the

men were kept fit by P.T., boxing and route marches; but new subjects were introduces which included M.T. driving, house-breaking, gangster methods, unarmed combat, and the use of various devices for sabotage purposes; whilst we arranged for visits and tours of inspection of aerodromes, W/T stations, Docks and factories.

Like the Canadian Battle Drill Training document, Fieldcraft was emphasized in a whole paragraph in the document whereas unarmed combat is given a very small mention and it is once again looped in with boxing and other subjects.

We know that the Fijian Commandos had already been experts in fieldcraft. But was that enough to put them in the same category as The Commandos? It would seem so. According to Dr. Fox, from what he knew from New Zealand sources, the New Zealanders and Fijians on Fiji operated similarly to armed adult boy scouts, with the emphasis on undetected movement, concealment and ambush. He pointed out that from Heinmiller's account of being a boy scout, he probably would have fit right in with that ethos.

We can recall that the Battle Drill Training document stated:

> Battle Drill training is founded upon the axiom that "until every soldier looks on himself as a ruthless killer, using cover with the facility of an animal, using his weapons with the practiced ease of a professional hunter and covering the ground on the move with the agility of a deer-stalker, infantry battle training will be based on false foundations"

On a final note, to show how valuable the knowledge was that the Fijians had, and that they were able to pass those things on, there is a mention of something in Tyler Webb's thesis. Although it's something more in the category of First Aid, it's worth pointing out that while the Buckeyes were fighting in Bougainville, during a relatively light period of action:

> the Buckeyes learned valuable lessons from Fijians assisting them on the island. The Fijian remedy for the painful bug bites was to open a small wound with a machete and simply pour water down the blade. Apparently, this was more effective than any treatment the medics could offer the soldiers.

As recently as 2022, New Zealand soldiers were training to survive in the Fijian bush. An article in the New Zealand Herald "Survival of the fittest: New Zealand soldiers training to survive in Fijian Bush" from June of that year stated:

> A group of Kiwi soldiers have gone bush in Fiji as part of an intense training programme designed to test their survival skills in the jungle.

> Students from the Officer Cadet School of NZ are in Fiji this month taking part in the Republic of Fiji Military Force's programme.

> Exercise Veitiutaki is an initiative that sees soldiers being placed in the jungle with minimal equipment and no food.

> The programme tests soldier's command, leadership and battle craft skills while in a jungle environment in the Nausori Highlands.

> They have been learning how to set up traps and snares, collect water, light a fire without matches, build shelter and understand how to effectively use items in a survival kit. They have also been taught what is edible in the jungle.

OCS senior instructor Captain Jonty Hooson said this part of the survival exercise was not only hugely beneficial to the cadets, but one they enjoyed.

"They caught eels, shrimp, water lobster – and learned more about one another," Hooson said.

"By exposing our cadets to this environment, they proved that they can survive with minimal equipment.

One imagines that this was the sort of training that Heinmiller the former Boy Scout would have fit right at home with.

Authors Note: The following two pages contain Notes on Fieldcraft Training by Captain Lord Lovat (No. 4 Commando) which were amongst Lucien Truscott's files.

Note the mention of the bushcraft and fieldcraft skills of the Aboriginal Australians and other cultures.

FIELDCRAFT.

Notes by Lord Lovat.

SOUNDS BY NIGHT: It is important that the trained men in a Commando, and particularly those qualified as Scouts, Snipers or Patrol personnel, should be able to interpret correctly the various noises which may be heard emanating from enemy positions. All ranks should have impressed upon them the carrying powers of the human voice. This applies particularly to mountain country and across water, where hills and sea act as sounding boards. This peculiarity has not escaped the less enlightened savage. The black fellow of the Australian bush, by pitching his voice, can pass messages over very remarkable distances: and I have heard Kaffirs in the Drakensburgs "throwing" their voices from hill to hill on an early morning when kraals had news to exchange, in the same way. Nearer home, the Swiss shepherd boys have made use of Yeodling ever since time immemorial.

Ignorance of this vox humana an le is particularly noticeable during practice landings, though it is not always the Army that is to blame. On a still night at Inveraray the vibrations of sound caused by knocking open the stiff door of a "sallyport" feels painfully loud at three quarters of a mile to the umpire on the beach. The hoarse instructions from one cox or bos'wain that invariably follow, though less audible, can generally be heard on a lee shore

PREPARED NOISES..

The following is a list of noises which can easily be produced for training purposes, and which I have found work successfully:

1. A party of men in F.S.M.O. crossing a wire fence.
2. Ditto digging trench.
3. Ditto revetting trench or fitting sandbags.
4. Hammering picket and angle irons.
5. Opening and closing rifle bolt, or changing magazines.
6. Posting of sentries.
7. Striking match, and glow of cigarette.
8. Talking whispering: sneeze and noseblow.
9. Walking down a road.
10. Cutting barbed wire.

...... and a dozen other experiments that any keen officer can think of. The only requirements are a still, dark night with no moon or wind.

The sound effects with untrained men should begin at 200 yards. Gradually work away and make more difficult as powers of observation improve.

It may be of interest to mention that I have never been far enough away not to see the strike of a match which at 600 yards looks like a searchlight. (How many lives have been thrown away both on exercises and active service by the careless smoker!)

Natives can smell water at a distance, and quite a number of six-and-eightpenny soldiers will wind a bad German cigar at 50 yards. This should be practised.

The noises and smells outlined above could all portend serious consequences, such as the enemy assembling for attack, men on a counter patrol, digging in, evacuating forward posts etc.

It is the business of Commando Scouts and Reconnaissance Patrols to obtain information of this kind. If the men are highly trained they will differentiate between sounds of offence and defence. For all concerned it is worth remembering that of the many noises heard at night on an occupied coast or No Man's Land, the majority will be caused by an evil-minded opposition!

.... Cont/

215

FIELDCRAFT (Continued)

Ears take the place of eyes in the dark. If an unidentified movement is heard there is only one thing to do; freeze into the ground. At close quarters the first man to move is the first man to die, since he will give his position away.

NIGHT WORK-GENERAL

WIND .. Always move upwind if possible. Movement can be heard better, and suspicious smells be detected (i.e. tobacco, wood-fires, cooking, farm buildings etc.)

MOON .. Keep the moon behind you always. If you are wearing a leather jerkin, turn it inside out on a bright night. It is as important to keep off skylines in the dark as it is in the daytime. If the moon is up, hollows and folds in the ground will be in intense shadow, while the ridges and bare hillsides will be clear and bright. Always check the moon before going out on patrol. (A number of people seem unaware that the moon rises and sets at different times.)

FOG ... Fog is the most unpredictable and the most difficult of all weather conditions. In foggy weather sounds are plainly heard and the direction of sound is very hard to locate.

CONCLUSION.

Finally, remember to halt and listen at frequent intervals, whatever the weather may be like. There is far too much bumming along by scouts who think their job has been well done when they are shot at close range on top of the enemy position. The super-scout should aim at just locating the enemy post and then either reporting its whereabouts, or leading his patrol past it - unobserved.

The halting or listening period has, in the case of untrained men, the severe drawback that it seems a signal for every man to cough, spit or clear his throat. Unfit men, heavy smokers, or those suffering from colds, must never do key work at night.

Colonel Logan E. Weston

Source: "The Fightin' Preacher", caption stated: newly commissioned officers (I'm back, left) on Fiji – 1942. Author's note: Lee Heinmiller believes that is his father Carl, standing to the right of Weston.

In his book *"The Fightin' Preacher"*, a man who knew Carl Heinmiller wrote about some of his experiences in Fiji during the war. Colonel Logan E. Weston later went on to become a part of Merrill's Marauders, another Commando-type organization.

Merrill's Marauders or Unit Galahad, which was officially named the 5307th Composite Unit (Provisional), had been a long range penetration special operations jungle warfare unit; which fought in the Southeast Asian theater of World War II, or the China-Burma-India Theater (CBI). It became famous for its deep-penetration missions behind Japanese lines, often engaging Japanese forces which had been superior in number.

A War Department Memorandum from the Operations Division (OPD), dated 18 September 1943, listed the proposed composition of the new all-volunteer unit.

The Caribbean Defense Command provided 960 jungle-trained officers and men, 970 jungle-trained officers and men also came from Army Ground Forces which had been based in the Continental United States. Another 674 "battle-tested" jungle troops from the South Pacific Command, who had been Army veterans of the Guadalcanal and Solomon Islands campaigns, also signed on.

It was from this group that Colonel Weston had arrived. He is important to the story of Heinmiller because they had been stationed together in Fiji. His book also discusses his feelings about the Japanese, and provides us with a glimpse of what the mindset was, concerning the enemy. Of his experience in Fiji, Weston wrote:

> We hadn't seen much action yet, other than a few minor skirmishes while on patrols to search out and destroy enemy radio relay stations. The Japanese had left behind small teams of soldiers hiding in the jungle whose job it was to provide information about allied ship and aircraft movements. When our naval intelligence picked up these signals, they would use direction-finding equipment to determine the general location of the enemy outposts and relay that information to us.
>
> We would run combat patrols in the locations identified by the navy, but our success seemed to depend as much on luck as skill. Occasionally we would find the posts abandoned, the Japanese soldiers fleeing only moments before we arrived. At two hundred and fifty pounds and measuring in at more than three feet, the radios on which they had broadcast information about our troops were disabled and left behind, too large and clumsy to carry with them.

On the few occasions when our patrols did surprise the Japanese at their posts, the enemy always fought to the death. We were instructed to take prisoners whenever possible for debriefing, but the Japanese had been told that the ruthless Americans tortured and executed their prisoners. Having seen the conduct of their own military in China and Korea, it is understandable that they would believe this.

When not on patrol, the majority of our time in Fiji consisted of fellowshipping with the Christian missionaries once our routine military duties were completed for the day. We had also done a bit of training with Fijian scouts, which we thoroughly enjoyed. These scouts were a carefree lot with a most peculiar sense of humor. They kept us entertained with their hilarious antics, and often sang lustily as they went about their various tasks. We were all amused, except when they continued their noisy serenades even on patrol in enemy territory.

The Fijians were very skillful in jungle craft and could move silently through the thickest jungle vegetation. We planned to use them as scouts in the Solomon Islands. On many of our maneuvers on Viti Levu, the American units would post heavy guards around their command installations. Even with a doubling of the guard, these Fijian pranksters would sneak in with white chalk and mark x's on the helmets, holsters, rifles, and pup tents of the sleeping American officers to prove how easily they could have been killed or captured in real warfare.

Many happy memories faded as the islands dropped over the horizon, and once again we were surrounded by the endless blue Pacific Ocean. I had recently obtained a battlefield commission, but there were no officer insignias yet available in the Pacific theater. As I stood there leaning on the railing, the sunlight glistened off the pair of second lieutenant bars which had been donated by an American nurses corps in Australia.

Ahead of us lay two thousand miles of open water before we would reach our destination in a small corner of the world that would come to symbolize a hell on earth for thousands of Japanese and Americans alike – Guadalcanal.

The book "The Jungle Survival Manual 1939-1945" discusses the efforts the British and Americans took to train their troops in jungle. According to the book's editor Alan Jeffreys:

> The Fourteenth Army prepared for the next phase of the fighting and a culture of training and continually learning lessons was instilled in the 7th Indian Division and across the Indian Army. Lessons were also learned by the US Marines and US Army fighting on Guadalcanal Island and in New Guinea. In 1942, Lieutenant Colonel Russell Reader interviewed fifty-nine officers and other ranks on Guadalcanal, and these interviews were published as *Notes on Jungle Warfare from the U.S. Marines and U.S. Infantry on Guadalcanal Island* and distributed at the Infantry School. As in India, he noted the importance of junior leadership, the importance of patrolling but there were differences as the Americans did not undertake night operations whereas the Indian Army underwent night training in all theatres. In New Guinea the need for training and experience was paramount (as demonstrated by 'Bill' Slim's quote in the introduction). Combat Lessons stated:

> The operations amply illustrated the need for thorough training of units and individuals in scouting and patrolling. They also proved, however, that there is no substitute for experience. It is therefore logical that in addition to training, every opportunity should be

taken to give our troops actual experience in scouting and patrolling against the enemy.

A training bulletin had been issued at Fort Benning on February 1st 1943, which was based off the *Notes on Jungle Warfare* document titled *Close-Up Of Guadalcanal October-November 1942 Verbatim Statements of Participants.* In the introduction of the bulletin it noted:

> The conclusions which follow the main body of the bulletin were prepared by Lieutenant Colonel Reeder and published as a part of the original document. They represent his views and not necessarily those of the Infantry School.

As a lead-up to the next chapter we are primarily concerned with two paragraphs. In the *Recommendations For Training* section there is a verbatim quote by a Platoon Sergeant George E. Aho, Company "F", 5th Marines who stated:

> HAND-TO-HAND COMBAT.—In our training for jungle warfare we had a great deal of work in hand-to-hand combat, use of the knife, jiu jitsu, etc. With the exception of bayonet fighting we have not used this work. I have been in many battles since I hit this island and I have never seen anyone use it.

In the *Equipment And Supply* section of the document Platoon Sergeant C. M. Feagin, Company "I", 5th Marines makes a statement which seems semi-contradictory to that of Sergeant George E. Aho. It seems the Marines may have not enjoyed the training aspect of knife fighting but they wanted access to the tool:

> The sabers which the Japanese officers carry have proved to be worthless. I killed two Japs who came at me with sabers and I got them first by shooting them, but I wished I had in reserve a good jungle knife. I don't mean a bolo, which we should have in cutting

trails, but a knife with a good 12-inch blade of good steel. We could use this against these Japanese as well as for cutting vines that catch on us at night.

There are many other good tidbits of information in the Notes document and for posterity I will include it with this book at the end of the chapter.

In Colonel Weston's book he wrote about the realities of war versus training he had received. He wrote:

> Although we had trained extensively on Guadalcanal, this jungle combat was unlike anything we had ever experienced before. The confusion and "fog" of war was only increased by the dense foliage and darkness of a triple canopy jungle. We advanced step by step, usually never able to see more than a few feet in any direction. Advancing in a jungle is like stretching out your hand in a dark room and feeling your way. Suddenly an enemy soldier would appear, and we often fired at almost point blank range. For us, survival required the quickness of an Old West gunfighter. We would instinctively drop to the dirt at the first crack of rifle and machine gun fire.
>
> The heat, humidity, and filth of the swampy jungle conspired to make the unseen Japanese take on an evil and brooding quality. The enemy would fight savagely one moment only to slip away into the jungle to ambush us once again a few yards further on. And still the battle raged on at a chaotic and constantly changing tempo.
>
> Our training paid off in spades that day. We quickly became experts at neutralizing Japanese machine gun nests. When we made contact, the Japanese would almost always open fire. Some of our men would pin them down with rifle and machine gun fire

while others maneuvered around to eliminate the threat with grenades or flame throwers.

Often we discovered, a Japanese soldier would lay in a foxhole or pull the body of a dead comrade on top of him and merely play dead. After our soldiers passed by, the supposedly dead Jap would jump up and fire at them from the rear. It was certain suicide, but it demonstrated the fanatical devotion of these soldiers to their emperor. Such experiences proved unnerving for our boys, and it was not unusual to see a soldier shoot or bayonet a fallen Japanese just to make sure he was really dead.

The marine unit on our right did not fare as well as we did. They advanced into a stronghold of Japanese forces dug in behind some coral formations. Though the marines fought valiantly, they were decimated. They began attack with eight hundred men, and by 3:30 that afternoon, less than two hundred and fifty remained in action.

I have always found it fascinating that most men fear the violence of combat only before the attack. Once the battle has begun, the action is so intense and consuming that all fear is forgotten. I have seen men fighting on, completely unaware that they had been severely wounded, only to collapse after being informed by a buddy that they were bleeding.

Casualties in our unit were low, only because we didn't get trapped by the enemy. We applied a principle I had learned regarding the spiritual enemy: never let him get out of sight. Our sector had kept the Japanese troops under surveillance even throughout the hours of darkness by the use of outposts and patrols.

It seemed that lessons such as these were learned on the job. They were building the plane while they were flying the plane.

One more thing worth mentioning from Colonel Weston's book, is the chapter in which he looks back on his life experiences. Weston discussed the Commando type training he had received while he had been stationed in India:

> One thing that often comes to mind is the motto of the British Commandos we were taught in India while we were preparing to march into Burma. We were indoctrinated with the philosophy that a commando unit must be endowed with a maximum of the offensive and imaginative spirit. The principle of commando success is that the whole area of guerrilla warfare lies in striking the enemy when he least expects it, where he is the most vulnerable. That means we have to take advantage of every opportunity, physical or spiritual, if we ever expect to be victorious over the enemy.

Commando was just as much about the mental conditioning in addition to physical. As the "Commando Training" document had put it, Commandos must have the ability to think and act independently and also to be endowed with the offensive spirit.

Circling back to the training aspect, it's interesting to point out what became important later on in terms of jungle warfare, during the Vietnam conflict. In a declassified Vietnam era MACV-SOG (Military Assistance Command, Vietnam – Studies and Observations Group) document concerning personnel and training and some of the challenges associated with that.

Activated in January 1964, SOG's real function was disguised by the cover name "Studies and Observation Group" with the mission to analyze lesosns learned in combat, but its real mission was to conduct strategic reconnaissance missions, sabotage, and psychological operations.

The author who wrote the comments on training, Colonel Stephen E. Cavanaugh, was a graduate of UCLA in ROTC. In 1942, Cavanaugh volunteered for parachute school, was assigned to a parachute regiment and spent World War Two in the Pacific, with that unit. He ended up as a Company Commander. During that time, he had two combat jumps with the 11th Airborne Division, fighting the Japanese in New Guinea and the Philippines. His second jump was on a North Luzon drop zone to link up with friendly guerrillas.

Cavanaugh next became an instructor at the Parachute school at Fort Benning, and was also stationed in Berlin and Taiwan before he wound up in Vietnam in 1961, on a MAAG (United States Military Assistance Advisory Group) tour where he served as the country's senior training officer.

In 1969 Cavanaugh wrote:

> The lack of proper training and qualification for this type of mission is, to my mind, the most serious deficiency which I have seen. Individuals trained at Fort Bragg in Special Forces techniques have, in the main, been qualified in a particular MOS and the techniques thereof and in counterinsurgency and revolutionary development type training. Few, if any, have had an opportunity to actually study or practice reconnaissance procedures and tactics.

> Graduates of the Ranger school at Fort Benning would appear to be a more suitable type of individual for this type of operation provided they have the motivation and interest. If the Army is going to continue to develop highly specialized reconnaissance elements for special operations, the individuals must be carefully

selected, must be volunteers, and must be trained in the proper tactics and techniques. Motivation is a key point and it is erroneous to believe that just because a man is directed to go to Ranger school or to some form of reconnaissance school that he automatically could be capable of the type of mission which SOG is currently involved in. It might suffice for an individual who is a member of a larger reconnaissance and patrol organization, such as the LRRPs, but not for the special operations, which involve an exceptionally small number of individuals, being conducted in an area which is entirely hostile.

To overcome the training deficiencies which are so obvious in our reconnaissance team personnel, a reconnaissance team leaders course was established at the SOG Training Center at Camp Long Tanh. It is a two week course prepared for and given specifically to reconnaissance team members. It stresses map reading, observation techniques, reporting procedures, communications, escape and evasion, trail watching, etc. No stress is given to those more exotic training concepts currently used by Special Forces to allegedly prepare people for combat, such as rapelling and hand-to-hand combat, and to exotic demolition training. While these subjects are considered to be necessary in certain instances, I feel that undue emphasis has been given to training in these areas and insufficient emphasis to fundamental aspects of ground reconnaissance and patrolling.

I have found that a great number of our new Special Forces personnel come into this program with no appreciation of these methods of observations and reporting sightings, cannot read a map, have never been taught the fundamentals of leadership and lack an understanding of joint air-ground procedures.

It was apparent that Cavanaugh thought that there was a lack of training in certain areas that needed to be addressed; areas which were better suited to the needs of Commando type warfare in a jungle environment.

Even during the Vietnam war it seemed as if individuals were learning things they actually needed to know on the job or in a fast course, rather than school.

Sometimes they learned things by trial and error. It still seemed as if these Commando types were building the plane as they were flying the plane, figuring out what was important and what was not as important.

Author's Note: the Close-Up Of Guadalcanal document is presented on the following pages.

CLOSE-UP OF GUADALCANAL

OCTOBER–NOVEMBER 1942

Verbatim Statements of Participants

FEBRUARY 1, 1943

CLOSE-UP OF GUADALCANAL
OCTOBER - NOVEMBER, 1942

VERBATIM STATEMENTS OF PARTICIPANTS

INTRODUCTION

1. The contents of this training bulletin are based entirely upon a document prepared by Lieutenant Colonel Russell P. Reeder, Jr., Infantry, entitled "Notes on Jungle Warfare from the U. S. Marines and U. S. Infantry on Guadalcanal Island".

2. The document prepared by Lieutenant Colonel Reeder presented the information in the form of a series of interviews with a total of 59 officers and enlisted men who had been and were engaged in combat just before and at the time they were interviewed.

3. The matter presented was so well selected, so timely and so responsive to a multitude of questions which have been asked by Infantry personnel in recent months that it was decided to produce it in this form.

4. It was the opinion of the School that the matter presented would have an enhanced training value if rearranged to assemble the opinions and conclusions of various individuals upon various subjects to facilitate comparison and thereby permit the reader more readily to draw his own conclusions.

5. At the same time, it was felt that the authenticity inherent in verbatim statements of those with recent combat experience should be retained. Accordingly, the main body of the bulletin which bears the title given it by the original author is made up of statements which are substantially verbatim. Each passage quoted from the statement of a particular individual is followed by a number in parentheses. The identity of the speaker can be established in each case by referring to the "References" immediately following this introduction.

6. The conclusions which follow the main body of the bulletin were prepared by Lieutenant Colonel Reeder and published as a part of the original document. They represent his views and not necessarily those of the Infantry School.

(1)

REFERENCES

The subject matter contained in this document consists entirely of substantially verbatim quotations from officers and enlisted men who have seen active service against the Japanese in New Guinea and Guadalcanal. Observations made by Lieutenant Colonel Russell P. Reeder, Jr., Infantry, who originally collected the information, are given in parentheses followed by the initial "R". Explanatory observations made by school personnel are given in parentheses with no signature. Each quoted statement is followed by a numeral, also in parentheses. The various numerals refer to the following personnel who were interviewed.

(1) Major General Archer A. Vandergrift, commanding 1st Marine Division.

(2) Colonel G. C. Thomas, U.S.M.C., C of S, 1st Marine Division.

(3) Colonel Merritt A. Edson, C.O., 5th Marines. Colonel Edson formerly commanded the Marine "Raider Battalion." He has been recommended by General Vandergrift for the Medal of Honor.

(4) Sergeant Major B. Metzger, 5th Marines. Sergeant Metzger, when interviewed, had recently been promoted from first sergeant.

(5) Platoon Sergeant H. R. Strong, Company "A", 5th Marines.

(6) Platoon Sergeant F. T. O'Fara, Company "B", 5th Marines.

(7) Platoon Sergeant R. A. Zullo, Company "C", 5th Marines.

(8) Corporal W. A. McCluskey, Company "D", 5th Marines.

(9) Second Lieutenant Andrew Chisick, 5th Marines.

(10) Marine Gunner E. S. Rust, 5th Marines.

(11) Gunnery Sergeant H. L. Beardsley, Company "G", 5th Marines.

(12) Platoon Sergeant J. C. L. Hollinsworth, Company "H", 5th Marines.

(13) Platoon Sergeant George E. Aho, Company "F", 5th Marines.

(14) Corporal J. S. Stankus, Company "E", 5th Marines.

(15) Second Lieutenant H. M. Davis, 5th Marines. Lt. Davis was promoted on the field of battle.

(16) Platoon Sergeant C. M. Feagin, Company "I", 5th Marines.

(17) Motor Section Sergeant T. E. Rumbley, Company "I", 5th Marines.

(18) Corporal Fred Carter, Company "I", 5th Marines.

(19) Sergeant O. J. Marion, Company "L", 5th Marines. Sergeant Marion was a platoon guide.

(20) Corporal E. J. Byrne, Company "L", 5th Marines.

(21) Corporal F. R. McAllan, Company "L", 5th Marines.

(2)

230

(22) Platoon Sergeant C. C. Arndt, Hq. and Serv. Company, 5th Marines.

(23) Colonel Demuth, Division Artillery Commander.

(24) Colonel Amor Le R. Sims, C.O., 7th Marines.

(25) Lieutenant Colonel L. B. Puller, C.O., 1st Bn., 7th Marines. Lieutenant Colonel Puller was recommended by General Vandergrift for the Medal of Honor for leading his battalion, with seven wounds, continually for 24 hours.

(26) Five noncommissioned officers of the 1st Bn., 7th Marines selected by Lieutenant Colonel Puller.

(27) Lieutenant Sheppard, 7th Marines. He was promoted on the field of battle.

(28) Master Gunnery Sergeant R. M. Fowle, 7th Marines. Sergeant Fowle had 24 years service with the Marines.

(29) Lieutenant Colonel Frisbee, Executive Officer, 7th Marines.

(30) A group of three second lieutenants and five old NCO's of the 2d Bn., 7th Marines.

(31) Second Lieutenant D. A. Clark, 7th Marines.

(32) Major Buse, Assistant G-3, 1st Marine Division.

(33) Brigadier General Ed Sebree, Assistant Division Commander.

(34) Major Ben J. Northridge, C.O., 2d Bn., 164th Infantry.

(35) Lieutenant Colonel Frank Richards, C.O., 1st Bn., 164th Infantry.

(36) Captain John O. Gossett, commanding Company "H", 164th Infantry.

(37) Captain John A. Dawson, commanding Company "B", 164th Infantry.

(38) Sergeant L. R. Lang, Platoon Sergeant, Company "E", 164th Infantry.

(39) Sergeant D. L. Golden, Company "F", 164th Infantry.

(40) Lieutenant John S. Graves, Platoon Leader, Company "C", 164th Infantry.

(41) Sergeant W. V. Demoss, Squad Leader, Company "C", 164th Infantry.

(42) Staff (Platoon) Sergeant A. L. Chapman, Company "G", 164th Infantry.

(43) Sergeant C. W. Arrowood, Company "F", 164th Infantry.

(44) Colonel B. E. Moore, commanding 164th Infantry.

(45) An unidentified Marine NCO.

(46) Major Lou Walt, C.O., 2d Bn., 5th Marines.

(47) Captain H. L. Crook, C.O., 3d Bn., 164th Infantry.

(48) Lieutenant Colonel N. H. Hannekan, C.O., 2d Bn., 7th Marines.

(3)

231

NOTES ON JUNGLE WARFARE FROM THE U. S. MARINES AND U. S. INFANTRY ON GUADALCANAL ISLAND

Section I

LEADERSHIP AND USE OF STAFF

1. COMMAND QUALITIES.—*a.* Our successful commanders are invariably those who understand the use of infantry weapons. (2)

b. This leadership business resolves itself down to being hard-boiled. By that I mean getting rid of the poor leaders, even if you like them personally, because this is a life and death affair. This goes right on down to the noncoms. (3)

c. I like the Marines better than the Army because the average Marine officer is closer to his men than the average Army officer whom I have observed. We have comradeship in the Marine Corps. (13)

d. Our battalion commander wants every last man in our battalion to know as much as *he* does about the situation. It pays. (13) Sometimes the information does not get down to us and then we are really in the dark. When we get the orders and information we can get in there and pitch better. (21)

e. Our battalion commanders know that if they need help they must ask for it and not just try to bull things through. That enables the regiments to act as teams in the right manner and in the right direction. (24)

f. Pick your officers for common sense. That is of greater value than all the words in the book. I am two deep in my battalions in regard to battalion C.O.'s. That is, each one of my battalion executives is a potential battalion commander. (24)

g. I back up my executive officer. I never see a battalion commander or a staff officer about administration unless they see the executive officer first. My executive officer and I are a team. (24)

h. A regimental commander cannot be impatient. Don't push your battalion commanders unless you feel there is a reluctance on their part. (24)

i. When handling my companies, I take the company commander's word for what is going on. You have to do this to get anywhere. (25)

j. Calling back commanding officers to battalion and regimental CPs to say "How are things going?" is awful! (25)

k. Officers and noncommissioned officers, during shelling, should move around and talk to the men. Quiet them down. If you don't do this, some of them will walk around with their fingers on their triggers and they get to imagining things. (28)

(4)

232

l. You gotta' have confidence in each other. When signals to move forward are given, you must have confidence that the men next to you will move forward even if you can't see them. We have that kind of confidence in this battalion. (30)

m. We have been in action continually here from August 7, 1942, until this date—November 26, 1942. What we all marvel at is how General Vandergrift can stand it so much better than we do. It must be his character. (32)

n. Teach the men how to handle men. I thought I knew how, but since I have been here I have learned a lot and revised my ideas. I have learned the primitive rough and tumble way. You can't pat all men on the back. You have to be rough with some men in order to get results. I have learned which men I can pat on the back and which I have to deal with in the hardest manner. (36)

o. (Note: When I saw Colonel Moore he was interviewing a patrol and patrol leader who had just come back. They had been on a reconnaissance for 15 hours. The patrol leader had been met at an advance position and, as he had valuable information of the enemy, he was conducted by jeep to the observation post of the artillery where he directed artillery fire; then returned to the colonel and made his report. The patrol and its leader were nearly exhausted. Colonel Moore had on hand small sample bottles of brandy which he issued one to each two men. One could not be around Colonel Moore very long without realizing that he is a leader in every sense of the word. (R)

p. The greatest problem is leaders, and you have to find some way to weed out the weak ones. The platoon leaders who cannot command, who cannot foresee things, and who cannot act on the spur of the moment in an emergency are a distinct detriment. It is hot here. Men straggle. They get heat exhaustion. They come out vomiting and throwing away equipment. The leaders must be leaders and they must be alert to stop this sort of thing. The men have been taught to take salt tablets but the leaders don't see to this. Many of the junior leaders have not used their heads at times. In their training I recommend you put them up against situations where they must use their heads. For example, C.O. Company .... reports he has only 35 men; that the rest had heat exhaustion. He did not have sense enough to rest his men, make them take salt, etc. The good leaders seem to get killed. The poor leaders get the men killed. The big problem is leadership and getting the shoulder straps on the right people. Not one man in 50 can lead a patrol in this jungle. If you can find out who the good patrol leaders are before you hit the combat zone, you have found out something. I have had to get rid of about 25 officers because they were just not leaders. I had to make the battalion commanders weed out the poor junior leaders. Our junior leaders are finding out that they must know more about their men. The good leaders do. (44)

(5)

2. USE OF STAFF.—*a*. I make my staff officers get out of this CP —not to snoop on the troops but to help the battalions and acquaint themselves with the general situation. (24)

b. The staffs are twice as large as they should be. The regimental staff is too large. I have five staff officers in the battalion and I could get along with less. (25)

Section II

CONTROL

3. *a*. This campaign has been fought with almost a total absence of paper work. We have gotten over that jump by continuous close personal contact, between troop commanders and the staff. (2)

b. Offensive action is the most difficult to support as you cannot tell exactly where your troops are. The principle of the command post up and to the front is certainly correct. (3)

c. In the advance in a jungle it is hard for a platoon leader to keep control of his men. Corporals and their men must be taught to act individually. (15)

d. In the jungle don't put troops into a skirmish line until actual physical contact is made. Keep them in squad columns with two scouts in front of each squad. Sometimes use connecting files between columns. Each man should know the objective. I make my platoon leaders designate an objective every hundred yards in the jungle, and they work to it and reorganize. They don't push off for the next objective until they get word from the company commander. I control my companies exactly the same way. I set up objectives for each company. When the companies reach their objective they report. After the reorganization we go ahead. (46)

e. This idea may sound strange to someone who reads your notes in an office far away, but it is a very practical means of controlling a march on a winding trail in this hot country. Marches here, where the air is hot and so steamy that there seems to be no air, takes a lot out of the men. The weak ones will say when the march gets tough, "Hold it up." This will be passed on up to the front and the column will stop when you don't want it to. We adopted the use of the letter "H" plus a numeral meaning to halt. The leaders and the point know what numeral we will use, and we change the numeral. For example, we will use "H2" the first two hours; then "H7" etc. (48)

f. The big problem which we have not solved completely yet to my mind, is maintaining contact in the attack between units in this jungle, especially between battalions. (31)

g. My flank men in each squad in the advance are responsible for maintaining contact with the squads on the right and left. Of course we have a base squad. (9)

(6)

234

Section III

CHARACTERISTICS OF THE INDIVIDUAL SOLDIER

4. JAPANESE.—*a.* The Japanese soldier fights with fanaticism and never surrenders. Officers about to be captured sometimes commit suicide. (2)

b. The Jap is no superman. With proper training our Americans are better, as they think better as individuals. Encourage your individuals and bring them out. (3)

c. We had nine men killed in one company in the last assault. Four were killed by a wounded sniper who had three holes in him. He was lying in thick brush 15 yards from my CP. He was camouflaged and had been passed over for dead. You have to kill them to put them out. (46)

d. The Japanese is not an individual fighter. He won't fight with a bayonet unless backed up by a dozen other Japs. (46)

e. You can tell Jap troops in the distance by their short, choppy step. (22) This is true and we think the reason for their short, choppy stride is that they wear wooden shoes in Japan. (3)

f. If you shoot the Japanese officers, the men mill around. Their noncoms are poor. You can tell their officers by their sabers and leather puttees. (26)

g. The Japanese do a lot of yelling at times, and at other times they are deadly silent. One night some Japs got in our marching column. We discovered them and bayoneted them. (27)

h. The Japs are man-monkeys and they run around considerably. In order to cope with these man-monkeys from Japan you have got to be in excellent shape and you got to be tough. We can lick them and we are doing it all the time. (28)

i. You have to kill these Japs before they will leave. Just turning a large volume of fire in his direction will not make him leave. (47)

5. AMERICAN.—*a.* I believe, sir, we baby our soldiers too much in peace time. I hope we are not doing this now. We should get rid of the gold bricks. It is better to be shorthanded with good men around than have a lot of undependables. (13)

b. If I could train my company again I would have some maneuvers on which the men were deprived of food, water and other comforts in order to find out which NCOs and men could take it. I would relieve those people who could not "take it." (37)

c. The Jap tricks, noises and infiltration have little effect on good troops. These hold their positions and fight them when they come up. (2)

d. Your men have to be rough and rugged, and to win they must learn to disregard politeness and to kill. (4)

e. I would like to tell you that a man's keenness or dullness of eye may determine whether he will live or die. Ten men in my platoon were killed because they walked up on a Japanese 37-mm gun. (7)

(7)

f. I have been in the Marines 16 years, in three expeditions to China and in five engagements since I have been in the Solomons. I will say this 1942 model recruit we are getting can drink more water than six old timers. We have too many noncoms in the Marines who are namby-pamby and beat around the bush. I think when officers make a noncom they should go over in their minds, "What kind of NCO will he make in the field?" (11)

g. The men have to be trained individually, for when the fire fight starts the corporal can't see all of his men. Further, when the order for the attack is given, any number of men are unable to see the men on their right or left. It takes guts for men to get up and move forward when the signal is given. The men have to depend on one another and have confidence in each other. (19)

h. This regiment can out-yell the Japs, out-fight them, out-bayonet them and out-shoot them. This yelling, as in hand-to-hand action, is important. (24)

i. Under stress men get nervous, particularly when alone. We learned to post double sentinels—one man to quiet the other. (28)

j. All my time in the Marines I have seen men bunch up. I have talked about this and made my noncoms talk about it all the time. The men seem to fear separation. (28)

k. A leader can be in only one spot at one time. Men must be trained to act correctly on their own. I have never seen this type of training. (40) I would like to say that there is no place for recruits here. We need trained soldiers who have initiative and know what is the right thing to do. The jungle here is so thick that the squad leaders cannot get around all the time to see the men and tell them what to do. (41)

(8)

236

Section IV

AMERICAN TACTICS AND METHODS

6. GENERAL.—*a*. In training for this type of warfare, go back to the tactics of the French and Indian days. This is not meant facetiously. Study their tactics and fit in our modern weapons and you have a solution. (1)

b. Most of the fighting here has been carried out at extremely close range and there has been as much throwing of hand grenades as firing of weapons. (2)

7. NIGHT OPERATIONS.—We have carefully avoided night attacks, making all of our offensive moves by day. Our officers feel that the Japs have placed so much stress on night fighting that they cannot or do not fight well at all in the daytime. (2)

8. INITIATIVE.—*a*. Try to get the Japs on the move; keep them bouncing around; don't let them get set. When you let them get set they are hard to get out. (24)

b. Sergeant Dietrich of Company "I", 5th Marines, recently used his head. One night when the Japs advanced, a Jap jumped into Sergeant Dietrich's foxhole. Dietrich pulled the pin of a hand grenade and jumped out. There was a hell of an explosion and one less Nip. (18)

c. After the Japs have been located, my platoon has gained surprise by moving in first with bayonets and grenades. (6)

9. COORDINATED ACTION.—We had the Japs surrounded with their backs to the river. (See figure 1). The three battalions were in close contact with the enemy. It was obvious that we had a large number surrounded and the best way to get them out was to put artillery and mortar fire on them. The problem was to put this fire on the enemy and not on our own troops. The movement which we executed was carefully coordinated with the artillery and the mortars. Each battalion, at a certain time, was to withdraw just before the firing started. We were careful to explain to the men what we were doing so they did not get a mistaken idea of the order for withdrawing. The maneuver was successful. Over 500 Japanese were killed in this action. We lost 44 killed and 63 wounded. Our men were not hurt by the artillery and mortar fire, of course, but were killed and wounded in the fighting which took place before the withdrawal. After the firing ceased, we went in and mopped up in hand-to-hand fighting. (24)

(9)

237

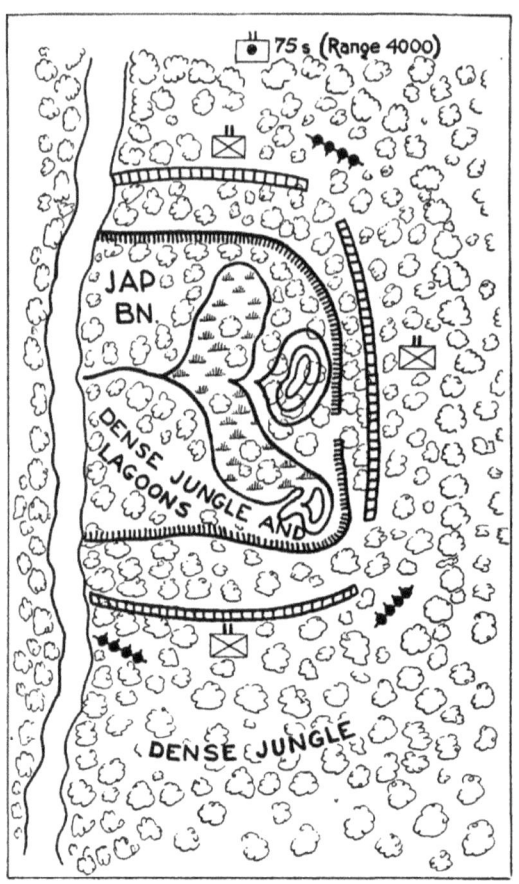

FIGURE 1.

10. COMBAT INTELLIGENCE.—*a.* Perhaps of greatest assistance to us have been captured orders and maps. A great deal of information has been gotten from captured diaries. Our interpreters on the spot were able to get, from captured orders, information on which we successfully operated at once. It causes me to want never to write another order. (2)

b. Our battalion commanders know that in reporting information at once they are enabling the regiment to act as a team. (24)

(10)

238

c. The forward observer of the artillery has furnished me with valuable information. Our system is to put the artillery observer group with each battalion and keep the liaison officer with the regiment. (24)

11. THE ADVANCE. — *a.* My battalion, moving through jungle country, acting alone, operates as follows (figure 2):

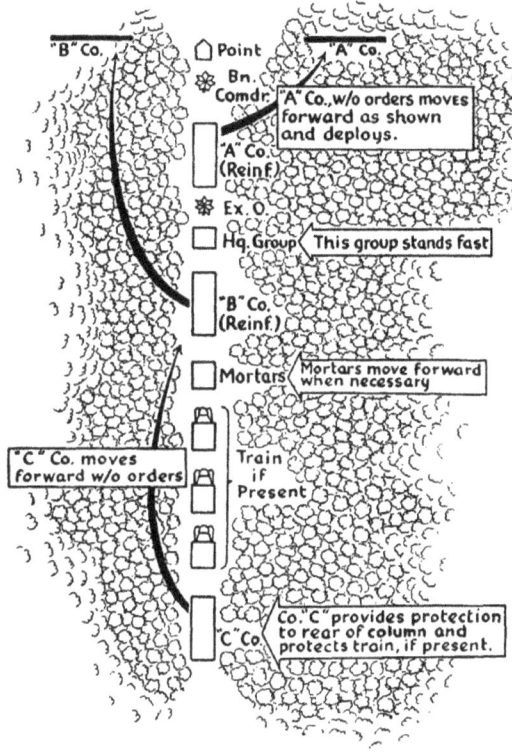

FIGURE 2.

A platoon of "D" Company (heavy machine guns) is attached to each rifle company because of the heavy country. "C" Company watches the rear. Each company is responsible for its flank. This is a time-tested and proven formation which works. If attacked from a flank, face and adjust. In marching or in camp we have learned that you must have an all-around defense. (25)

b. We have learned that when we get off the beaten trails it seems to confuse the Japs and we have better success. (10)

c. After contact you crawl in the advance—unless you are to charge and make it. The reason for this is that all men hit are hit from the knees up except for ricochets. We have crawled up to within 25 yards of a machine gun firing over our backs. The Japs don't depress their machine guns. (19)

12. CHANGE OF MISSION FOR UNIT IN CONTACT.—Our battalion commanders have learned not to pull a company out of action to use it elsewhere. Send another company from somewhere else. If you make the mistake of milling around, as we call it, you will expend men's lives. I have never seen it fail to cost twice as much as an original commitment would. (24)

13. SUPPORTING ARMS.—*a. Artillery.* (1) The work of our artillery has been exceptional. Our forward observers have been right in the front line and artillery fire has caused the enemy many casualties. (2)

(2) We have learned we have to fire a 360 degree traverse here. Also, due to the way these Japs crawl around in the jungle, we have to pay much attention to the local security of artillery positions. (23)

(3) Don't spare your artillery. Every time you get enough information, even if the target is not profitable, get artillery fire on it. They hate it. (24)

(4) Are you teaching your regimental commanders to understand how to use artillery? (24)

(5) We have found it profitable to bring successful patrol leaders back to the OPs of the mortar and artillery and let them direct the fire. We get them back as soon as possible. The basis of this method of operation is scouting and patrolling. (33)

b. Aviation. The time to have air observation is when we attack. At other times when our planes go over, the Japs keep down and keep still. (47)

14. RESERVES.—*a.* I think reserves in the attack should be kept up close so they can be committed immediately. The reserve company commander continually reconnoiters and is ready to commit his company at once when ordered. If the reserve company is not on its toes, and must take time out for reconnaissance, the delay may make their effort useless. The situation may change. I keep my best company commander in reserve. (46)

b. The Japanese attacks have come on a narrow front at rather widely separated points. Captured orders and operations maps have shown they were intended to be, but were not, simultaneous attacks. This lack of coordination has permitted us to shift our all too small reserves from one area to another. (2)

c. You cannot clear out all the snipers before you advance. You can get those that are left by the use of small groups from the reserves. (3)

(12)

15. DEFENSE.—*a*. Our orders to Marines on the perimeter defense are: "You stay on your position and do not pull back. If they bust through you, we will plug the hole, but you stay there." (24)

b. When we take a defensive position, as we have now to protect the air field, due to the dense jungle we do not take up a formation which we would use on more open terrain, such as that in the States. Here we generally do not establish strong points. We have a shoulder-to-shoulder defense with mobile reserves in the rear. (32)

c. (1) We have learned from the Nips to make the "stand up covered Japanese spider hole." (15) See figure 3.

FIGURE 3.

(2) We learned to dig small, covered foxholes. Slit trenches are best. We had men smother to death in holes that were too large. Don't put more than three men in any hole unless the hole has a support on top big enough to stop a 500-pound bomb. (28) We insist on overhead cover for foxholes because of the Jap mortar fire. In doing this you have to guard against the men building these foxholes up too high above the level of the ground. (29)

16. DECEPTION.—*a*. The Japanese night attacks have limited objectives. Sometimes withdrawing after dark as much as 50 yards will fool them and they won't know where you are. (3)

b. A Japanese trick to draw our fire was for the hidden Jap to work his bolt back and forth. Men who got sucked in on this and fired without seeing what they were firing at, generally drew automatic fire from another direction. (18) **(13)**

17. SECURITY.—*a.* When we move around on these jungle trails we have learned to put men with light loads at the rear of each platoon so they can get their weapons into action quickly to help overcome ambush fire from the rear. (12) I was in one advance when the Japs let us come through and then rose up out of covered foxholes and shot us in the back. The best cure for that is a rear guard looking toward the rear. (19)

b. We have learned to make reconnaissance before moving into an area. We have learned to be quiet, listen and look. We sure like to see that artillery come down on an area before we move into it. (31)

18. SECRECY.—*a.* Unnecessary firing gives your position away and when you give your position away here you pay for it. (14)

b. Discontinue the use of the tracer for night firing. They give away your position. (3)

c. Smoking stops at dark and you have got to be quiet. (3) We have learned to be quiet, listen and look. (31) We are learning the hard way to move quietly in this jungle. (16)

d. We have to use flashlights at night sometimes because we have no luminous sights on the mortars. This flashlight business is dangerous. (17)

e. We have two American Indians whom we use to talk on the telephone or voice radio when we want to transmit secret or important messages. (30)

f. In the Raiders we used nicknames for the officers. All ranks used them. We did this because the Nips caught on to the names of the officers and would yell or speak in the night, "This is Captain Joe Smith talking; "A" Company withdraw to the next hill." So we adopted nicknames as code words. Captain Walt became "Silent Lou." My nickname was "Red Knight." An example of the use of these nicknames as code words is: One night the Japs put down smoke and yelled, "Gas." We were green at that time and two of our companies withdrew leaving "A" Company exposed on both flanks. In this instance I was a battalion commander. Captain Walt called me on the voice radio to inform me of the situation. He was cautious and used the nickname as follows: He said, "Who is speaking?" and I said, "Red." He said, "What name do you identify with 'Silent'?" I said, "Lou." He said, "That is correct." So we both knew that we were talking to each other and were not talking to the enemy. He explained the situation to me. At the end of his conversation a voice broke in and said in perfect English, "Our situation here, Colonel Edson, is excellent. Thank you, sir." This was the enemy speaking. (3)

(14)

242

Section V

JAPANESE TACTICS AND METHODS

19. *a.* All of the Japanese attacks have been on a narrow front at rather widely separated points. These were mass attacks and although captured orders and operations maps show that they were intended to be simultaneous, they were not. Our feeling is that his failure to estimate the terrain difficulties caused the lack of coordination. We believe the enemy has dispersed his efforts and therefore has failed to make any gain at any one point. When given his choice, he operates exclusively at night. He attacks practically en masse. The result for him has been almost complete annihilation in every case. As far as we can determine, these various attacking groups are started out, and there are indications that they pass out of real control of their higher leaders. We have never seen anything to indicate that any effort has been reinforced after the initial push has been made. (2)

b. Here is an example of a Japanese attack. We were on the Matanikau river. (See figure 4).

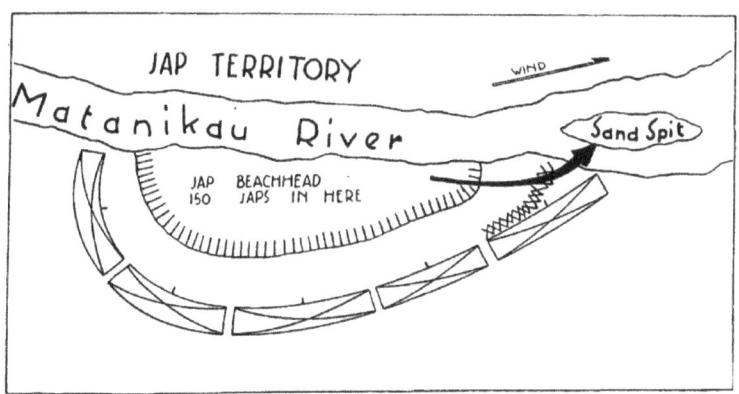

FIGURE 4.

Our companies were at half strength. This was a Raider battalion, plus two companies of the 3rd Battalion, 5th Marines. The Japanese beachhead was a thick jungle with camouflaged, standing-type foxholes. They had with them in their beachhead six heavy machine guns and eight light machine guns which we captured in this action. At 6:30 PM they smoked our two light companies and when the smoke had enveloped these companies the Japs broke out. They came in mass formation, 20 abreast, yelling, bayonets fixed, automatic weapons working, rear ranks throwing hand grenades. They were trying to escape to the sand pit at the mouth of the river in order to cross the river and get back. Our right front company had

(15)

243

just completed a double-apron, barbed wire fence. When the Japs hit the left flank of the right company they killed nine out of the first 11 men they met. Then they hit the barbed wire. Two of our machine guns opened up, shooting down along this barbed wire fence, and dispersed their attack. It got dark—quickly, as it does here. There were smoke, Japs and Marines all mixed up. Three Jap officers were swinging their two-handed swords. There was hand-to-hand fighting all night long. We mopped them up at daybreak. We killed 78 Japs. They killed 12 Marines and wounded 26 of us. (46)

c. The Japs hit hell out of our advance guard points. They don't wait with the idea of getting more men. They seek to delay us. When the point goes down, teach men to get behind big trees if close by, not behind saplings. (26)

20. DEFENSE.—a. The Japs defend on the low ground in the jungles. They dig standing trenches, extremely well camouflaged.   (3)

b. When we first got here the Japs fooled us, as they like to place their machine guns on the reverse slope of a ridge, shooting upward.   (47)

c. Their outpost at times is in trees. I saw one tree which was rotten inside. The Japs had a light machine gun and gunner down inside and they had built a trap door on our side. Every once in a while the door would open, and they would poke the machine gun out and fire. We took care of this.   (26)

21. FIRING METHODS.—a. The Japanese fire is not always aimed. It is harassing fire and scares recruits. Get the recruits so they are used to overhead fire.   (26)

b. The Japs sometimes put their machine guns in trees. On one occasion a 60-mm mortar crew was firing from a reverse slope. They fired two or three rounds. Then a Jap machine gun opened up from a banyan tree which was high enough to look down on the mortar position and killed three and wounded two of the crew.   (26)

22. Japs who have infiltrated, signal to each other with their rifles by the number of shots. We get these birds by constant patrolling. A lot of these Japs who infiltrate have radios. Think of the advantage of this in respect to artillery fire, mortar fire, location of troops, etc. My platoon found nine Japs slipping behind our lines.   (26)   We have killed 38 Japs behind our lines, during the period August 7 to November 29, 1942.   (29)

23. SNIPERS.—a. The Japanese infiltrate as many snipers as it is reported they did in Bataan and Malaya. These things have little effect on good troops who hold their position, which they can do with safety, and fight them when they come up. So far as I have been able to determine, though we have had hundreds of snipers in our position, only one man has been killed by a sniper. We usually get every one of them. Don't worry about them. They are ducks on the pond when daylight comes.   (2)   Sir,

(16)

the first thing I would like to say is that this Japanese sniper business has been overemphasized. They talked and talked about them and made these young men of mine jittery. You can't see the sniper anyway until you start your attack, and as his fire, until the attack starts, is very inaccurate there is no use to worry. I think this sniper business should be debunked. They hide under a banyan tree and just poke their muzzles through a hole and fire indiscriminately. When the attack starts they will come out. Those you by-pass in the attack must be mopped up later. (28) The Japanese snipers are really annoying. You can't clear them all out before you advance, but they won't be particularly effective. Some Japanese snipers, by-passed in the attack, hid for two or three days and then quit. Some will hang around inside your lines for a month. (3)

b. Every scout should be taught to look in the trees. I was a scout and got shot in the shoulder by a Jap in a tree. I look in the trees now. (18)

c. The snipers tie their guns in the trees so they can't drop them carelessly or if wounded. In putting their light machine guns in the trees, they lash them in and have relief men ready to go up the tree. (26)

24. DECEPTION.—*a.* I was on my first patrol here, and we were moving up a dry stream bed. We saw three Japs come down the river bed out of the jungle. The one in front was carrying a white flag. We thought they were surrendering. When they got up to us, they dropped the white flag and all threw hand grenades. We killed two of these Japs but one got away. (31)

b. Some of our men got killed because they examined Japanese mortar shells. There were hundreds of these shot at us which turned out to be duds. The recruits pushed the plungers. Result—instant death. (28)

c. We learned not to get excited or go off half-cocked because of noise. The Japs make noise to mislead us. They shot off some fire crackers at the start, but we have learned that where the noise is, he ain't. You never hear him move. He sleeps in the daytime and does his work at night. (28)

25. SECRECY.—When we cease firing, they cease firing. When we fire, they open up. They do this to conceal their positions. (26)

Section VI

RECOMMENDATIONS FOR TRAINING

26. GENERAL.—If I had my regiment to train over again I would stress small group training and the training of the individual even more than we did when we were in training. (3)

27. JUNGLE WARFARE.—If I were training my unit again I would like to have a minimum of 90 days training in jungle warfare. I would stress in this training, teamwork between the leaders in all units; liaison between supporting units and all leaders; and liaison between artillery and infantry. (27)

(17)

28. DISCIPLINE.—*a.* (1) For Pete's sake teach the men not to be "trigger happy." (38) (Note: Expression used on Guadalcanal for men who are very nervous and who fire without seeing the enemy. This type of man is dangerous and has caused a lot of trouble. He has also given the position away. R.)

(2) On the Matanikau River we got to firing at each other because of careless leadership by the junior leaders. We are curing ourselves of promiscuous firing, but I think new units should get training to make the men careful. (18)

(3) Teach not to waste ammunition. Learn to make every shot count. (24)

b. (1) It must be impressed upon and drilled into young soldiers not to throw away their equipment. Our young men did this at first, and we regretted it, as later we needed the equipment. We actually found some of our new equipment, which had been thrown away, in the hands of the enemy. (28)

(2) Some of my men thought their hand grenades were too heavy. They tossed them aside when no one was looking. Later they would have given six months' pay for one hand grenade. (5)

c. Some men used to lag behind in the advance. They have finally learned to keep up as lagging is unsafe for all. (21)

d. (1) All my time in the Marines I have seen men bunch up. I have talked about this and made my NCO's talk about it all the time. The men seem to fear separation. (28)

(2) We have trouble with men bunching up in order to talk to each other. They seem to do this even though it means death. (31)

e. (1) Men get killed rushing to help a wounded man. If the wounded man would crawl about ten yards to his flank he can generally be aided in safety, as the Japanese seem to fire down lanes in the jungle. (19)

(2) We have taught our men that the best way to aid a wounded man is to push ahead so that he can be cared for by the corps man. (3)

(3) I notice, and I pointed this out to my platoon, that when men get hit, the men close by get to yelling, "Corps man, Corps man" and they get so excited sometimes that they actually forget to use first aid packets. (12)

(4) Teach your soldiers, sir, that when a man is hit in the assault to leave him there. (4)

f. We have a lot of trouble in my platoon with water discipline. (31)

29. HAND-TO-HAND COMBAT.—In our training for jungle warfare we had a great deal of work in hand-to-hand combat, use of the knife, jiu jitsu, etc. With the exception of bayonet fighting we have not used this work. I have been in many battles since I hit this island and I have never seen anyone use it. (13)

30. CAMOUFLAGE.—The biggest thing I have learned since I hit Guadalcanal is that the Japanese camouflage is miles ahead of ours. Their

(18)

246

individual can camouflage himself a lot better than ours. We must practice and train in this. (39)

31. BATTLE REALISM.—*a.* If I could train my men over again, I would put officers and men in slit trenches and drop bombs nearby to overcome fear. We were all scared to death at first. Let's overcome this fear. How about firing some captured 25 caliber ammunition out of captured rifles to let officers and men know the sound; also captured Japanese machine-gun ammunition out of captured machine guns. (34)

b. If I could train my battalion again I would have some maneuvers in which things were made to go wrong—communications upset, etc. I would observe which leaders are no good and replace them on the spot—not later. (34)

32. CONDITIONING.—*a.* I hope the Army is being toughened up. We toughened up by bivouacking—not camping—at the combat ranges. In order to teach our platoons to keep off the road, we made them march in the fields alongside the road when they moved from one combat area to another. (29)

b. How about training in the field with short rations? Put your patrols out for from three to five days; every officer in the unit to participate. Make them go across country without maps or compasses. (27)

33. SCOUTING AND PATROLLING.—*a.* (Note: After I had interviewed a number of men in one regiment selected as the best fighters, two of them came up to me and said, "Sir, you did not see Sergeant Arndt. He has been on more patrols and does more scouting than any man in the regiment." They got him for me. R.) (The following comment is from the interview with Sergeant Arndt.)

I practice walking quietly over rocks, twigs, grass, leaves, through vines, etc. I practice this around this bivouac area. I received instruction in scouting and patrolling at Quantico, but I still practice. I believe this is the reason I am still alive. Some of the other NCO's laughed at me because I am always seeing how quietly I can walk around and because I go out and practice on my own. They have stopped laughing because I have been on more patrols than any man in the regiment and I am still alive. (22)

b. (1) Our basic training is all right. Emphasize scouting and patrolling and really learn it and apply it. Put your time and emphasis on the squad and platoon. (3)

(2) Stress real scouting and patrolling and teach them to go the hard way. (43)

c. (1) In your scouting and patrolling, and your "training in patience" (which you should have) have the men work against each other. Same thing for squads and platooons in their problems. (3)

(2) Train patrols in stalking certain positions. I consider this very important. If I were training my battalion again I would have train-

(19)

ing in patience. I would have patrols wait for the enemy to expose himself. They move around too. I would have the men in this patience training be made to stay still for hours at a time. (35)

d. If I were training my unit again I would really have some high class patrol training. I would do everything with these patrols I could possibly think of, to include losing them and making them go across country without maps or compasses. (27)

e. (1) There must be training in difficult observation, which is needed for offense. It is my observation that only about 5% of the men can really see while observing. (3)

(2) We need better trained scouts. The poor scouts lose their lives. (47)

(3) Teach the young fellows to look over the ground and look in the trees and to learn where the enemy probably will be. The Japanese will be in the toughest places and naturally on the best ground. (28)

(4) Every scout should be taught to look in the trees. I was a scout and got shot in the shoulder by a Jap in a tree. I look in the trees now. We take turns being scouts; so all should be trained as scouts. (18)

(5) When I am scouting and come to an opening in the jungle and have to cross it I generally run across quietly and quickly. Going slow may cost a scout his life. Different types of terrain call for different methods. Here is the way the Japs patrol. I was out on the bank of the river with another man. We were observing and were carefully camouflaged. We heard a little sound and then saw two Japs crawl by about seven feet away from us. These Japs were unarmed. We started to shoot them, but did not do so as we remembered our mission. Then 15 yards behind came eight armed Japs. They were walking slowly and carefully. We did not shoot as our mission was to gain information. When we got back we had a lot of discussion as to why the two Japs in front were not armed. Some of the fellows said maybe it was a form of Japanese company punishment. I believe they were the point of the patrol and were unarmed so they could crawl better. (22)

34. COMPASS.—Every man must know how to use the compass. The dumbbells who don't, have to be helped instead of being able to help themselves. (39)

35. USE OF WEAPONS IN COMBAT.—a. How about some training in shooting at vague targets, at close ranges, in dense woods? (42)

b. I understand in the U. S. troops in training for this type of warfare are practicing firing at short ranges. That is fine. (34)

c. We should develop better snipers. (3)

d. The men in my squad fire low at the base of the trees. There is too much high firing going on. (14)

e. It is important that the entire squad know the BAR; not just two men. Think of the BAR men who are wounded, get killed, and become sick and have to be evacuated. (37) I think that Japanese snipers look for BAR men. (6)

(20)

f. (1) The 60-mm mortar was not stressed enough in our training. I love that mortar. (17)

(2) Give more attention to the training with the 81-mm mortar and the coordination of these weapons with the foot troops. We were too slow in getting the 81's into action when they were needed. Get 'em into action fast. (48)

(3) The BFM's state that a mortar round must not be opened until it is ready to be fired. This, in my opinion, is impracticable during battle, because to deliver a large volume of fire, you have to have hundreds of rounds opened and prepared for firing. Some of the containers for the mortar rounds get wet and have to be cut in order to get the round out. This takes time. On occasion it takes the entire ammunition squad and all available hands to cut open ammunition. Result may be, when "cease firing" is given, you have numerous rounds open. These rounds, when exposed to the atmosphere, become wet or damp, making them dangerous to fire later because the increments won't burn uniformly and the round falls short. We have had a round fall short as much as 600 yards, firing at a range of 2700. I recommend that additional increments be issued in water-proof containers in order to remedy this condition. Also, we need additional cartridges for misfires. (28)

g. (1) I would suggest some training in throwing hand grenades in the woods. (42)

(2) Some of the men were so scared of our hand grenades when they were first issued that they jammed down the cotter pin. Then later, in action, they could not pull out the pin. (12)

(3) After you pull the pin of a hand grenade (and release the safety lever), don't forget to count, "One Jap dead, two Japs dead" before throwing the grenade. We had a Marine killed in this battalion because he forgot to count and a Jap picked up the hand grenade and threw it back. (30)

36. TEAMWORK.—I think men in these rifle companies should receive training in the work and the mission of the machine-gun company. The other day, on "Bloody Ridge," riflemen protecting our light machine guns pulled out and left us. We were doing O.K. at the time, but their pulling out caused our whole outfit to withdraw. (8)

37. AMMUNITION AND PIONEER PLATOON.—Our battalion pioneer section must have better and more complete training in carrying food, water and ammunition, and in cutting trails. (37)

(21)

249

Section VII

WEAPONS

38. GENERAL.—*a.* Put the big, rugged men into the Heavy Weapons Company (in order that they may keep up with the advance while carrying the weapons). (12)

b. Both our riflemen and machine gunners must be taught to shoot low. (3)

39. GRENADES.—*a.* We need the rifle grenade or some weapon to fill the gap between hand grenade and mortar. We need to dig the Nip out of his hole under banyan trees, etc. (3) I consider it imperative that the Army and Marines carry only one type of grenade. Have the hand grenade fit a knee mortar and be of use as a hand grenade and also as a rifle grenade. You need a rifle grenadier in each squad for use against enemy machine-gun nests. (25)

b. Our rifle grenades (presumably antitank) have been effective against hidden machine-gun positions. (47) The rifle grenade demoralizes the Jap. A Japanese prisoner told me in English, "That 30 caliber cannon is terrible, sir." (26)

c. We had to multiply our unit of fire in hand grenades by five. The yellow color on hand grenades is poor. Why can't they be painted black? The yellow color enables the Japs to (find them readily and) throw them back. (32)

40. MORTARS.—*a.* (1) (The so-called "knee mortar" of the Japanese apparently made a great impression upon American forces.)

(2) We need the knee mortar badly. The name "knee mortar" is a misnomer. It is not fired from the knee. One of my men tried this and broke his leg. The following are reasons in its favor:

(a) The weapon with 10 rounds of ammunition is a one-man load.
(b) It has a high rate of fire.
(c) It gives the platoon commander a weapon of this type immediately available.
(d) The Japs use the mortar as an all-purpose grenade—ranges from 50 yards to 650. It can be lowered to a low angle and placed against a log and shot straight out. I would recommend one change in the projectile. The Japs have too much high explosive in it and the case is too thin. We get a lot of casualties from it but they are minor wounds. The Japs have three of these mortars in a mortar squad in each rifle platoon. They have two ammunition carriers per mortar. (3)

(3) I consider it imperative that the Army and Marines be equipped with knee mortars. (25)

(4) Sir, tell the Army to get the knee mortar. It's hell. (13) The Japanese knee mortar gives us hell. They come in fast, thick, and accurate. Can't we have one? (43)

(22)

b. The mortars are very effective here. An example: We were moving up a trail and were stopped by machine-gun fire. I withdrew the platoon and spread out off the trail, forming a skirmish line. I sent word back to the mortars to set up. They had to cut down some trees in order to set up properly. The OP man comes forward and gets the azimuth and paces off the range as best he can. Then the mortars open up (presumably, with success). (31)

c. I think that the heavy weapons company should have the 60-mm mortar to use in addition to the 81. I like the 81, but it cannot keep up in certain situations because of its weight and its heavy ammunition. (3)

d. If the numbers on the mortar sight were luminous, with a luminous strip on the stick, we would not have to use the flashlight. This flashlight business is dangerous. (17)

41. MACHINE GUNS.—I recommend substituting the M1919-A4 (light machine gun) for the heavy machine gun for offensive operations in the jungle. The heavy machine guns are needed and are very valuable in the defense. I am even considering substituting BAR's for the light machine guns in the offensive. (3) It pays in the attack in the jungle to use the heavy machine guns. There is a difference of opinion, as you have noticed, on this matter. It is hard work, yes, but don't overlook the value—morale and otherwise—and don't forget about the high rate of fire. If you ditch the heavy machine guns and substitute the lights in their place, you must remember that you will be up against the Japanese machine gun. (48) We love the heavy machine gun. (30)

42. BROWNING AUTOMATIC RIFLE.—I think the Japanese snipers look for BAR men. (6) No doubt about this. In one engagement, in one platoon, every BAR man was hit. (3) This BAR I have here is my best friend. (21)

43. RIFLE.—The M1 is a fine rifle. It is doing fine work here. (44) We like the M1 but we don't like the way the front end shines. (34) Are we getting a glass sight (presumably telescopic) for the M1 for sniper work? (38)

44. CLOSE RANGE WEAPONS.—The Thompson submachine gun or carbine is needed as the Japanese execute their attacks en masse. We understand the carbine will have more penetrating power than the Thompson. (30)

(23)

251

Section VIII

EQUIPMENT AND SUPPLY

45. GENERAL.—*a.* Is the Army stripping down to essentials in equipment? (24)

b. It has been impressed upon us here that logistics have to be correctly planned. The science of logistics turns out to be your life. I have a fine, forceful executive officer. I use him in the rear echelon seeing that the S-4 functions and that supplies get up. Don't misunderstand me. The executive officer lets the S-4 run his job. He checks and aids him if he needs help. (24)

c. The tendency is to overload the infantry with ammunition. It seems to be standard practice to start out with the belt full plus two bandoleers. We soon found that 25 rounds was enough for two or three days if you do not have targets to shoot at. (3) (Note: Our infantrymen approaching Buna in the jungles of New Guinea were carrying 40 rounds. R.)

46. CLASS I SUPPLY.—I have seen awful attempts at individual cooking, however, some of my men have got to the point where they can make jam tarts. (28) You asked about individual cooking. Yes, in my opinion the troops should know this but it is not practical for units who are not close to water to cook that way as they cannot clean their mess gear properly and dysentery results. These units put the "C" ration (stew or bean) can to their mouth and eat that way. (33) How to carry water and rations around in this jungle to the troops on the line is a big problem. (35) I hear that in the new jungle kits the men will get water-sterilizing tablets. These will help as my men dip water out of streams. (5) I think that in the regimental supply there should be extra canteens so when an outfit gets in a place like the "Table Plateau" where there is no water an extra canteen can be issued. (9) This idea is being used in some places here. The turnover in the canteens will be great, but it would be a big help at times. At one time we had a battalion without water for 24 hours but only two men were evacuated because of heat exhaustion. (3)

47. MISCELLANEOUS.—*a.* Two ammunition pockets in the belt should be converted to grenade pockets. Each man should have two hand grenades. If you don't do that, develop slip-open pockets which can be quickly opened and will carry two hand grenades. (3)

b. We don't have enough ammunition carrying bags. We should have this for the mortars. We need these bags for other types of ammunition too. I don't know how many as we have not experimented—all I know is we need them. We need grenade carriers too. (35)

c. The Japanese powder is more smokeless than ours. We need smokeless powder. (34) (Note: The reason the Japanese rifle when it is fired does not make as much smoke is probably because not as much powder is needed to propel a 25 caliber bullet as is needed to send a 30 caliber bullet on its way. R.)

(24)

d. The sabers which the Japanese officers carry have proved to be worthless. I killed two Japs who came at me with sabers and I got them first by shooting them, but I wished I had in reserve a good jungle knife. I don't mean a bolo, which we should have in cutting trails, but a knife with a 12-inch blade of good steel. We could use this against these Japanese as well as for cutting vines that catch on us at night. (16)

(Note: Many men express their wish for a jungle knife such as that described. This desire is not repeated in further remarks. R.)

e. Every man should be equipped with a compass. (39)

f. We want better field glasses. Can't we get a glass for spotting men in foliage? (42)

g. I have been on 15 patrols, and each time the patrol was fired on, the man with a net on his helmet drew the fire. I have seen 25 caliber bullets go through our new helmet; so, as for me, I use a fatigue field hat. (43)

(Note: I talked to a man who showed me his steel helmet with a 25 caliber bullet hole in it. The man received a slight head wound. He was convinced, and so am I, that if he had not had on his steel helmet when this bullet was fired at him he would have been killed. R.)

h. We need more intrenching shovels. Give shovels to men who have wire cutters. You need both the wire cutter and shovels. (25)

i. I am screaming for gloves to use in handling barbed wire. You cannot put up a barbed wire fence in a hurry if you are barehanded. (48)

j. Our Marine field shoes have too heavy a top which chafes. It should have a type of hobnail as it slips on the jungle grasses. Rubber shoes are needed for night work. (3) I would give $75.00 for a pair of tennis shoes to rest my feet and for use in night work. (12)

k. At Tulagi the Japanese used wooden bullets. I saw some of them. My theory for their use is that they were developed for troops which were to infiltrate behind our lines and shoot us in the back. These wooden bullets could not carry far enough to injure their attacking troops. (3)

Section IX

SANITATION AND FIRST AID

48. *a.* (1) The regimental commander must make it his personal duty to watch and be greatly interested in sanitation. Because of our great interest in sanitation our sick list is below 40 men per battalion—lower than normal. (24)

(2) Sanitation—I know it is right! To violate it causes billions of flies, and sickness. When you occupy a position for several days in the tropics the sanitation problem becomes tremendous. The young officers and NCO's must get after this at the start and keep after it all the time. (28)

b. Put "bug dope" in your jungle equipment. (14)

c. In first aid training, teach your men the correct method of injecting morphine and procedure of tagging, because what you gonna' do when the corps man gets hit? (12)

(25)

253

Section X

COMMUNICATIONS

49. GENERAL.—*a.* Concentrate on communications. I have had to loan the communications regimental section men, to help carry wire through tough places, but I want communications. Your information has to be timely and properly evaluated. (24)

b. I have been on 20 patrols in the last 40 days and in most all of these patrols we went out from two to five miles. Getting communications back to the gun position is an awful problem. Can you help us? (39)

50. EQUIPMENT NEEDED.—*a.* Are we getting more small, hand radios? Man, they are sure needed, for communication within the company and within the battalion is tough. (38) The walkie-talkie the Japs have operates. Why can't we have a similar one? (25)

b. Bring back the signal flags; they are badly needed. (13)

51. USE OF WIRE.—We depend to a large extent on wire communications. It is tough work but it can be done. (24) In an attack we always use the telephones from regiment to battalion. The jungle is thick, but the wire can be made to keep up. The wire is supplemented by the TBX Radio. If we get held up, the radio goes right out to the companies from the battalion. (46)

52. USE OF SPECIAL SIGNALS.—We have developed signals in our battalion which are not recorded in any textbook. I recommend that all troops do the same. (30)

CONCLUSIONS

The following is a *digest* of lessons learned in the tactics of Jungle Warfare as a result of interviews which are attached:

1. Troops must receive a high degree of individual training to prepare for jungle warfare. The individual in combat will be required to act on his own a large part of the time. This is due to the dense foliage. However, individuals must feel the very presence of their squad leaders and other leaders, and know that they are important members of a team which can lick the enemy. The leaders must take pains carefully to explain to the privates what their responsibilities are, and what is expected of them in each situation. Furthermore, weak individuals who cannot be trusted to act correctly without supervision must be weeded out, preferably before they arrive in the combat zone.

Individuals must have thorough practice in throwing hand grenades in woods. They must reach a much higher degree of proficiency in the art of camouflage. This will require constant application in the training period.

By realistic training a large amount of fear can be overcome in the individual. He should know before he reaches the combat zone what it

(26)

feels like to have bombs explode near him, what a sniper's bullet sounds like, and what overhead machine-gun and artillery fire sound like.

The prowess of the enemy must NOT be overemphasized. American soldiers and marines can whip the Jap and they are doing so every day. Many men stated that they had been talked to so much about the Japanese snipers that at first they were afraid.

Individual riflemen must know the tactical relationship between the machine gun and their rifle in order to be able to act intelligently.

Training in observing and firing at vague targets must be emphasized.

2. In training, scouting and patrolling must be emphasized. Major General Vandergrift, commanding the First Marine Division, states that jungle warfare against the Japanese is a question of going back to the tactics of the French and Indian days, with these tactics adjusted to fit in with our modern weapons.

Men should receive training in *patience*. Our national character is foreign to this idea. We are an impetuous people. Training in patience is needed as sometimes the men will be required to remain motionless and quiet for hours at a time.

3. Not every man can lead a patrol successfully in the jungle. The good patrol leaders should be discovered in the training period.

In training, patrols should be sent out from 10 to 15 hours at a time. Due to the slow way in which a patrol moves, it is necessary to keep patrols out for long periods of time. The problem of getting communication back from the patrol to friendly territory in the jungle is a hard one. It must be made easier by training. Patrols should be confronted with unusual situations.

4. The Japanese knee mortar is needed. An all-purpose hand grenade, which, in addition to being used as a hand grenade, can be used in the knee mortar and as a rifle grenade, should be adopted.

Mortar squads must learn to set up quickly and be able to operate in wooded terrain.

5. All units must receive practice in the problem of maintaining contact in the advance in the jungle.

6. In the interviews there are many remarks on leadership. The leadership shown by the 5th and 7th Regiments of the U. S. Marines stands out because of their great wealth in experienced officers and NCO's. On the other hand the remark of Colonel B. E. Moore, Commanding Officer of the 164th Infantry, emphasizes the great problems in the leadership which confronted a partially trained regiment which had been rushed to the combat zone.

(27)

The Pacific Knife-Fighter

I had touched on unarmed combat systems in a previous chapter. I will discuss one more related thing in this chapter for the action-oriented individuals. Although it appeared that unarmed combat seemed to be of lesser importance than other things in the field, it did seem that having access to a good knife was of great importance to many individuals. So it made perfect sense that something was taught about how to handle one.

It's important to dispel the notion that everything taught during the World War Two stemmed from the Fairbairn and Sykes school of Gutter-Fighting. They had a great deal of influence on Commando type training but they could not be everywhere at once, and they certainly were not the only people teaching those things during that time period.

In Fairbairn's close combat syllabus in the knife-fighting section he stated:

> The repugnance of killing with a knife as compared to killing with a pistol is one of the most difficult problems facing the instructor.

The difference is mainly psychological and a good instructor will be able to break it down and also to immediately build up confidence in the knife, not only as a method of attack, but as the best, and we might say the only method of defense. (That is of course where fire-arms, etc. are not used.

An article in The Valley Enterprise, September 16th 1943 titled "Lt. McCarthy Says Japs Are Biggest Enemy" described one man's experience utilizing edged weapons to battle the Japanese in Attu, Alaska. Of course it's a different climate than what Heinmiller had to experience, but the article demonstrates that similar training came into play. Journalist Ronnie Mullally wrote:

> What are the knives we have been asked to donate to the armed forces being used for? Are the stories we hear of Jap treachery really true, or are they told for propaganda purposes? Are we soon to end this war, now that Italy is out of the picture and the nazis are being bombed regularly?
>
> These are a few of the questions that one might put to a commando leader who took his men onto Attu island and saw 82 per cent of their names on a casualty list. And here are some of the answers from that man—Lt. Thomas L. McCarthy of Omaha, who led the volunteer commandos into the "valley of death" that is the rocky, fog-ridden island of Attu.
>
> McCarthy, who with his wife, is visiting in this vicinity, was recently dismissed from an army hospital at Walla Walla, Wash., where he was treated for frozen feet, sustained in the battle of Attu. He also suffered a stomach injury on the island when he tried to "lend a hand" to a fallen comrade who stepped off a steep rock on the island.

On May 11, McCarthy (who by the way is as Irish as the name implies) with his picked company, was put out of an American submarine off the coast of Attu. The sub came to the surface long enough to let the men get into their rubber boats. "And" said McCarthy, "if you think that you don't get left with a funny feeling out on the water all on your own after the sub disappears under the surface, you're mistaken. After the sub goes down, the boats, each of which holds ten men, are absolutely on their own. So you paddle to find yourself a nice enemy shore."

A total of 3,700 Japs was scattered on Attu island when Lt. McCarthy's picked group landed. McCarthy's job was to make the Japs believe that he had a much larger, number of men than he had, and to keep the enemy occupied while the main allied task force landed on another part of the island. This they did. With casualties of 82 per cent.

The fogs which come like huge waves over the island of Attu proved of value to the Americans when they found that the strange muggy weather could be used as a screen. Every time the fog rolled down the Americans advanced. Unable to see their advance, the enemy did not know where they lay.

Equipped only with ammunition—three knives, a light machine gun and an automatic rifle, apiece, the men fought off the cold as well as the Japs. No blankets are in the commandos' kit when he lands on a combat mission such as that of Attu. His job is to strike and strike often, the leader said. The commando clothing consisted of a reversible uniform, olive drab on one side and white on the other, which can be work either way just so it blends in with the surrounding area, be it green foliage or snow-capped mountains. On Attu they wore fur-lined caps and high shoes.

For 36 hours the commandos fought before the task force arrived. Calmly McCarthy told of the manner in which a man uses a knife "to kill a Jap" in combat. Three types of knives are used by the commando. The bolo, a curved weapon, the stiletto and the double edged blade knife which will cut in any direction are in his fighting equipment.

"One does not aim at the heart," McCarthy said, "for it is too easy to miss. Under the arm or under the collar bone is a better aim.' A good commando can throw a knife from 15 to 20 feet and hit his mark, he said.

"When you are fighting Japs," the commando leader said, "you do not stop to think that they are human, for they do not act that way. When you see the men you have worked with and fought with being hewed down you just want to kill. And the knife is the quickest and the quietest way."

Through my connections I was given a course whose author is unidentified and its source undetermined. I believe the course is of the era because of the attire of the participants in the drawings.

If I had to venture a guess I would say it's a course that belonged to the United States Marines. The fact that the participants are shirtless leads me to believe that the training is being conducted somewhere tropical. The most logical conclusion is that it was training geared for fighting in the Pacific. I have decided to include the course in this book as an illustration of what Carl Heinmiller may have been exposed to in terms of his own training.

I am also including it with the hope that somebody will be able to provide me with some background or further information on it. The course is titled Hand To Hand Fighting Tactics and it appears to be a section from a wider course of instruction; probably with other subject matter similar to what was taught to the Commandos.   Perhaps even including a section on Jungle-Fighting.

Two instructors demonstrate knife fighting tactics while other Marine Raiders watch.

Author's Note: an unattributed course from World War Two, which presents knife-fighting tactics, titled "Hand-To-Hand Fighting" is presented on the next fifteen pages.

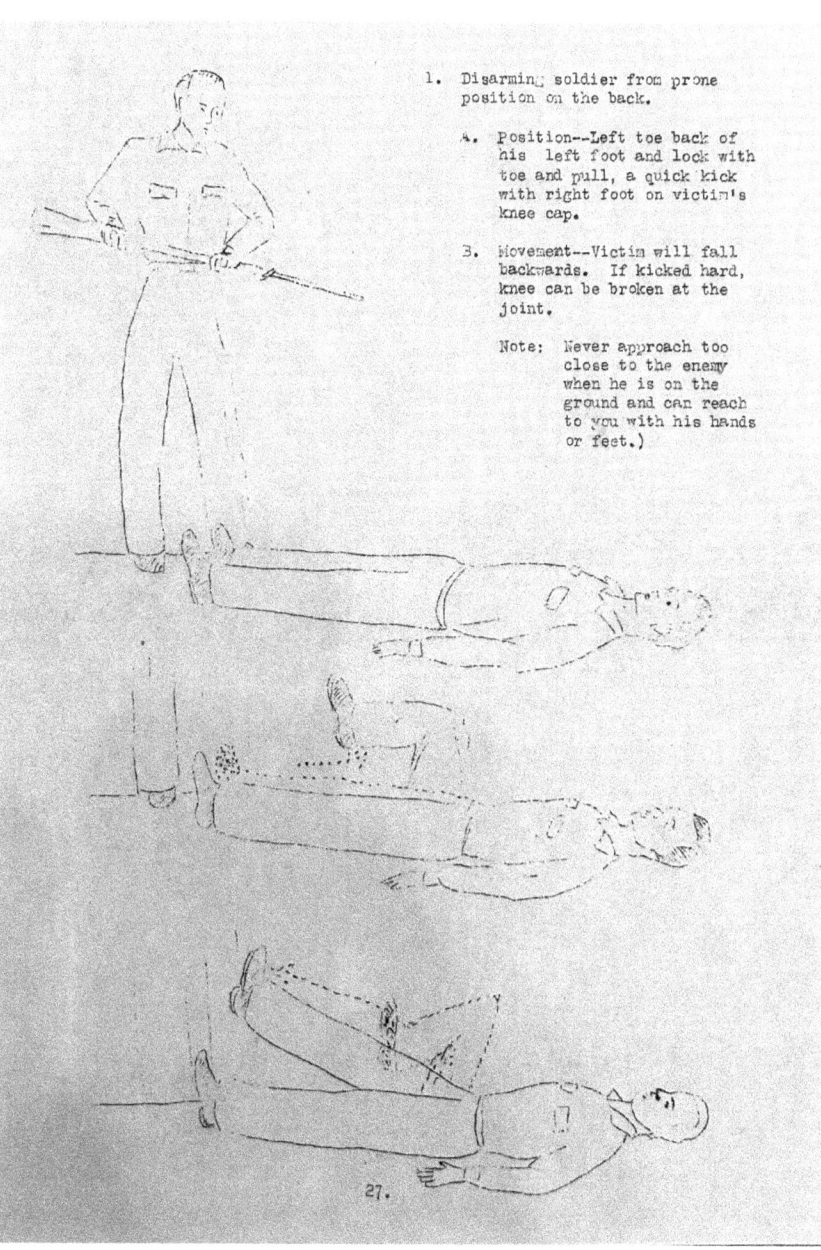

1. Disarming soldier from prone position on the back.

    A. Position--Left toe back of his left foot and lock with toe and pull, a quick kick with right foot on victim's knee cap.

    B. Movement--Victim will fall backwards. If kicked hard, knee can be broken at the joint.

        Note: Never approach too close to the enemy when he is on the ground and can reach to you with his hands or feet.)

27.

261

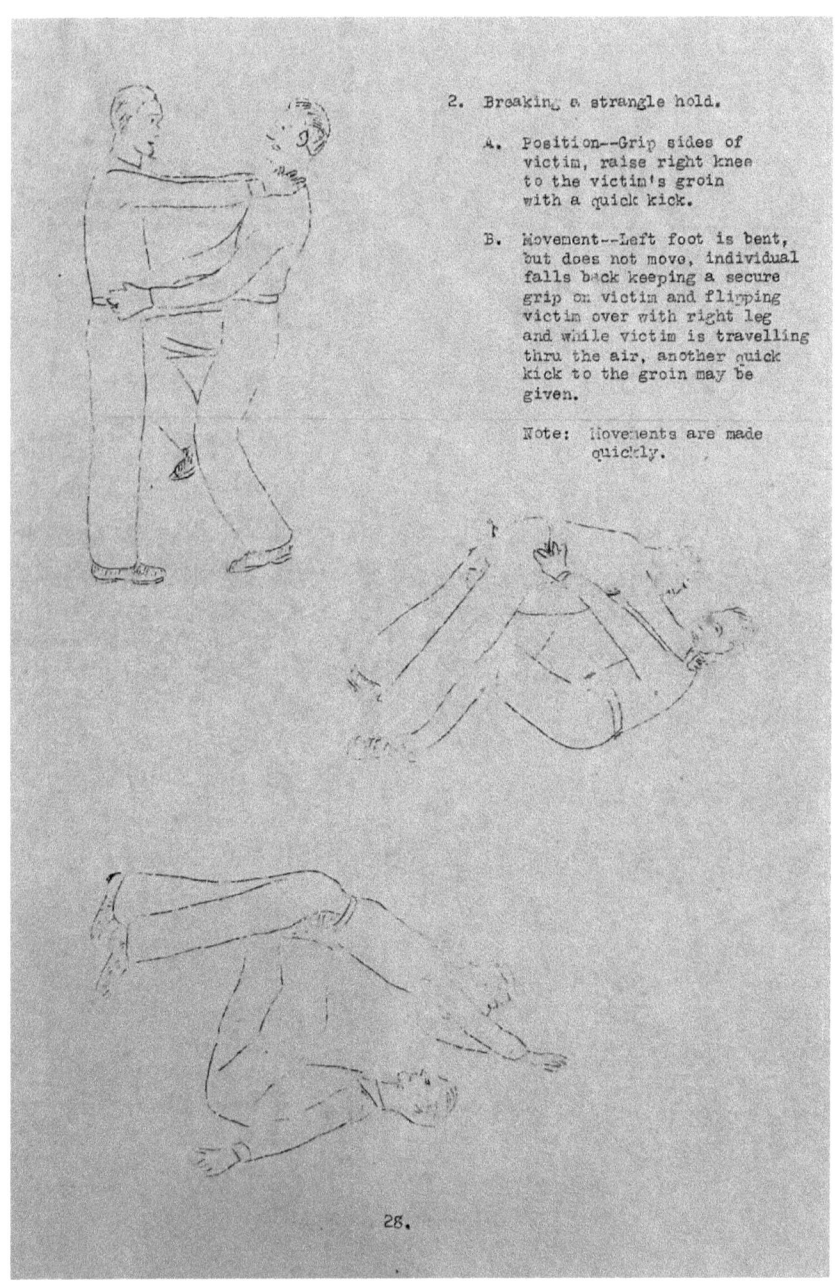

2. Breaking a strangle hold.

   A. Position--Grip sides of
      victim, raise right knee
      to the victim's groin
      with a quick kick.

   B. Movement--Left foot is bent,
      but does not move, individual
      falls back keeping a secure
      grip on victim and flipping
      victim over with right leg
      and while victim is travelling
      thru the air, another quick
      kick to the groin may be
      given.

      Note: Movements are made
            quickly.

28.

262

3. Killing sentry before he can make an outcry.

    A. Position--All clothing removed, short knife is placed
        in teeth.

    B. Movement--Creeping slowly, at the same time removing all
        twigs and placing them to the side as you move. Within a
        1 ft. of the guard, grasp knife in right hand, place palm
        of left hand over victim's mouth, digging fingers into
        skin and eyes, pull head over to the left with right hand
        and plunge knife in eye, throat, or back of ear.
        (as shown in following sketches).

29.

263

264

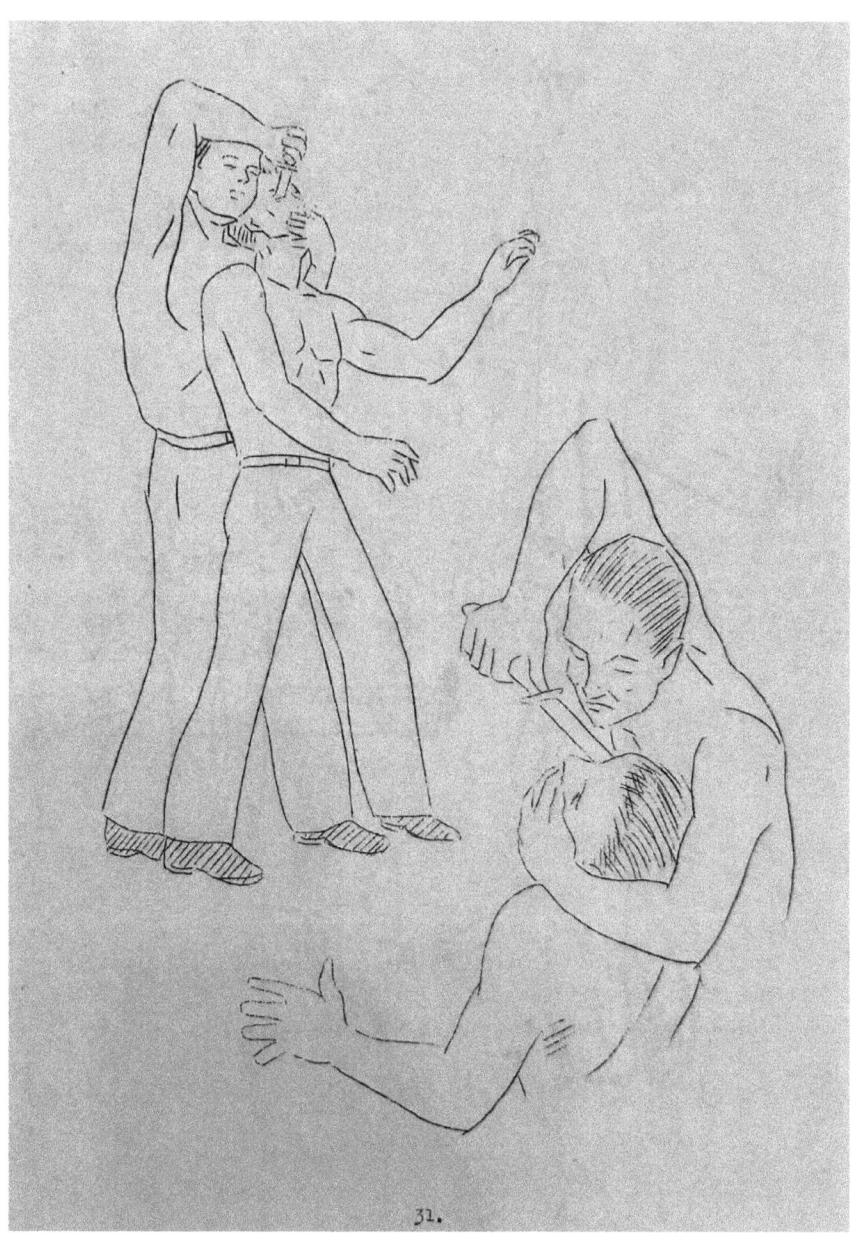

31.

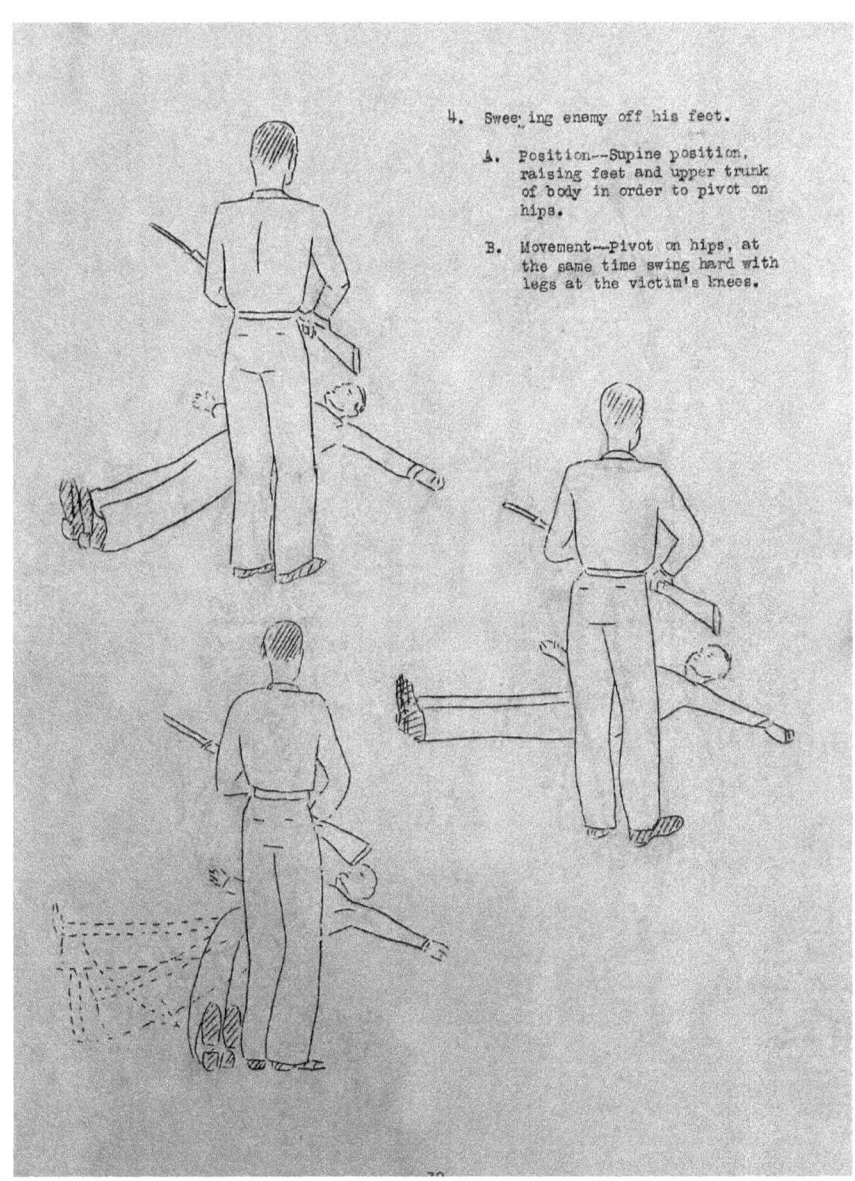

4. Sweeping enemy off his feet.

   A. Position—Supine position,
      raising feet and upper trunk
      of body in order to pivot on
      hips.

   B. Movement—Pivot on hips, at
      the same time swing hard with
      legs at the victim's knees.

5. Wrestling gun from enemy.

 . A. Position--As enemy runs toward you, start for him in a
      zig and zag motion; within 6 ft. of the enemy spring
      and swing legs to the side at the same time grasp the
      rifle he has close to his hands. The swing and pull
      will pull the victim down in the position as shown in
      figure No. 2.

   B. Movement--Throw left leg over keeping left arm straight;
      roll over with rifle pressed across victim's throat.

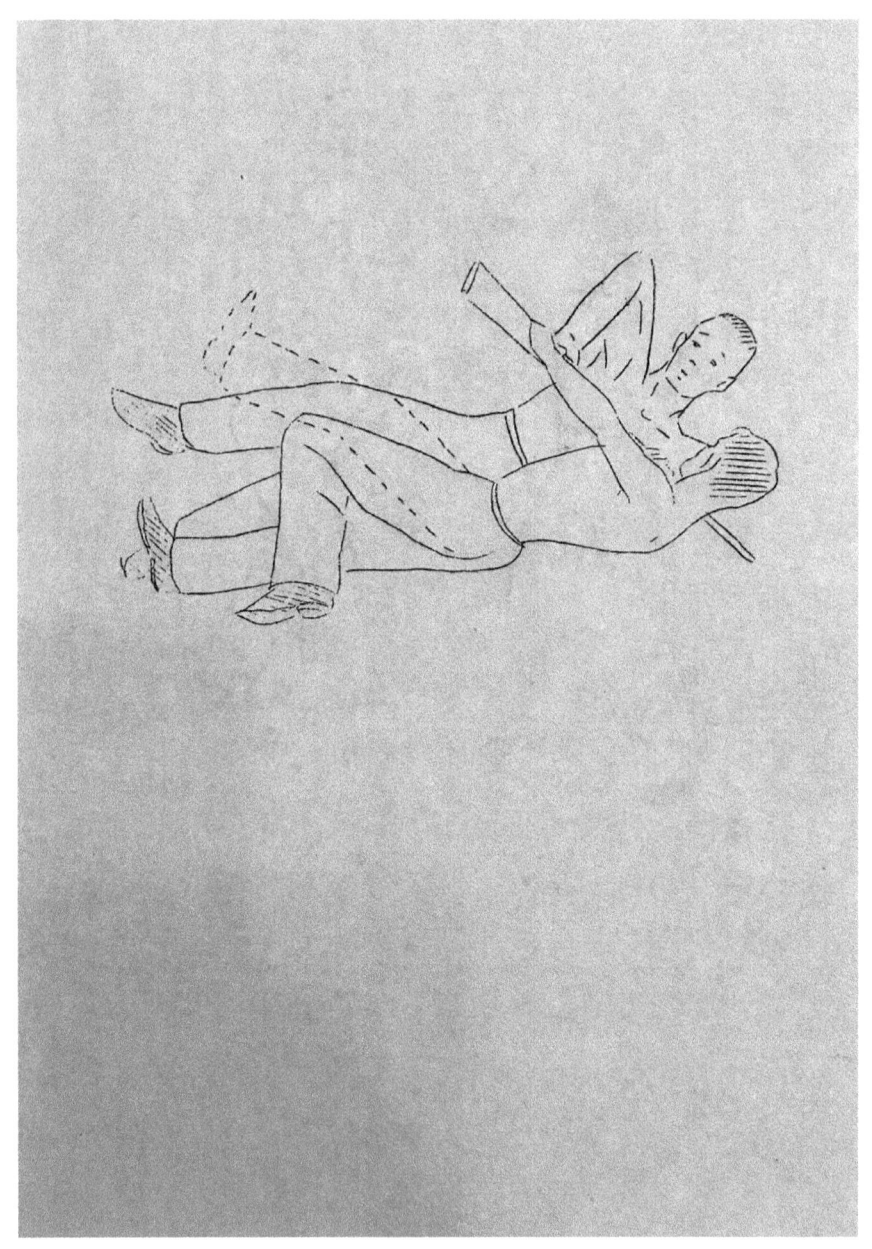

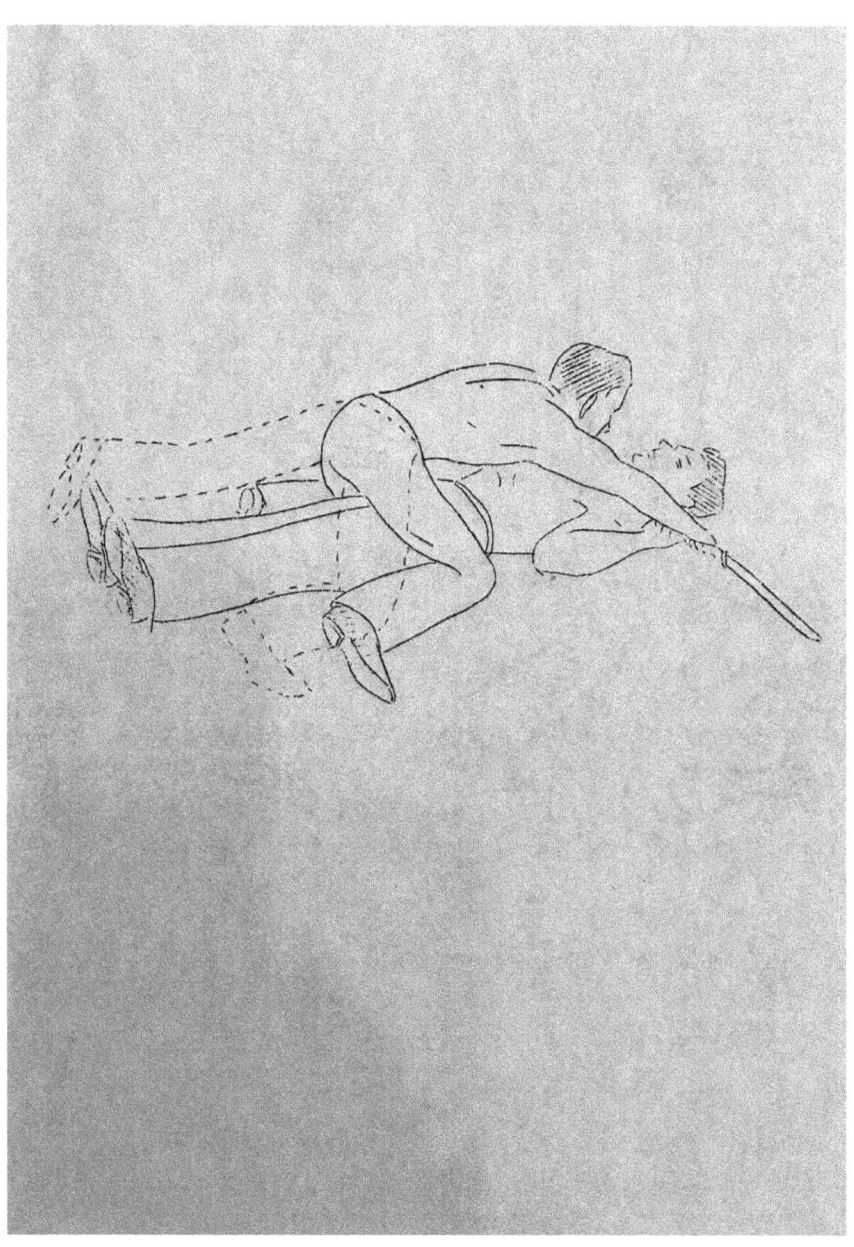

6. Using bayonet from the rear.

    A. Position—Bayonet point placed below the belt.

    B. Movement— Thrust forward and at the same time pry upward with rifle. This causes a collapse of the spinal cord.

7. Breaking a strangle hold.

   A. Position--Hand on victim's throat with thumb down.

   B. Movement--Grasping victim's "Adams Apple", squeezing fingers
      together, and twisting to right; at same time gouging
      out victim's eye with thumb of other hand.

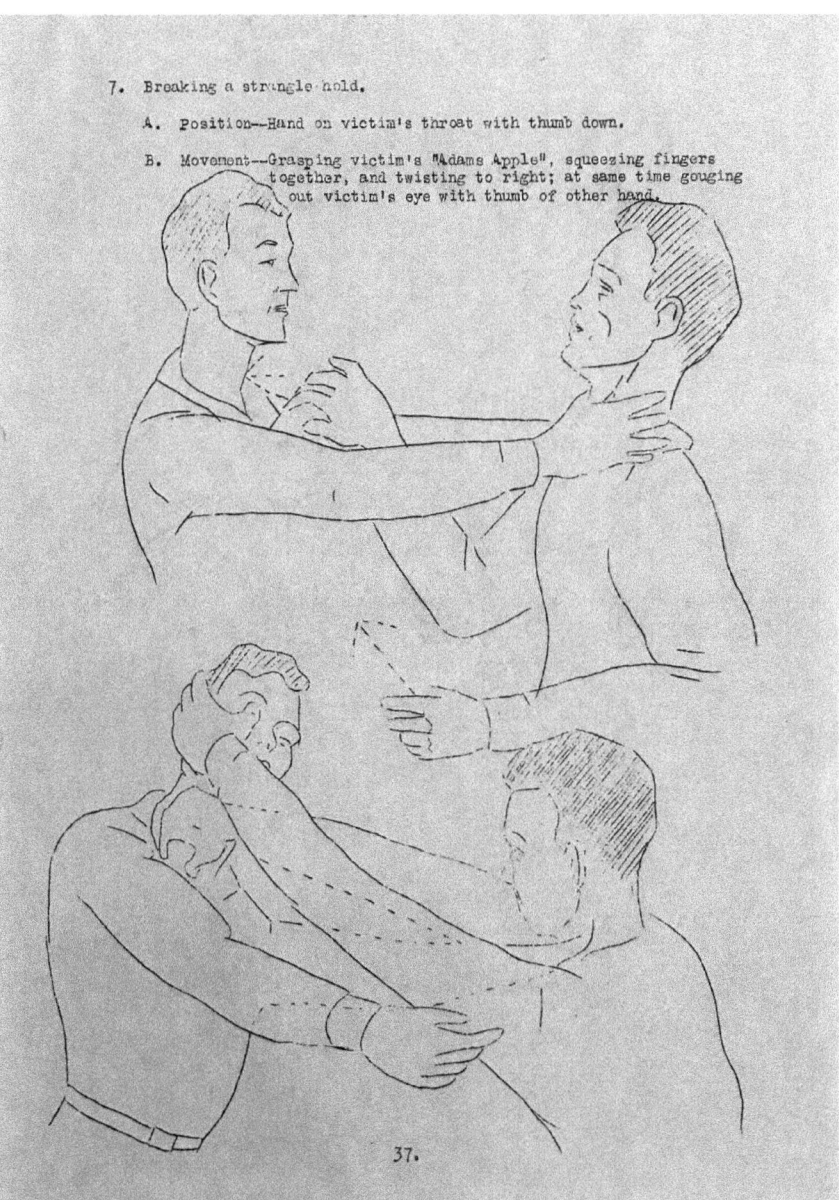

37.

271

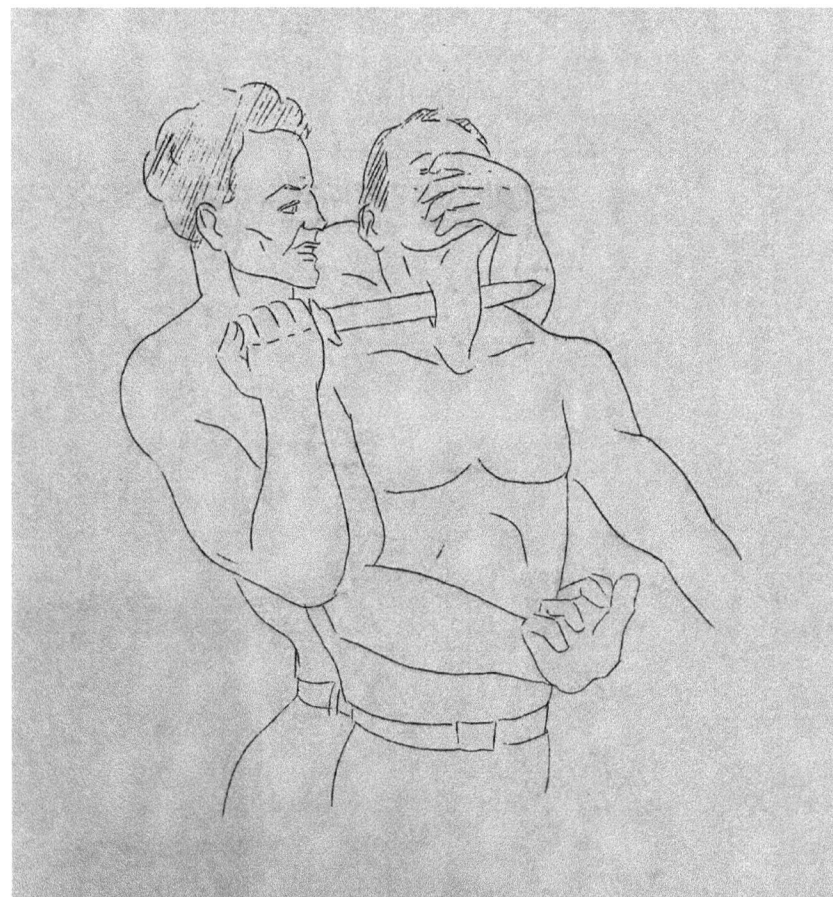

8. Keeping guard from making outcry.

    A. Position--Grasp chin with left hand, pull victim's head to the side.

    B. Movement--Thrust bayonet in back of "Adams Apple" with upward thrust.

9. Disarming man with knife or gun.

   A. Position—when attacker asks you to raise hands,
      do not put them above your head, but put them
      as shown in Figure #1.

   B. Movement—move right hand to attract attacker's
      eyes. When the eyes move over make a fast grab
      at the right wrist with your left hand. Grab
      his elbow with your right hand; at the same time,
      take one step forward to his left and make an
      about-face. Bend forward snapping the arm and
      the attacker over your head.

      Note: Remember to always look the attacker in
      the eye. His eyes are your go signal. In throwing
      attacker, his arm may be broken with a quick snap.

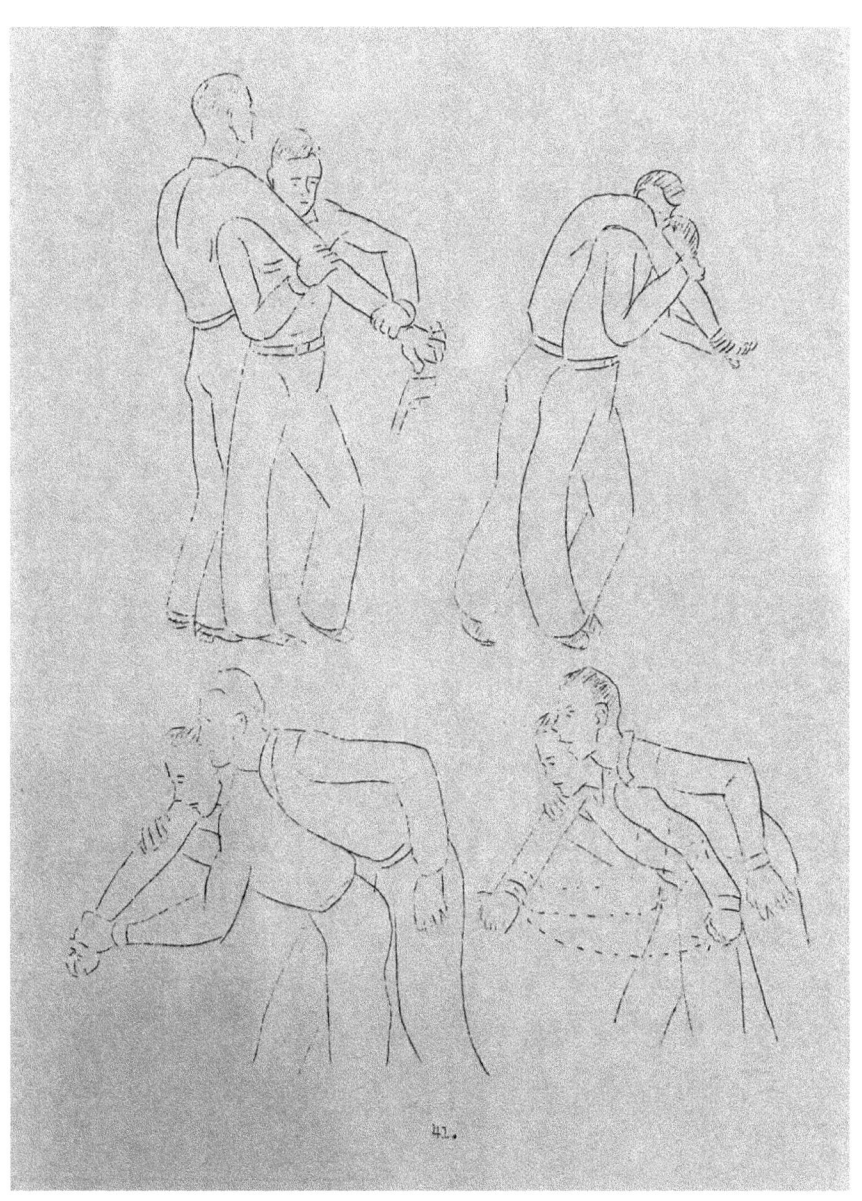

41.

275

David D. Duncan

Besides Weston and Heinmiller there had been other individuals who were greatly impressed by the Fijians. One such individual was U. S. Marine First Lieutenant, David D. Duncan.

In the January 1945 there was an article which appeared in National Geographic written by Duncan, while he had been on assignment for the Marine Corps. The article "Fiji Patrol on Bougainville" also contained several photographs of Fijian Commandos.

In an interview later in life at the age of 88, Duncan who became an accomplished photographer after the war, described how he came to be on Bougainville with the Fijians during the war.

In 1940, National Geographic Magazine had bought a picture essay on big-game fishing in the Humboldt Current off Peru, from Duncan; who had primarily been an amateur photographer up until that point. He soon found himself in a career as a photojournalist. In 1941 while Duncan had been working for Nelson Rockefeller's Office of Inter-American Affairs as part of an effort to improve U.S. relations in that region; the Japanese attacked Pearl Harbor. That cut his career short. When he got back to Washington he used his contacts at the National Geographic to help him get a job with the Marine Corps.

After training at Quantico, Duncan became the photo officer with Marine aircraft group (MAG)-23 on Oahu, but had very little to do there. For a time, he volunteered to photograph the Guatemalan coast as part of effort to locate Nazi U-boats. However, he did not have training in aerial photography and so he soon switched to the South Pacific Combat Air Transport Command (SCAT). It was there that Colonel Al Koonce, the commander, cut orders which enabled Duncan to photograph SCAT operations in New Zealand and Australia.

When Duncan found out that SCAT was dropping supplies to Fijian guerrillas of the 1st Battalion Fiji Infantry Regiment which had been operating behind Japanese lines on Bougainville, he asked to be sent there. It was where he would meet future President Richard Nixon. In his interview for the December 2004 issue of Naval History, Duncan stated:

> On Bougainville, there was a Piper Club outfit (at Torokina) flying supplies to Ibu, which was in the center of the island under the volcano called Bagana. The base officer at Torokina for the Piper Clubs was Dick Nixon, a lieutenant (j.g.) in the Navy. He had about four planes flying artillery-spotting missions and supplying Ibu for the Fijians. One of his Marine pilots flew me in.

It was there that he met Lieutenant Colonel Geoffrey Upton, who had been commanding the Fijian battalion. According to Duncan, what began as a one-time photo shoot turned into something more, when the Japanese counterattacked. He stated:

They drove us off the top of the mountain. It took five days and four nights to get out of the place and back to the coast. Landing craft took us back to Torokina and that's where Nixon made the shot.

Nixon had taken a photo of Duncan holding his carbine. The events which occurred prior to that; which Duncan wrote about in his article, were of note because they described the Fijians who were scouts but also the Papuan scouts that the Fijians employed. Duncan wrote:

Had Hollywood created Ibu as the background for a guerrilla band, the setting could not have been wilder. Dense, forbidding jungle pressed in from every side. An old lattice-walled mission house served as headquarters. Steps were hewn from tree trunks.

The clearing around the house was a profusion of ferns, bamboo, palms, and wild ginger. Mount Balbi, the 10,171-foot volcano, towered over the vine-festooned trees.

Dramatically dressed in multihued silks of discarded parachutes, heavily armed Fijians roamed the camp, completing the illusion of a scene from movieland.

"Do we surprise you, Lieutenant?" queried a soft voice at my shoulder.

I was startled. No one had been near me a moment before. Whirling, I stared into a vast, coppery chest, from which deep laughter rolled. Towering over me stood one of the most powerful men I have ever seen.

Under one arm he carried a log of telephone-pole dimensions. In the other, a submachine gun. Around his waist this bearded giant wore a bright-blue skirt!

"Permit me, Lieutenant, to assist with your equipment. I am going that way with this rafter for the medical dugout." I was dumbfounded, first because of his English, then that he could carry still more.

After supper that evening, as rain beat down over the jungle, I sat back from the lamplight, listening to the conversation. Matches flared, momentarily high-lighting the faces. The major was speaking earnestly, so low that I could scarcely hear.

"Tomorrow we do it again. This morning new Japanese troops moved in near the deserted village of Pipipaia. They still have no natives to guide them. They may have forgotten our last little party; so we'll give them another."

No one smiled, not even the major. That "last party" had trapped and killed twenty-two Japs. One Fijian also lost his life. It was no picnic.
"Now, let's check the setup." Pushing back his packing-crate chair, he stepped to the cart table. After a glance at the large-scale map, he called to his batman in the darkness. "Go down to the camp and tell Bero, the Papuan scout, that we must see him immediately."

While the major waited, other officers crowded around. Flashlights traced lines across the battle chart, as though each was silently choosing an ambush along the network of trails.

Soon bare feet whispering over the floor announced the arrival of Bero. Squat, barrel-chested, tattooing around his eyes, he was of the jungle. A pair of khaki shorts, with a kris at his waist, was all that he wore. But what held me was a feeling of something untamed prowling that veranda. Only a thread of civilization seemed to hold him in check.

While I oiled and cleaned my carbine, a junior officer beside me on the bunk told me about this sinister-looking soldier.

"He's tough, that bloke. Massive shoulders, powerful legs, unlimited endurance, and chopped from mahogany. Not much like a Solomon islander, is he?'

"But what place does he fill in your Fiji battalion?" I asked.

"Before the Japanese came, the Australian Government conducted a police school at Rabaul, New Britain," he explained. "the most intelligent and toughest men from New Guinea, boys like Bero, were trained as a constabulary force to maintain law and order throughout the Australian Mandated Islands."

"Like you Marines, we Fijians had never seen Bougainville until a short time ago. To campaign behind enemy lines, we needed scouts who knew the country. The police boys were the answer. Bero and his Papuan friends, who were stationed on Bougainville, know the island like the floor of their homes and are invaluable to us."

Later, I asked Bero how many Japs he had killed and he gave two answers: first, those he had shot with his carbine; then, with a laugh, those he had finished in the way of the jungle, using only his kris or his bare hands. He had several dozen Japs to his credit.

When the major had completed briefing his officers for the next day's action, he came over and sat on the bunk.

"Tell me about your Fijians," I said. "Is it true that no men in the Pacific make better jungle fighters?"

"Correct!" he replied. "These men possess three remarkable assets. First, their uncanny sense of perception. Out in the jungle, they see, hear, and even smell things beyond the powers of you or me.

"Second, their tremendous good nature. Whether the day is sunny or rainy, they will convulse each other with stories and jokes, then sing the rest of the time. It isn't that they can't be serious. Wait until you have lain in ambush or made an attack with them.

"Finally, their complete lack of fear of the enemy and their indifferent attitude toward death. No Fijian worries about being killed any more than he questions the sun's not rising. Thorough training, too, has molded their natural abilities into a hard-hitting machine, capable of stalking the enemy in any jungle of the Pacific."

"What about your officers? They are not all Fijians?" I asked.

"No," he replied. "Some are Fijians; the majority, though are New Zealanders. For jungle sense, the Fijians beat us Kiwis every time! But enough of this—tomorrow we have a big job to do! Good night."

According to the Naval History article, in a letter to the squadron's skipper, Upton had described Duncan's role in an engagement near Sisivie:

> "When the enemy finally attacked, 2/Lieut. Duncan proceeded
> with the advanced elements and was in the thick of the fight…
> He was by chance the first officer I encountered and he was able
> to give me a clear picture of the situation. From then on he
> acted on my invitation as assistant-adjutant…and was of the
> utmost help. On the long march back over the Crown Prince

range he rendered many services and I cannot speak too highly of him both as an official photographer and an honorary member of my Battalion staff."

According to the article, the SCAT orders got him to Sydney, Australia, where he spent a month at the *The Sydney Sun*, developing film and making prints.

He mailed the Fijian prints to Upton, who sent him the regimental patch, reminding him it was "worn as square" and saying how proud the regiment would be if he wore it. Duncan had sewed it on his Marine greens.

"Their campaign would never become famous," he wrote later, "but Colonel Upton and his guerrillas had planted the seed of a legend of black ghosts in the Solomon Islands." The legend grew as it was retold, but "no one could ever tell the story better than simply the way it was up at Ibu with the Fijian guerrillas." Although he was awarded the Distinguished Flying Cross later in the war, the patch seems to mean more to him than any of his decorations.

Before closing out the chapter I thought it would be appropriate to provide some further background on Colonel Upton and his guerrilla fighters. The newspaper The Advertiser, December 2nd 1944 stated the following about them:

The hard-fought battalion which Lieutenant-Colonel Upton now commands went into action on Bougainville under the command of a capable World War I veteran, Lieut.-Col. J. B. K. Taylor, of Auckland. A 25-lb bomb came through his tent one night. Colonel Taylor is still under treatment for severe head wounds in the Auckland Hospital. When Colonel Taylor was wounded. Upton was a major, second in command of the battalion.

It is said that the famous Māori Battalion, of the New Zealand Division, in Italy, is the best-decorated battalion in the 2nd NZEF. Most people think it unlikely that the Māori could have taught the Fijians anything as soldiers—and the Fijians have medals to show, too.

Lieutenant Isireli Korovulavula won the Military Cross, Sgt. Peni Setuata, the Distinguished Conduct Medal; Sgt. George Mate, Cpl. Kalipate Bainivalu and Pte. Jeke Vakararawa, the Military Medal. Six others were mentioned in despatches. Sairusi Koto won the American Silver Star for capturing a machine-gun and a mortar on Bougainville.

And recently came the long-delayed announcement of the post-humous award of the Victoria Cross to Cpl. Sefanaia Sukanajvalu, the first non-European soldier from the colonies to be so decorated in this war. His act of valor was the selfless bravery of the martyr—he died that his companions might live.

On June 23, when his platoon was ambushed at Bougainville, Sukanaivailu was struck down while bringing in two wounded men. Several vain attempts were made to rescue him. He urged his comrades to leave him. When they persisted in their attempts to save him he deliberately raised himself in front of a Japanese machinegun and fell riddled with bullets.

Lt-Col Upton won his Distinguished Service Order on Bougainville. An official report covering the award stated that his unit saw active service there with United States forces. The commanding officer of the United States corps specially commended Col. Upton on the skillful withdrawal of his battalion across country during an engagement with strong Japanese forces. Col. Upton's battalion killed 120 of the enemy and wounded a large number, while itself suffering only one casualty—a man slightly wounded.

During the withdrawal the battalion successfully evacuated 200 friendly natives, who would otherwise have been subjected to Japanese reprisals. The American general said the success of the operation must be credited to the commander of the battalion.

After the withdrawal the commanding American general described it as "a classic in miniature of modern warfare." Brig. J. G. C. Wales, formerly officer commanding the Fiji Military Forces, stated in an address recently that the withdrawal was now quoted in American Army schools of instruction.

High praise was given Col. Upton in General Orders of the headquarters of South Pacific Base Command, announcing the award of the Bronze Star medal. The citation stated:

"The Bronze Star medal is awarded to Lt-Col. Upton for heroic achievements against the enemy at Bougainville, Solomon Islands, from January 12 to April 30, 1944, while serving as the commander of the battalion which successfully occupied an outpost at Ibu, 20 miles beyond the American perimeter, and constructed the Kameli strip for air supply and evacuation.

"Col Upton also submitted valuable information concerning Japanese preparation for an assault on our perimeter defences, enabling American commanders to take counter-measures, which contributed materially to the repulse of the hostile effort when it was launched. He performed gallantly on numerous reconnaissance-in-force missions, leading his battalion into strongly-held Japanese territory. Throughout this prolonged period of intense activity he exhibited aggressive leadership, keen foresight and superior devotion to duty."

Maj. C. W. H. Tripp, of Geraldine, South Canterbury, who commanded the First Commando, Fiji Guerillas, also known among American troops as South Sea Scouts, was also awarded the Distinguished Service Order.

As for Wales, Gillespie wrote in his book that he handed over his command and was succeeded by Brigadier G. Dittmer, DSO, MBE, MC, after commanding the Fiji Military Forces for 14 months, during which he had molded them into a highly efficient organization. Gillespie wrote:

> Malaria had taken its toll, and many of the commandos were too ill to undertake further patrol work. The whole unit was therefore withdrawn from Vella Lavella on 25 September and returned to Guadalcanal, where it remained until 5 October and then moved to Florida Island. Brigade Headquarters, however, in the interests of morale and health, decided to withdraw the unit from the combat zone and replace it with another group. In November 1 Commando returned to Fiji and was finally disbanded on 27 May 1944.

Portrait of Lieutenant Colonel Geoffrey Thomson Upton, taken in the Pacific on May 1944.

An Unfortunate Incident

Colonel Weston wrote about an unfortunate event which occurred in Heinmiller's life, toward the end of the war. Weston had been stationed Stateside, and was tasked with training infantry replacements. He wrote:

> I was notified that my orders had been changed and I was to report to the Infantry Replacement Training Center (IRTC) at Anniston, Alabama, a week early, so I said my goodbyes and boarded a south-bound train. An old friend of mine from South Pacific days was also stationed there, Lieutenant Carl Heinmiller. Carl and I were both going to be training infantry replacements. We looked forward to working together again.
>
> About two months into the training program, I went to visit carl in the hospital. In all the fighting we had done in the South Pacific, Carl had never received so much as a scratch. Yet here he was, victim of a grenade explosion.
>
> He had been showing the trainees how to handle grenades on the fragmentation hand grenade range. Army grenades had a five-second delay fuse, which meant that they wouldn't explode until five seconds after the pin was pulled. Our experiences from the South Pacific taught us that when we pulled the pin it was necessary to hold the grenade for a couple of seconds before throwing it. Otherwise, the enemy would have time to pick it up and throw it back. By holding a grenade for two seconds before throwing it, we were able to time the explosion for just about the time a Japanese soldier picked up the grenade to throw it back.
> Carl was teaching these recruits the tactics we had had learned in handling the five-second delay grenades. By mistake, he had been given a crate of marine three-second fuse grenades. He pulled the pin, held the grenade for two seconds, and as he was reaching back to throw, the grenade exploded taking his right hand.

I asked Lee about the incident and he told me:

> He lost an eye and thumb, index, and middle finger (all to middle knuckle) on his right hand doing a booby trap demo in the States!! He was showing a bunch of guys one of his triggers for an explosive on a blasting cap, a jerk bumped him and set it off. He only had time to bury it at his feet in sandy soil, didn't want to toss it into the crowd of recruits!! As a Judge later in life, he made a lot of jokes about Justice being only Half Blind!!

In 1944, aside from his duties as an instructor, and likely because of the injuries sustained from the training accident, Heinmiller was also contributing to the war effort in other ways. He was helping to promote the selling of war bonds.

Perhaps his injuries were being utilized in a way to emphasize the point that War Is Hell, as the quote attributed to the Civil war general Tecumseh Sherman went.

An article in the Statesville Daily Record, June 10th, stated:

> Captain Carl Heinmiller, who has had months of combat duty in our present war, and bears many scars as a result, will be in Statesville Thursday, June 15th in connection with the WAC War Bond Day. He will be featured during the opening ceremonies at one o'clock on the Square, as well as during the evening Army musical variety show, which will take place at eight o'clock in the high school stadium. In case of rain, the show will be held in the high school auditorium.
>
> Captain Carl Heinmiller's experiences as commanding officer of his company of men in battle, are of vital interest to all. These men have gone through, and are going through, unbelievable days of pain, hunger, and physical exhaustion from sleeplessness and

nervous strain. The message that Captain Heinmiller has for the citizens of Iredell County is one that should not be missed by any man, woman or child.

Another article that same year described a similar event in which Heinmiller used his experiences during the war to sell war bonds. The article in the Anniston Star, December 15th titled "Pacific Veteran Talks on War" stated:

> Experiences that he and members of his outfits endured fighting the Japanese in Guadalcanal and New Georgia were related to members of the Kiwanis Club at the luncheon meeting Thursday at the Jefferson Davis Hotel by Capt. Carl Heinmiller of Fort McClellan.

> The things that Captain Heinmiller told about are things that go on in every battle by thousands of others. They are the experiences that bring death constantly to thousands and that bring permanent injuries to thousands of others.

> The speaker did not plead with the Kiwanians to buy War Bonds. He did ask, however, "you wouldn't put a baby out on the street without proper clothing, food and care, would you?"

> As serious and horrible as the war is, Captain Heinmiller recalled some events, the telling of which made his audience laugh.

> Part of his duties at Fort McClellan call for lectures to trainees at Fort McClellan on the importance of doing their best in training and Captain Heinmiller devoted a few minutes to incidents of battle in which there was a direct influence of training upon the individuals.

Wac War Bond Day!

COME ONE; COME ALL · · · ·
YOUNG AND OLD, FOR A GALA
COMMUNITY DAY OF FUN

Program

1:00 P. M.—OFFICIAL OPENING CEREMONIES AT SQUARE BY MAYOR J. WESLEY JONES
Memorial Services For Boys Of Iredell County Lost In War.

1:30 TO 3:45 P. M.—AT THE SQUARE.
1. Booths Selling Bonds Manned By WACS.
2. Jeep Rides For Purchase Of $25 Bond.

4:00 P. M.—PARADE — STARTS AT CITY HALL — DISBANDS AT STADIUM.

5:00 P. M.—ACTIVITIES AT STADIUM — FREE ADMISSION.
1. Picnic Supper. Bring The Family.
2. Auction Box Suppers — War Bonds.
3. Auction — Gifts — War Bonds.
4. Games And Field Events — Open To All.
5. Jeep Rides — For Purchasers Of Bonds.

8:00 P. M.—ARMY AIR FORCES VARIETY SHOW — FREE OF CHARGE.
1. Camp Sutton Band Concert.
2. Camp Sutton WAC Syncopators.
3. Blues Singers.
4. Comedy Skits.
Capt. Carl Heinmiller, Back From Combat, Will Be A Star Feature.

The Invasion Has Started — Invade Your Pockets — Buy War Bonds

BOND 'DAY

FRIDAY June 16th

A New Army Air Forces Show
On the Stage of The Playhouse Theater
At 8:15 P.M.

SOLDIER SHOW

"There's Something About A Soldier"
— WITH A CAST OF 75 —

TICKETS ARE ISSUED TO BOND PURCHASERS

BUY YOUR BOND NOW — OR BEFORE JUNE 16th!

(Proper Evidence Of Having Purchased Bond To Be Shown For Ticket)

SEATS ARE LIMITED—FIRST COME—FIRST SERVED

SECTIONS RESERVED FOR BOND PURCHASERS — $25 BONDS UP.

THIS PATRIOTIC MESSAGE SPONSORED BY

FANJOY & BOWLES

Note: Capt. Carl Heinmiller, the star feature. Source: Statesville Daily Record, June 12th, 1944.

A few more articles show that Heinmiller was doing much of the same in the final year of the war. An article in the Aniston Star, April 19th 1945 stated:

> With a goal of $2,969,000 to shoot at during the Seventh War Loan drive. 200 Anniston business men learned last night the part they are expected to play in putting across the drive at Calhoun County at a short, peppy meeting which followed an appetizing barbecue dinner provided for the occasion by the Coca-Cola Bottling Company. Served on the plant grounds by Manager Joe Rutledge and his staff, the meal was thoroughly enjoyed by the scores of men and women present.
>
> War Finance Committee Chairman Howard W. Cater presided over the informal meeting and before introducing the first speaker he pointed out that the Calhoun County quota is set by Secretary of the Treasury Henry Morgenthau Jr., is the largest task ever handed to business men and citizens of the county. Of the total of $2,969,000 which has been set as the goal for Calhoun, $1,876,000 is in "E" bonds. Mr. Cater said. He then called on Capt. Carl Heinmiller, special service officer of the IRTC at Fort McClellan to tell those present a few things about the big War Bond Boxing Show to be staged at Memorial Stadium next Wednesday night, when a War Bond purchase will be the entrance fee.
>
> Captain Heinmiller, an old boxer himself, told the crowd that the boxing card will be made up of bouts featuring some of the best boxers that it has ever been his good fortune to see in action. Many of them, he said, are either A. A. U. champions or runners-up in their respective classes, but all are top-notch fighters who really fight for the love of it. The bouts, he said, will be dedicated to the memory of the late Ernie Pyle, war correspondent pal of GI's the world over.

It appeared that Heinmiller was once again utilizing his knowledge and love of boxing to contribute to the war effort.

Another Aniston Star article from June of that year, showed that Heinmiller was utilizing demonstrations of unarmed combat to sell war bonds. The article "M'Clellan Show Aids Bond Sale In Birmingham, Boxing, Judo, Dirty Fighting And Vocalists Thrill Magic City Crowd" stated:

> The highly publicized judo and dirty-fighting exhibition was highlighted by the battle between tiny Cpl. Helen Mieleska, a 105-pound WAC from the Fort McClellan Regional Hospital, and Capt. Carl W. Heinmiller, IRTC special services officer and famous South Pacific knife and dirty fighting expert. The crowd, which paid up to $1,000 a seat in War Bond purchases for each seat, howled with glee as the little WAC slammed husky Capt. Hienmiller to the mat time after time with judo holds and throws, putting to shame a wrestling match between two Birmingham professional grunters and groaners, which opened the show.

> Corporal Mieleska was coached for the contest by S/Sgt. Richard C. Hunt of the IRTC public relations office, one of the few Americans ever to become a member of the Koda Kwan, official Japanese jui jitsu society.

> Lieut. John D. Archer, hand-to-hand fighting expert, and S/Sgt. Raymond King, both from the Eighth Battalion here, gave a fast demonstration of bayonet fighting, disarming and hand-to-hand battling that kept the spectators on their feet.

> Sgt. Louis A. Sahley of the IRTC special service officer was the "victim" of Capt. Heinmiller in a demonstration of knife and machete blows.

Heinmiller later turned up in a strange article in the Atlanta Constitution, on August 24th. The article titled "Spunky Jo Jo, GI Cub Stationed At Park Zoo" stated:

> Atlanta's Grant Park zoo possesses its first veteran of World War II, a 56-pound Canadian black bear cub, GI Jo Jo, who barely won his honorable discharge before his owner, Maj. Carl H. Heinmiller, special service officer of the Infantry Replacement Training Center at Ft. McClellan, Ala., separated him from the unit after six months' service and gave him to George J. Simons, general manager of city parks.
>
> Jo Jo's penchant for food resulted in his downfall and in the indignity of being consigned to a zoo rather than having the run of the camp, where he was the most popular of all GI's. Described as "one of the orneriest, but most lovable infantrymen ever to hit camp," Jo Jo was "discharged" and presented to the city after his impish pranks, spurred by a voracious appetite for forbidden food, backfired and kept his keepers in hot water with commissary officials.
>
> At the zoo yesterday, Jo Jo turned his nose up a little higher in the air as he scorned civilian chow. When Simons and Johnnie Dilbeck, zoo keeper, informed him that he was no longer in the Army and that impromptu riads on his major objective—food— were over, he looked disdainfully at them and ended the conversation with a disgusted grunt.
>
> On the night before he was mustered out, he displayed the true spirit of an over-trained infantryman by taking by storm and holding four bags of popcorn, a pack of hard-to-get cigarets, two stogies, better than civilian issue; a box of ice cream, an umbrella without ribs, and a part of a young woman's skirt, according to reports from the camp.

This was the last straw, Maj. Heinmiller "broke" him, reducing him from a private's rating to that of a "yardbird," docile type. He spoils for a fight, and enjoys mixing it with all and sundry. Simons and Dilbeck learned promptly to respect him as he stalked about his cage, daring them to approach too closely.

"He's an imp, but I like him." Simons said. "He has spunk, and he probably got it honestly because of his environment. No group ever had more fight or courage than the boys of the infantry. We are proud to welcome a fighting member of Ft. McClelland to Atlanta. He will be a favorite of the thousands who visit the zoo, and will become one of Johnnie's pampered pets."

One final article in the Anniston Star, dated November 21st titled "Major Speaks On Pacific War" stated:

Telling of his experiences in the Southwest Pacific, Maj. Carl Heinmiller, for several years in Special Services at Fort McClellan, was a guest speaker at the Rotary Club luncheon yesterday at Jefferson Davis Hotel.

A. C. Cater introduced the speaker, stating that Major Heinmiller would leave McClellan next week for Washington where he will be stationed in the Special Information Section.

Major Heinmiller will be succeeded in Special Services at the post by Maj. C. W. Armstrong of Knoxville, Tenn., who was overseas with the 75th Division.

Going overseas with the 37th Division, Major Heinmiller told of landing in the Fiji Islands and of organizing a commando patrol in the jungles inhabited by headhunters.

He related experiences of his service on Guadalcanal and on New Georgia Island.

The major declared that when the planes left Guadalcanal on the mission to kill Admiral Yammamoto every GI on the island, in some manner, knew of the mission; and that, when the planes returned, and success of the mission became known, the cheers could be heard traversing the island.

The officer prefaced his experiences by urging all to see the War Department film "True Glory," actual battle scenes from D-Day in Europe to the final victory over the Germans.

Constitution Staff Photos—B. W. Callaway

GI JO JO and G. I. SIMONS

Postwar Venture

Leaders of the Veterans Alaska Co-operative Company examine map and model of Chilkoot Barracks area, which they have purchased for "planned settlement." They are (left to right) Steve Larssen Homer, Carl Heinmiller and Tresham D. Gregg. Source: Oakland Tribune.

As mentioned, Weston wrote about events which occurred in Heinmiller's life after they had crossed paths again at the end of the war. In his book he wrote the following regarding Heinmiller:

> After he was released from the hospital, the army discharged him for medical reasons. He decided to pursue a longtime dream of his, developing a homestead colony in the Yukan. I was intrigued by this plan, and planned to join the colony when I was released

from active duty. Carl moved back to Toledo, Ohio, to organize and plan for his colony.

In the same chapter Weston later described what occured:

> At the end of World War II, I was transferred to Fort Bragg, North Carolina, where I received a discharge from active duty. I had been looking forward to joining Carl Heinmiller in Alaska. Quite a few people had joined his colony, and they had made their way up through the Yukon Territory. They traveled several miles by boat, cleared a tract of land to serve as their homestead, and raised cabbage the size of small washtubs and potatoes as big as a person's head. It was a very successful harvest. Then the rivers froze and they found it impossible to get their produce to market fast enough, so everything spoiled. The colony was a failure. Carl and his group returned to the lower forty-eight.

According to Lee Heinmiller, it was U. S. Navy Reserve Steve Homer, who initiated what later became the Alaska Marine Highway System, who had spent several summers in Southeast Alaska and shared his dream of living there. This was what generated interest in the veterans moving there. On October 14th 1946, there was an article in The Times Leader which discussed the beginnings of that enterprise. The article "200 Clevelanders Leaving To Start Town in Alaska" stated:

> A party of 200 persons—including a doctor, a dentist, and nurses—expect to leave within two weeks to get a new town started in Alaska, in the Chilkoot Barracks 15 miles south of Skagway.

> Major Carl W. Heinmiller of nearby Berea, a founder of the Veteran's Alaska Cooperative Company, which bought the fully equipped barracks from the Interior Department as surplus

property for $105,000, expressed hope today of having a thriving community there by spring.

The cooperative obtained title to the 400-acre settlement after a spirited hearing in Washington over the merits of a similar bid by Kenneth O'Harra, operator of the O'Harra Bus Line, the biggest in Alaska. O'Harra, a former Ohio State University student, was known as "the richest corporal in the Army."

"Chilkoot is an ideal spot," Maj. Heinmiller said. "We have everything ready to move in—the town has all utilities. Many of the houses are furnished and we have running water and oil heat, sewage and other conveniences."

Sixty-six of the 400 acres are cleared and there are 86 buildings, including a 13-bed hospital, two barracks buildings and a fire station.

All of the first settlers—veterans and their families—have purchased a $100 share of common stock in the cooperative. Maj. Heinmiller, now on terminal leave after six years in the Army, said 800 applications were received.

The company plans to operate a cooperative retail store and aid members to get started in business. A tank landing craft and a five-passenger plane already have been purchased to help bring in supplies.

Eventually, the group expects to start similar enterprises in other parts of Alaska.

"However, it is a pioneering set-up," Heinmiller added. "It won't be too easy at the start, but with two or three years we should have a thriving community of 1,000 families."

Non-veterans recommended by members may join as well as veterans. All must purchase stock and all have a vote in the running of the organization.

Members are required to have at least $2,000 to tide them over until the project becomes self-sustaining, Maj. Heinmiller said.

The Oakland Tribune, November 3rd 1946 contained an article titled "Veterans Form Co-op Colony" which also discussed Heinmiller's venture.

A group of young people in this country is convinced Alaska is a land of opportunity. It has contracted to buy for $105,000 a 400-acre abandoned Army camp in the southeastern strip of the territory.

The group is the Veterans Alaska Co-operative Company (VACCO), organized last January by five young veterans.

President of the company and one of its founders is Steve Larssen Homer of Fairfield, Conn., ex-Navy lieutenant (J.G.) and former Alaska traveler.

The other four are: Tresham D. Gregg of New York City and Martin L. Cordez of Kokiak, Alaska, both former Navy lieutenants; James N. Trelford, Ashland, Wis., a former Navy chief petty office; and ex-Army major Carl Heinmiller, Cleveland, O.

Heinmiller, who lost an eye and two fingers fighting on New Guinea, is executive vice-president. All are members of the board of directors.

VACCO is a co-operative only to the extent that each member must but one $100 share of common stock in the company. This investment entitles him to share in low cost buying of food through a co-op store, operated by the company for the benefit of all its members.

Members will also be able to purchase wholesale supplies through the co-op with which to operate their own small businesses. Profits made by the co-op will be returned to members as a dividend.

VACCO has received 1000 applications for membership and currently has 60 members in good standing. Every stock owner has one vote in the co-operative regardless of the amount of stock he owns.

VACCO's aim is "planned settlement." Its members must be U.S. citizens sincerely eager to go to the territory, set up housekeeping, raise families and become a permanent part of the community.

Two months ago VACCO made a $10,500 down payment on the 400-acre tract of land at Chilkoot, an abandoned Army installation. Chilkoot is in the long, narrow southeastern strip of Alaska bordering British Columbia, 73 miles northwest of Juneau, Alaskan capital. It is located at the northern tip of one of the largest stands of virgin timber in North America.

Six members of the company are already at Chilkoot preparing it for the arrival of 50 VACCO families in early Spring.

Eighty-six buildings, one of them a fully equipped 13-bed hospital, dot the landscape at Chilkoot. A complete sewerage system, water system, electrical plant and oil-heating unit are ready for operation. These utilities will be run by the co-op as a whole.

Homer says the land and installations are actually worth "1,000,000. Members of the co-op will share in the decreased cost of consumers items resulting from mass purchase by the co-op. Beyond that the co-op will not enter extensively into the set-up. Members will own their own stores, filling stations, movie houses, restaurants and the like, free from any co-op control. The co-op will provide a guaranteed market for owners of these small businesses. Retail businesses will be restricted in number by the expected needs of the population.

Four main activities are expected to supply employment for all hands at Chilkoot. They are lumber, shipping, tourist and fishing.

The company is not accepting as members any applicants who don't have at least $2000 cash. The board of directors feels each member should have that much cash to get himself organized, to meet the initial cost of living and to start up a small business.

According to Lee, after winning the bid to purchase the Fort, the veterans arrived only to discover the ready-made "town" they had purchased was not precisely in the condition they had been led to believe. It was lacking quite a few of the 68 buildings which had been advertised.

Lee explained that the Army numbered everything.

So if the building was gone, there was still a number there…the little eight-by-eight shed in the yard that had oil storage…the flagpole. A whole lot of the things that weren't nailed down on officer's row, like some of the clawfoot tubs and the refrigerators and the stoves and stuff…was pretty much gone.

According to Lee, an FBI investigation discovered that most of the items had either been sold to or scavenged by the town, and demanding them back wouldn't make any friends, so Carl decided not to pursue it. But he still needed to repay the Fort loan and find a way to generate funds.

Carl would play many roles within the Fort, Haines and Klukwan communities over time. Not only did Carl serve the area as a magistrate for over 20 years, he also knew first aid from his time in the military. He performed basic medical care for the community, who had lost their doctors when the Fort closed.

Lee recounted how his father filled the gap:

> People would come in with a hatchet sticking out of their shin from chopping wood… and he'd patch 'em up. Carl was called to Klukwan in order to help deliver a set of twins…and made some close contacts with the families up there. That was still the period of time where the City of Haines was taking people's property here for…quote unquote 'back taxes.' And so my dad was helping some of those people with their legal issues. In the course of making friends with people in Klukwan, they ended up adopting him into the Wale house.

In August of 1954, Heinmiller turned up in an article in the Daily Boston Globe. The article "One-Eyed Ex-Army Man "Doctor" to 700 People", was written by Evan Hill, a Boston University Professor who had been touring the Territory. Hill wrote:

> There is a one-eyed seven-fingered retired Army major here who would be a candidate for a "doctor of the year" award if he were a doctor, but he isn't.

> Tall, friendly Carl Heinmiller, who lost an eye and three fingers in a training accident in the States after fighting with the famous Fiji scouts in the Pacific in World War II, is constantly patching

up people here in this doctorless area. Heinmiller learned his first aid in the Army and applies it almost daily here.

He is manager of the Port Chilkoot Company, land development firm that owns the former Army post of Chilkoot Barracks here, and he has his fingers in about as many pies as there are hereabouts.

But his unpaid, most-important job is that of midwife, diagnostician, surgeon, and sometimes psychiatrist to the area which contains about 700 people.

I have been with this fantastic man, now for 48 hours, and I'd be just as happy if I never see another person sewed up, given a shot or put into a splint.

On a single night he was called to a construction engineer's house, where he stitched a two-inch gash in the foot of a 9-year-old boy who had slashed the member with a hatchet. A few hours later he was bandaging a young Indian wife who had cut her hand badly on a swinging glass door in an unlighted hallway.

The next morning Heinmiller gave one of a four-shot series to an infant with an infected ear. That afternoon, while preparing to take his family on a picnic, a man in a speeding car shouted that a girl was on the road nearby, writhing in pain. With his young wife, Betty, and a backseat load of splints, medicines and blankets, he gave aid to the girl, a 16-year-old Indian, who apparently had dislocated her knee.

He gave her a sedative, splinted her leg with his blonde wife's help, and arranged for her transportation to Juneau, 90miles away by plane. Then he telephoned Juneau and told the doctor who would treat her what he had done, what drugs had been administered.

Once he helped deliver twins; he has diagnosed appendicitis, has treated two children badly burned in a blazing tent; has given artificial respiration to an Indian infant who had been dead for several hours before the parents called him.

He has spent hours on the telephone talking with Juneau doctors, describing in minute detail the symptoms of suffering patients, both white and Indian, and the doctors have told him what to do until the patient could be rushed to the Juneau hospital.

Because he has only one eye, his depth perception is bad, if existent at all, and much of his work is with surgical needle and thread sewing up wounds and gashes.

He works with the remarkable strength of the stubs of his fingers on his right hand and refuses to let the one eye interfere with his work. He has developed the technique of watching shadows to tell when the needle is where he wants it, and sometimes he slides the needle across the flesh before he takes a stitch.

He has treated broken legs and arms, children who have gotten into the sleeping pill bottle, men with ulcers and people who were seriously ill. No one has been refused help, and no one has been charged.

There is a public health nurse assigned to the vicinity, but she cannot be here all the time. She has other villages to visit, and local emergencies do not wait for her presence here.

The Indians seem to prefer Heinmiller's first aid, and perhaps it is old custom, because Heinmiller's house is the former headquarters of the Army post and the building next to his is the hospital where Indians have been treated for a half century.

There is no doctor in this area although there is one in Skagway 15 miles away and several in Juneau, where there is an excellent hospital. Most of the patients to whom Heinmiller gives first aid prefer to go to Juneau.

Heinmiller's wife once said she could not stand the sight of blood, and asked to be relieved of any help in such cases after they were married.

"But the first time she saw me sewing one up," Heinmiller laughs, "she started telling me how to make the second stitch."

Today Betty Heinmiller is an old hand at this pioneer first aid and doctoring. She works with her husband in many cases, but their two-year-old son takes up a lot of her time. She has only one complaint and it's from a woman's practical viewpoint.

"Well, mainly it's the blankets," she says. "We've lost 12 so far, I do wish they'd return them."

They are lost when a Heinmiller patient is put aboard a plane for Juneau and they just don't return.

In 1958, Carl Heinmiller made an appearance in a column written by Anne Bradford, for the North Virginia Sun. The article "Alaska Beckons to American Youth" started off with an editor's note by Bradford:

The following story of high adventure in the Alaska wilds is told by a former Arlington resident who is in the United States now to present and to stress the vista of opportunity open to American youth in the U. S. territory. In Alaska, we feel, is a chance for the rugged, out-of-doors-type lad to live (for a varying period) as he yearns in his secret heart to live.

Bradford then wrote about Carl Heinmiller and an incident with a bear.

"He had left his gun behind—after all it was ten pounds he would just as soon not carry—and gone into the brush. He had seen the skin of a dead animal there the day before, but it was all covered up. An old kill, he figured. He had just started to poke at the skin when, all of a sudden, he heard a roar.

"Turning, he saw a grizzly bear—800 or 900 pounds—coming. He had nothing – no weapons—so he started up a tree. But the bear grabbed him by the back of his thigh."

This was the start of a true Alaskan bear story told to a SUN reporter by Carl Heinmiller, former Arlington resident, now mayor and chief of police of Port Chilkoot (near Haines), newest city in Alaska.

Mr. Heinmiller, with his wife Betty, and two children, Lee, five, and Judith, three, is staying at the Marriot Hotel, on Route 50 in Arlington, until tomorrow when he will return to Alaska.

His purpose here has been to explore with Department of Interior officials, and others, ways for promoting "Alaska youth, Inc.," a non-profit vocational training school in southeast Alaska.

Learning Indian lore, and such occupations as seafood production, lumber, construction and tourism—all vital to the Alaskan economy—would be part of the youth training.

"Here is a wonderful opportunity to learn a trade—frontier opportunity where individual initiative pays off," stated Mr.

Heinmiller, now initiating a five month youth program where trainees would be paid for their labor while learning.

"Here too, is a program geared to youth not planning on college, or for boys in need of vocational opportunities in summer months. Alaska Youth, Inc., will provide training for a segment of today's youth generally forgotten in an era intent upon higher education.

But to get back to the bear story, as told by this rugged outdoor Scout leader, who wears a black patch over one eye (service in World War II) and who was recently made an Indian Chief by the Chilkat Indians at Klukwan for his service to them:

Forest Young, 50 an Alaskan construction worker, was the hunter attacked by the bear.

Mr. Heinmiller continued:

"The bear pinned him down with one paw, broke his hand. Forest punched him… but finally, as the mauling continued, he decided to play dead. The bear walked off. Then Forest moved his head just a little.

"The bear rushed back, grabbed him and flung him around. Forest fell, crushing part of his chest. Again he played dead; then, made the mistake of opening his eyes to see where the bear had gone.

"Back in a flash, the bear bit his back, his thigh, his chest, dislodging, two ribs, causing splintered bones to fall into the diaphragm, puncturing a hole.

"He was found lying semi-conscious an hour later by his hunting companion Martin Cordes.

(Cordes, also a former Arlington resident, had come to Alaska with Carl and his group of veterans to develop a town on the Chilkoot Army barracks location. Their group had purchased this property from the government.)

"Well—to make a long story short," Mr. Heinmiller continued, "Marty had to leave Forest lying there, in a sleeping bag with a Coleman lantern to keep the bear away. He came back to Port Chilkoot to help.

"Since I was in charge of rescue teams and first aid," Carl explained. "I grabbed a bag of surgical supplies, morphine, homostats, sodium, caffeine, etc. We took blankets and a stretcher.

"Through the black of night, we paddled up the hazardous Chilkat river, sloshed through a ravine, following a trail of toilet paper Marty had left—and found Forest just as the Coleman lantern flickered out. It took us three-and-a-half hours to carry him one-and-a-half miles by stretcher to a hunter's cabin.

"I sewed Forest to his sleeping bag to close up the hole in his chest that made his breathing difficult.

"Next morning a Royal Canadian Air Force helicopter from White Horse landed and completed the rescue. By a miracle, Forest lived, and in three months was nearly recovered.

Mr. Heinmiller smiled thoughtfully, and added as a post-script, "Forest has been an enemy of mine. We had clashed on everything. But when I found him that night, lying on the Coleman lantern he looked up and said:

"Heinmiller, you old so-and-so, I knew you'd come."

309

The next article in which Heinmiller appears is dated August 30th 1960. That article "Alaska At Port Chilkoot" written for The Herald-News, by someone called "The Vagabond" stated:

> After an amazingly beautiful flight in a Grumman Goose amphibian on which we flew over a score of glaciers, above the Inside Passage and over hundreds of snow-capped mountains we arrived in Haines. We were taken to Port Chilkoot where we stayed at the Hotel Helsingland (Swedish). At Port Chilkoot we met one of Alaska's most engaging personalities – Carl Heinmiller.

> During World War II Carl organized and trained the Fiji Commandos and was wounded in action several times. He lost an eye and part of a hand as he threw himself over a grenade which had been poorly thrown thus sparing many others from injury. Yet several years later he is an energetic, enthusiastic and vigorous leader in the program of saving the 15,000 Indians who reside in southeastern Alaska.

> With five other ex-servicemen he bought old Fort William Seward, sold in 1947 as government surplus. They incorporated the city of Port Chilkoot and Carl is mayor, manager of the light plant, a ferry terminus, a salmon smoking plant and several other projects.

> His non-profit Alaska Youth, Inc., is an attempt to save the youth of the Chilkoot Indian tribe for the U.S.A. Because of his efforts in behalf of the tribe he has been made a member of the Chilkoot nation.

> In 1959 he took his Indian dance group to the Indian reservation ceremonials at Gallup, New Mexico There at the National Indian

Dance contests among 400 contestants and over 40 groups his group won national honors as the best interpretive group.

At the National Girl Scout Roundup in Colorado Springs, Colorado last summer it was his four Girl Scouts who presented the new U.S.A. flag with its 49th star to the national president.

Being immediately adjacent to Haines, the terminus of the Alaska Highway as well as the Army oil pipe line, this area presents real promise. The U. S. Steel Corporation is working on the development of the Kluckwon iron ore region.

With the return of several thousand Indians to the area and the withdrawal of the Presbyterians from their Haines House project the Alaska Youth, Inc. becomes all the more imperative. This vicinity is rich in natural resources, scenery, tourist possibilities, game, and the Indians who present a new challenge to our nation. We met a number of Indian young people, high school graduates who were going to college next year in "the downeast states" majoring in art, music and the sciences.

Carl Heinmiller in Alaska, February 1949. Source: National Archives.

ELECT
Carl W. Heinmiller

of HAINES

Republican Candidate for the

House of
Representatives

"Tired of Poor Government?
V O T E !"

Source: Daily Sitka Sentinel, April 16th 1954.

Color postcard photo by Carl W. Heinmiller. Caption on the back states: Parade ground at Port Chilkoot, Alaska, formerly Chilkoot Barracks, showing former officers' quarters and the newly erected Totem Village.

A Legendary White Warrior

Source: Fairbanks Daily News Miner, photo credit Alaska Airlines, by Bob and Ira Spring

As we have seen in the preceding chapter, Heinmiller was quite active in his adopted hometown during the postwar era. He wore multiple hats. I think it's safe to say that he was not a person who would let any physical limitations get in the way of the important work that had to be done.

Heinmiller liked to be involved in many things all at once. That was especially so with the Native American community he had been involved with. Heinmiller also appeared to be a highly respected individual in the town he lived in.

While he had been stationed in Fiji, Carl was exposed to indigenous art and dance. His contact with the local Tlingit people renewed his interest in Native culture. Fort Seward would eventually house the fruition of that interest – Alaska Indian Arts.

An article "Legendary White Warrior Leads Native Dancers" in the Fairbanks Daily News-Miner, April 7th 1969, stated:

> Friendlier Indians than Chilkats are hard to find. Yet, a hundred years ago this fiercest clan of war-waging Tlingits was the scourge of pioneers and Indians alike. They jealously guarded mountain passes and waterways, and clobbered gold and fur seeking invaders of their Southwest Alaska corner.
>
> However, one look at this Eden on the upper reaches of Lynn Canal and you can't blame them. Their ancestral home nestles among snow-capped peaks, game-filled forests and sparkling fjords teeming with salmon. The Chilkats lived an affluent, leisurely life, with time for artistic pursuits including dancing and fine woodcarving.
>
> Friendly? Then why drums, spears and war dances in the tribal house? And how about the loud singing, drumbeating paleface "chief"? It's all for fun now, and for visitors!
>
> With drumbeat and stirring chants, Chilkat Dancers perform age-old story dances. Some tell origins of mosquitoes and tides; others describe deeds of derring-do. All ages and races participate. Cute, costumed preschoolers follow old customs and learn steps watching from the sidelines. Some costumes are museum pieces

(especially famous Chilkat blankets), the rest have been meticulously fashioned by participants.

Today's Indian story starts with white chief Carl Heinmiller, a legendary figure who came to Port Chilkoot 20 years ago. He was dismayed at the plight of local Indians, especially the young people.

One of Carl's first efforts was to organize a scout troop. As many youngsters were Indian, a logical project was Indian dancing. Learning authentic dances from Chilkats at nearby Klukwan Village seemed a reasonable step. But Carl found traditional dances and mask designs are inherited and private clan property. Older Indians had to be convinced their young people—and Carl—were seriously interested.

The Chilkats finally brought out their most prized artifacts. Under Carl's skilled guidance, the youths studied and crafted intricate, elaborate dance costumes. Girls joined the group. There was no doubt about the youngster's enthusiasm.

First venture of these Chilkat Dancers into competition was major league, the Inter-tribal Indian Ceremonies at Gallup, New Mexico. Challenging the best dancers from East, West, Canada and Mexico, they took first place.

Major Heinmiller (ret.) is a warrior from way back. He has scars to prove it. Tangling with a land mine while leading Fiji Islanders in guerrilla tactics in World War II, and diving onto a hand grenade dropped by a terrified recruit while training commandos left him with a game back, missing eye and half a hand. (To this day he claims he tripped accidentally; witnesses and medal givers disagreed.)

Chilkat Dancers are only the most visible result of Heinmiller's fight for natives. He also organized Alaska Indian Arts, a school to rekindle native's interest in their crafts and heritage. Travelers can wander through informal classrooms and watch natives teach and work at various crafts: carving Alaska soapstone, ivory, wood; etching silver; buffing copper; making costumes. Outside, Tlingits may be carving a 30 foot totem pole.

With scanty help of the government agencies, Carl teaches new trades to seasonal fishermen, handicapped and unemployed. Handiwork is for sale in "Cache" next to the Trible House.

Heinmiller appeared in that same newspaper on July 8th 1972. This time in an article titled "Chilkat Dancers reproducing aboriginal art" written by Downs Matthews. In that article Mathews discussed in further detail, what Heinmiller had accomplished in his community. Matthews wrote:

In time with a tom-tom's slow thumping, a dancer garbed magnificently in a Chilkat chieftain's tunic pantomimes a bear hunt for his charmed audience of tourists visiting Alaska from the Lower 49.

He grapples fiercely with a hulking figure wearing a carved wooden bear mask. Killed in the struggle, the chief is borne away by his tribesmen on a blanket of mountain goat's wool.

Then come the hunters to avenge his death. They search long and unsuccessfully until a friendly raven leads them to the killer.

Around about the dancers wheel, slaying the bear. The raven, with his sharp-beaked mask, hovers apocalyptically over the scene.

They are the Chilkat Dancers performing their Bear and Raven Dance, a classic among the Tlingit Indians of the Alaskan coast.

Their tunics, cloaks, headdresses, masks and the dance itself, are products of an artistic heritage which one expert described as "unique among the world's art traditions."

It is a tradition, however, on the verge of extinction. Today, it is being kept alive by a handful of talented natives working together as Alaska Indian Arts, Inc., under the direction of a former Ohioan named Carl Heinmiller.

When Heinmiller arrived at Port-Chilkoot-Haines in 1947, he found fewer than a hundred members remaining of two Tlingit villages that a century ago numbered around 3,500.

Decimated by foreign disease and demoralized by cultural shock, the Tlingits could not cope with 20th Century change. The survivors lapsed into hopelessness, poverty and renounced an artistic heritage considered to be the richest and most highly developed of any aboriginal group in North America.

But Heinmiller, who had worked with tribesmen in the Fiji Islands, befriended the Tlingits. To give the children something to do, he formed a Boy Scout troop. As a project, he assigned them to learn the dances and ceremonies by which tribal history and mythology were expressed.

He persuaded the tribe's elders to teach their young the ancient and almost forgotten skills of dance and art which would have perished with them. Thus, the Chilkat Dancers came into being.

Performing for tourists traveling to Port Chilkoot from Juneau or Skagway, the dancers have achieved nationwide fame for the unusual beauty and authenticity of their performances and costumes.

The extraordinary aptitude of the young Tlingits, who had to learn to carve the wooden masks by which various roles are symbolized, led Heinmiller to start a program to teach the craftsmanship to unemployed and handicapped natives of the area.

In 1957, Alaska Indian Ars was incorporated with funds from the Indian Arts and Crafts Board of the Department of the Interior; the Alaska Rural Development Agency, and the Manpower Development and Training Administration. Over 40 natives have learned valuable skills in the program; of these, a gifted half-dozen have developed into artists of unusual ability.

Their output ranges from totem poles (including a 132-foot skyscraper, the tallest in the world) to block prints of traditional motifs. Achieving a high degree of expertise, the artisans of Alaska Indian Arts produce carvings which the tribe's elders say equal the work of master carvers of bygone years.

As an outgrowth of their accomplishments, Heinmiller suggested still another project to recapture and invigorate native culture: the reproducing of Northwest Coast Indian art contained in Russian collections.

"The best and most authentic examples in the world are in Russian museums," says Heinmiller, who has examined the collections personally.

"The Russians owned Alaska from 1741 to 1867," Heinmiller points out. "Their explorers and traders assembled some superb collections when aboriginal Alaskan art was at its peak. We felt that if Alaska Indian Arts could reproduce these masterpieces, we could bring back some of our lost heritage to Alaska."

A grant made it possible for Heinmiller to realize his ambition. Working from a reference work by a Russian ethnologist, Heinmiller selected for reproduction seven masks and a halibut hook from a collection housed in the Museum of Anthropology and Ethnography of the Academy of Sciences in Leningrad, and two masks from the Anthropological Museum of the Lomonosov State University in Moscow.

He decided to add two unusual masks of Chilkat origin to provide variety in motifs and ethnic traditions.

Completed, the 12-piece collection is being exhibited throughout Alaska and at selected museums in the Lower 48 under the auspices of Humble Oil & Refining Company, who made the original grant.

Included are representations of the moon, its luminescent countenance decorated on top of sprigs of human hair; an old woman, her face heavily carved with wrinkles; a bear with eyebrows of copper and eyes, nostrils and teeth of abalone shell; an eagle with teeth of snail shells; a killer whale; a mosquito with decorations of feathers, walrus whiskers and abalone, and several masks of men and women.

A halibut hook, used in fishing, also is included and is an example of the artistic carving which Alaskan aboriginals lavished on even workaday objects.

"Masks were important in the social and ceremonial life of the Northwest Coast Indians," Heinmiller says. "Artists who created them were among the most honored personages of the tribe. They were exempt from military service and other tribal responsibilities."

Carving red cedar or birch with wooden hasps tipped with shell, stone, or beaver teeth, the artists ornamented their work with natural pigments, beaten copper strips, abalone shell, walrus and seal whiskers, feathers, fur, and sometimes human hair. The masks represented totem animals, spirits, and mythological beings, and were handed down from generation to generation within each clan.

Secret societies performed dances to enliven the winter months and commemorate events. The dancers used masks to represent specific animal and spirit characters. The clan's shaman, or medicine man, had a particularly large number which he would use in healing ceremonies.

Some masks covered the wearer's face, while others were attached to ceremonial headdresses or to helmets worn in battle. Art motifs stressed the close relationship between man and animal, and the masks frequently combined both human and animal features.

Symbols characterized specific animals: A long straight beak indicated a raven; a hooked beak was the eagle's symbol; a hooked beak curving to touch the mouth was the sign of the hawk. Bear, beaver, whale, wolf, mountain goat, and sometimes fish and insects played a role in tribal mythology.

Heinmiller recognized and saw the value in a tribe's cultural heritage and their knowledge. probably due to his time embedded amongst the Fijians. He saw that it was dying out and he sought to preserve it. Once the knowledge is lost, it's usually lost for good. It's important to preserve it for future generations as the knowledge has the potential be valuable someday. It even has the potential to save lives, like the Fijian's bushcraft skills.

Forgotten Warriors and Nice Fellows

I recently had a conversation with a fellow researcher regarding a book I wrote about Skeeter Vaughan, otherwise known as Grey Otter, the legendary tomahawk and knife thrower. I specifically wrote about a tomahawk fighting system that is attributed to him. Along with his knife throwing skills, that hawk system helped him to survive the war and therefore it was valuable knowledge that he later sought to pass it on to others who were willing to listen and learn.

While writing that book I also took the opportunity to bring some necessary exposure to some of the Native American warriors from World War Two. A researcher I spoke with, who is from the UK, told me that he found the book very interesting because he had not thought about the Native Americans and their contribution to the war effort; and the fact that they had been more or less airbrushed out of that history. He mentioned the same happened in his country with regard to their Colonial troops.

The researcher told me that he had learned a lot of other stuff he did not know about tomahawks, and that I also made him think about the nature of being a warrior.

If I am able to provide people with new information that is not readily available; and also bring exposure to some of the unknown hand-to-hand combat instructors, warriors, and veterans from the past, then I feel I accomplished what I set out to do.

If I have been able to help someone like me, who wants to know about as much as one can possibly know about the history of this subject matter; and perhaps one day they will use my books as a reference in the same way that I have used people like Larsen's works, then I believe that I was successful in my goal.

But it's also the knowledge of some of the systems I have discussed in my books that I want to bring attention to, because they have helped others survive and live through hairy situations. As Ed Don George, one instructor I wrote about called them, these skills are life-saving skills.

At this point I have written twelve books, attempting to explore unarmed combat systems and the instructors who have taught them. With my previous book, Commando Craze, and this book, I attempted to take things a step further and explore what was necessary for those individuals, who were tasked with instructing Commando "type" tactics, to accomplish that goal.

I specifically looked at what the commandos of the Pacific needed to learn, in order to survive in a jungle environment, as opposed to what the Commandos in the European theater of operations needed.

One major question which arose, was exactly who was training who? The Fijians, the New Zealanders and the Americans all contributed something, but it was a question of how much they contributed and what.

As my fellow researcher had noted, the "Colonial" or indigenous troops and their contributions were often overlooked after the war; although they oftentimes played a very important role during it. The truth of the matter is that it was the New Zealand and American officers who got all the accolades; but it was the Fijians, who did a lot of the heavy lifting who tend to get forgotten about.

Heinmiller had been the catalyst for me in wanting to write this book, but it turned out that his time during the war was only one part of the whole story.

Carl Heinmiller, the Boy Scout, became involved with Fijians on a tiny island on the other side of the world. He may have not been directly responsible for their training overall, but he saw an opportunity to learn from them and also to help make their training better. He assisted where he could and he had the drive to want to help people. He helped by passing on the knowledge he had learned from the Fijians and their officers from New Zealand, to his fellow soldiers and by doing so he helped many of them to survive.

Who trained who? It became apparent to me that the New Zealanders, the Americans and the Fijians all learned valuable lessons from each other.

The Fijians were not any less influential than the New Zealanders, and the New Zealanders were not any less influential than the Americans. Perhaps the Americans learned more from the Fijians and the New Zealanders but they also had things to offer in return. The vital knowledge that they passed on to each other was valuable knowledge. It was ancient knowledge (such as the Fijian's bushcraft survival skills) or it was knowledge learned on the job. For example, Heinmiller had received the commendation for inventing an elevated machine gun platform in the mangrove swamp, as Lee put it. Lee said:

> He was just a Boy Scout dealing with staying dry!! He thought the citation was sorta stupid, just for thinking on your feet!!!"

It was knowledge that helped all of them to win the war and to survive.

Being the physically active type and having an interest in sports, Heinmiller had utilized those interests as well, in order to help with the war effort.

We all draw upon our experiences in life. In Heinmiller's case he utilized the things that he knew from his youth, to carry him through the war (a prime example, his boy scout hatchet). Later, he utilized some of that same knowledge to help the people from his community, in his adopted hometown in Alaska.

Heinmiller's story didn't just begin or end with the war. He was a warrior in all aspects of his life, through and through. He utilized all his learned knowledge and experience to help elevate other's lives.

It's always admirable when people utilize their knowledge in order to make the world a better place. They seek to affect positive change. There are countless stories of people like Heinmiller doing that during the war, when it seemed like all hope was lost. They also continued to do those things in order to make a difference later on, when they went back to civilian life.

Don't let a people's history and their knowledge disappear. Seek to preserve it like Heinmiller did.

That should be the main takeaway from this book. Men such as Heinmiller and Tripp sought practical solutions to problems and overcame obstacles by utilizing the knowledge that they had learned. And once it had been learned they did not hoard it, they passed it onto their fellow man.

Another question which arose was, does getting things done Quick and Dirty sum up the content and context of Commando training? What exactly made a Commando a Commando?

Larsen stated that the Fijians were called Commandos but that the name "commando" was used in its older sense and applied to those units because they were independent companies, almost self-contained.

According to an article by David Thomas regarding "The Importance of Commando Operations in Modern Warfare 1939-82", written for the Journal of Contemporary History, October 1983, the British concept of commando operations derived from the English tradition of maritime raiding and seaborne assaults, and from the experience of irregular warfare in the Peninsular War and the Boer War. He stated:

> However, before Dunkirk, there was no coherent appreciation in the British army at the command level of the tactical or strategic value of special forces and commando operations and almost no systematic development of specialised units for any purpose.

We can see that illustrated in the Laycock document when he points out that there was no uniformity in the training of the different Commando units. Thomas continued:

> From 1940, it transpired that commando forces were established in each major theatre of the war, northwest Europe, the

Mediterranean, and the Far East, in response to the operational requirements of the theatre command, but in general without any reference to preexisting doctrine or a systematic plan formulated by the General Staff in Britain. Every British military commando force was essentially an inspired improvisation or invention in the face of necessity or expediency. The several forces which came into existence between 1940 and 1942 owed their formation not to British army strategy and doctrine, nor to any far-reaching conception of commando warfare, but to the fertile imagination of Prime Minister Churchill and a number of gifted officers.

Does getting things done quick and dirty make a Commando? I think it all depends on your interpretation of things. I believe getting things done *Quick and Dirty* but also *Independently* was essentially what it was all about, and that was the reason why "Commando" became a global "craze" or a fad in some senses. People respected that "Get Shit Done" attitude.

Thomas continued:

The first commando force, the Army Commandos, was an *ad hoc* unit, for which the regular military establishment originally could foresee no useful or permanent function beyond the one assigned to it by the Prime Minster at the time of formation, namely, to serve as a reserve, mobile strike-force in the defence of Britain against the expected invasion.

That is essentially what the Fiji Commandos were functioning as on Fiji, they were meant to be stay-behind units. Larsen wrote that they were more strictly speaking, "guerrillas," and had the Japanese actually landed in Fiji they would have adopted a harassing role.

Thomas wrote:

Thus, when the threat of invasion passed, the Commandos at first had no well-defined military function. However they were shortly re-deployed as amphibious raiding forces for operations against occupied Europe designed to bolster military and civilian morale

326

and regain a measure of the tactical initiative at a time when the army was confined to the strategic defensive. The numerous pin-prick missions conducted in 1940 and 1941 otherwise had no serious military value. In terms of the resources expended upon them, the amount of training and rehearsal, and the casualties suffered, the costs of these coastal raids were quite out of proportion to the minimal results achieved. However, these operations represented a form of psychological warfare, and they were less important for what they attained in terms of losses inflicted on the Germans and information obtained, than for their effect upon the psychology of the British and German armies.

A similar thing occurred with the Fijians when they undertook operations outside of Fiji. Thomas later wrote:

Summing up the importance of British commando forces in general in the second world war, it must be said that the contribution of commando operations has perhaps, been overestimated with the passage of time. One commando unit, the SAS, did achieve results out of all proportion to its size and the resources expended upon it. However, no commando operation in any theatre of war can be said to have made an indispensable contribution to the tactical or strategic success of the regular army in any battle. Except in the case of intelligence and reconnaissance missions, which may have been the most valuable types of operations undertaken by the various commando units, commando operations provided the British armed forces with a welcome, though not essential, bonus, whether as the result of successful sabotage and diversion or of the capture of fortified objectives that otherwise might have delayed the advance of the infantry inland after a landing. The German army certainly took notice of commando operations, and Hitler became obsessed with British commando warfare, as witness the infamous Commando Order. Yet, no commando operation had a decisive effect upon any German military operation in the war.

Were the Fijian Commandos also Commandos? Yes they absolutely were, they fit the bill. They had a high level of physical fitness. They were subject matter experts in fieldcraft and survival in the bush. They were able to function independently if they had needed to. They came from a warrior culture and were therefore comfortable with being ruthless killers when they had to be. They also made a psychological impact.

As the Battle Drill Training document had pointed out:

> Battle Drill training is founded upon the axiom that "until every soldier looks on himself as a ruthless killer, using cover with the facility of an animal, using his weapons with the practiced ease of a professional hunter and covering the ground on the move with the agility of a deer-stalker, infantry battle training will be based on false foundations"

The Commando Training document also stated something similar:

> Field-craft and the art of the hunter are the next to be developed and the would-be Commando expert must learn to see without being seen. He must receive training in the use of ground, in concealment and camouflage and in the use of the stalking glass, but he must bear in mind that these are only a means to an end, and are the methods by which he will achieve his objective, get to grips with the enemy and eventually make good his escape.

The Fijians certainly did not have it easy by any means. They had to prove that they too could be Commandos.

An article in the Sydney Morning Herald, April 23rd 1954, "Fijians: Fighters and Footballers" stated:

> Fijians have a reputation both as jungle fighters and as Rugby Union footballers. But they had to fight hard against prejudice and indifference for recognition in both spheres.

Australians, who generally know a great deal about the war in the South-West Pacific, know distressingly little about the South Pacific, know distressingly little about the South Pacific theatre, where first Vice Admiral Ghormley and then, after October, 1942, Vice-Admiral "Bill" Halsey were in command.

In New Zealand the position is reversed. The New Zealanders whose 3rd Division served in the Solomons, were the first to recognize and encourage the Fijians, both as Rugby footballers and as jungle fighters.

Eleven thousand men served in the Fiji military forces, during the war. Of these 1,500 were New Zealanders—in the main officers and N.C.O.'s from the 2nd N.Z. Expeditionary Force.

For, early in 1942, the New Zealanders augmented their forces for the defence of Fiji, and wholeheartedly engaged in strengthening the Fijian Defence Forces. They moulded the untrained, but highly willing, Fijians into disciplined army units.

In the end their disciples gave back as good as they got. It was perhaps inevitable, seeing what useful scouts they proved on their own island terrain, that someone should conceive the plan of training the New Zealanders in jungle tactics using the Fijians as instructors. And the Fijians taught their visitors a great deal of their own lore.

Then the catch came. I am indebted for the story to the Historic Section of USAFISPA, headquarters of the U.S. Army, who generously allowed me to use their files, and facilities at the Pentagon building, Noumea.

The catch was that, although the Fijians were anxious to go into action, and although their use was being pressed by the British High Commissioner for the Western Pacific, backed by the British Government, the Americans were reluctant to use them.

The Americans thought the Fijians might not be equal to the task, and contended that, anyway, they had been formed only for local defence on the flank of the Allied offensive.

In October, 1942, the British High Commissioner arrived in Noumea to consult Admiral Ghormley, and then went to Auckland for discussions with the New Zealand Government.

Major-General Robert S. Beightler, the U.S. commander in Fiji, was in sympathy with the proposal to use the more highly trained Fijian troops and commandos in the Solomons.

But the U.S. Army's commanding general in the area, Lieut-General M. F. Harmon, who had tactical land command in the Solomons once the Army replaced the Marines, had still to be persuaded.

On November, 7, 1942, Admiral Halsey sent General Harmon a memorandum, saying that a brigade of native troops and three companies of native commandos from Fiji had been offered for combat use on Guadalcanal. He asked for views on their probable combat value and the effect their detachment would have on the security of Fiji, and the probable value of native commandos.

On November 15 General Harmon replied, recommending against the use of Fiji forces outside the Fiji group. He said the commandos had been developed only for patriotic coastal watching duties and their combat capacity as commando parties was considered doubtful.

"This matter of the use of natives from one area or group of islands in a combat capacity in another area has been discussed by me with an Australian commando officer of excellent repute," General Harmon said.

"This officer recommends definitely against, stating that clashes would inevitably result; and that Australian attempts of similar usage in New Guinea had failed for the same reason."

It would be a risky experiment, General Harmon continued, because the detachment of any or all of the Brigade could have an adverse effect on the security of Fiji's defence, entirely disproportionate to his estimate of their combat value in the Solomons.

He said United States Forces were concentrated there to defend a critical island area with Fiji troops in the essential task of outposting half of the island shore line. If the Fijians were moved elsewhere, it would be necessary to disperse the already inadequate American forces.

But pressure by the British side was not relaxed, and soon afterwards General Harmon agreed that "it would be fair to try out a small sample force of Fijians in the Guadalcanal campaign," which was then causing heavy losses to the United States Army.

The so-called "special party" was the thin edge of the wedge that opened the Solomons campaign to more commandos and two battalions of Fijian troops, who proved a great success.

The party comprised seven New Zealanders and 20 Fijians. They were landed by United States boats for behind the Japanese lines in the Visale area on Guadalcanal. They took the enemy in the rear, playing havoc with his defences, destroying guns, infiltrating into Japanese positions at night, and paving the way by demoralization for the American drive along the coast.

These "South Pacific Scouts," as the Americans called them, were next assigned to lead the first contingent of Allied troops to invade the Japanese-controlled Russell Islands, and they went on from island to island and from success to success, on their own, or leading American patrols.

Finally, early the following January, the general on the spot, General Alexander M. Patch, in command of the American Division, asked; "Have you any more at home like these?"

He requested priority for a completely trained Fiji commando unit, which soon arrived—40 New Zealanders and 165 natives, including 28 Tongans.

Their numbers grew considerably in April, the additions including a number of Solomon islanders.

The results were magnificent, and led to the demand for, and the arrival of, two trained Fiji Battalions. Their achievements too became legendary on Bougainville and the lesser islands.

In the first two months of patrol actions one battalion alone killed 125 Japanese for a loss of one Fijian killed and two wounded.

We in Eastern Australia now know the Fijians on the football field. They were here in 1952 and they are coming again next month.

Their combat battalions and commandos include some of their finest footballers of twelve years ago; and their battalion at present in Malaya is just as strong in this respect.

Some of the footballers who are coming to Australia have served in Malaya and have played in battalion teams which have been very successful in the Far East generally. They held almost an unbeaten record in Malaya and made successful trips to Hong Kong and Indo-China. Some of them have come back on leave especially to join the team for Australia.

On Bougainville was Lieut. Isireli Korovulavula, "the smiling fullback" who led their first Ruby Tour of New Zealand in 1939.

He was shot down when out on air observation at Bougainville and was given up for dead when after 32 days in the jungle, he struggled back to his unit. During the last 20 of those days he had nothing to eat.

Korovulavula rejoined the Army a year or two ago and went to Malaya with the 1st Battalion, Fiji Infantry Regiment. He came back with the rank of major and joined the staff of the Prisons Department. He has recently been appointed an overseer, the first Fijian to attain that rank.

Fiji's fighting men won many decorations, British and American, including a posthumous VC (Cakau Sailasa's). Sturdy islanders, many over six foot, broad shouldered and muscular and slimmer in the waist than Polynesians of comparable stature, they made a fine impression in war as on the Rugby field.

Training by competition paid off.

In closing, I think people should take a page from the Fijian Commando's book and have integrity in everything that they do. Don't just sit around and think about stuff, get out of the comfort zone and do it.

The Fijians could not wait to take the fight to the enemy to prove themselves. Take the initiative upon yourself and be more "Commando" about things. Be decisive.

Accomplish what you set out to do and give it your all. Put all your best efforts into whatever task lies ahead of you. Live in the moment but also live to fight another day.

In other words, keep a Positive Mental Attitude. It's not all bad. Learn from the experience. Like the Fijians you too might then be remembered fondly, as one of the nicest fellows, because of your good nature and your good attitude.

Learn the lessons. Gain the knowledge. Even if you don't succeed, you can be comfortable that you made the best decisions that you could, by using the best information you had available to you at the time.

Knowledge is Power. Know your stuff.

In some of the training camps in World War One and again in World War Two, there was a slogan that was utilized for the training of the troops in hand-to-hand combat and bayonet tactics. It was:

If You Don't Know You Get Killed

Carl Heinmiller's Photographs

A map belonging to Carl Heinmiller, which he used during Guadalcanal.

Fiji Commandos patch, author's personal collection.

Major Heinmiller with General Omar Bradley and his wife Mary at the
Dutch Embassy, Washington, D. C.

Presenting the original manuscript of "The Ballad of Rodger Young" at the White House in 1945. Front Row: Senator Huffman (Ohio), President Truman, Song writer Frank Loesser. Second Row: Major Heinmiller, Major General Beightler, Lieutenant General "Lightning Joe" Collins (Infantry School Fort Benning, Georgia), General Jake Deavers, HQ, Army Ground Forces, Major Putnam, Deaver's Aide.

Carl Heinmiller's first trip back to Fiji in 1977, since the War. Heinmiller presented the Tlingit War Club/Slave Killer to the Governor General.

Carl with three Chilkat Dancers.

www.ingramcontent.com/pod-product-compliance
Lightning Source LLC
Chambersburg PA
CBHW040149010726
47475CB00040B/502